A
CONCISE
GUIDE
TO THE
CATHOLIC
CHURCH

A CONCISE GUIDE TO THE CATHOLIC CHURCH

Felician A. Foy, O.F.M.
Rose M. Avato

Our Sunday Visitor, Inc.
200 Noll Plaza, Huntington, IN 46750

Imprimi Potest: Rev. Alban A. Maguire, O.F.M.
Minister Provincial
Province of the Most Holy Name

Nihil Obstat:
Rev. Herbert K. Tillyer
Censor Librorum

Imprimatur: ✝Frank J. Rodimer, D.D.
Bishop of Paterson
April 18, 1984

The Nihil Obstat and Imprimatur are official declarations that a book or pamphlet is free of doctrinal or moral error. No implication is contained therein that those who have granted the Nihil Obstat or Imprimatur agree with the contents, opinions or statements expressed.

Acknowledgments: *The Documents of Vatican II,* ed. W.M. Abbott, S.J. (Herder and Herder, America Press: New York, 1966; copyright © 1966 by The America Press; all rights reserved), for quotations of conciliar documents; *Code of Canon Law, Latin-English Translation* (Copyright © 1983 by the Canon Law Society of America; all rights reserved), for quotation of portions of Canon 844; Rev. John J. Manning, O.F.M., for theological consulation and editorial assistance.

Library of Congress Catalogue No: 83-63170
ISBN 0-87973-616-X

Printed in the United States of America

Dedicated to Mary,
Mother of the Church

Contents

Foreword • viii

The Catholic Church • 1

Revelation • 3

The Bible • 6

Teaching Authority and Infallibility • 10

Apostles and Evangelists • 14

Ecumenical Councils • 17

Fathers and Doctors of the Church • 22

Catholic Beliefs • 27

Moral Obligations • 31

Social Doctrine • 35

Liturgy • 47

Mass, the Eucharistic Sacrifice • 52

The Church Building • 60

Sacraments • 64

Marriage Laws of the Church • 72

Liturgical Year and Calendar • 75

Mary, Mother of Jesus • 85

Saints • 87

Devotions • 90

Eastern Catholic Churches • 94

Organization and Government of the Church • 99

Papal Representatives • 108

The Vatican • 110

Code of Canon Law • 115

Apostolate of Lay Persons • 122

Religious: Men and Women • 124

Interfaith Relations • 130

Appendix. Popes: Chronological List • 138

    Antipopes, The Western Schism • 145

Titles and Forms of Address • 146

General Index • 147

Foreword

This book, in line with its title, is intended to serve as a concise guide to the Catholic Church, with coverage of its origin, nature and mission; its beliefs and moral teachings; its sacraments and forms of worship; its people, in all categories, and their respective roles in the Church; its saints; its organization, and its relations to other religious bodies and society in general.

The Catholic Church

The Catholic Church is the society whose members, baptized and incorporated in Christ, profess the same faith, partake of the same sacraments and are in communion with and under the government of the successor of St. Peter, the pope, and the bishops in union with him.

"The unique Church of Christ which . . . we avow as one, holy, catholic and apostolic . . . constituted and organized in the world as a society, subsists in the Catholic Church, which is governed by the successor of Peter and by the bishops in union with that successor" (*Dogmatic Constitution on the Church*, Second Vatican Council).

Established by Christ: The Catholic Church, prefigured in the Old Testament, was instituted by Jesus Christ. He selected, trained and commissioned the Apostles to preach the Good News of salvation, to baptize and form the community of faith in His name. It is the one Church instituted by Christ.

The Church is "the initial budding forth" of the Kingdom of God which was proclaimed by Christ and will reach perfection at the end of time. It is the Mystical Body of Christ. It is a kind of sacrament and instrument for the salvation of all people. Its members are the People of God. They are all equal in virtue of their baptism but are differentiated in various ways by their respective vocations. They comprise the communion of saints — the union of those on earth, in heavenly glory and in purgatory with Christ and one another in grace, prayer and good works.

Necessary for Salvation: The Church is necessary for salvation, and all persons are called to the catholic unity of the People of God. All are related to this people in some way because of the universal call to salvation — the Catholic faithful, fully; catechumens; other Christians; those who have not yet received the Gospel and those who do not know the Gospel or the Church but who sincerely strive to seek and to carry out the will of God as it is known to them.

Salvation is possible for all persons except (1) those who know the Church is necessary for salvation but deliberately reject it by refusing to enter it or remain in it, and (2) those who, although part of the body of the Church, do not persevere in charity.

MARKS OF THE CHURCH

The Church, as professed in the Apostles' Creed, is one, holy, catholic and apostolic.

Unity: The Church has unity in doctrine, worship and government along with appropriate diversity or pluralism in theology, liturgy and discipline, which is clearly evident in different rites and cultures.

Holiness: The Church is holy because of the indwelling of the Holy Spirit, in its sacraments and worship, in the thrust of its doctrine and discipline, and in the lives of its members in grace. While ever holy in its divine element, the Church is in constant need of renewal and reform because of the human imperfections of its members.

Catholicity: The Church, which proclaims the whole body of divine revelation, is universal also in its embrace of people in all times, places and cultural settings.

Apostolicity: The Church is apostolic from its origin in the succession of its bishops, through the bishop of Rome, from St. Peter and the college of the Apostles, and also in fidelity to the doctrine received from the Apostles.

CREED, CODE AND CULT

The Church possesses the fullness of divine revelation in the Bible, tradition and doctrine proclaimed by the magisterium (official teaching authority). Flowing from the doctrine emanating from these sources are the creed, mission, moral code, official worship and structure of the Church. Its teaching is preserved from error by the abiding presence of the Holy Spirit.

The Church, in conjunction with recognition of itself as the unique community of salvation instituted by Christ, acknowledges that there are elements of sanctification and truth outside of its visible structure. Such elements, "as gifts properly belonging to the Church of Christ, possess an inner dynamism toward Catholic unity," according to the Second Vatican Council.

Revelation

Revelation is (1) the act by which God makes known himself and truth pertaining to salvation, and (2) the whole body of truth so revealed.

Scripture and tradition form the one and only sacred deposit of revelation, whose authentic interpretation has been entrusted to the magisterium (official teaching authority) of the Church.

Scripture: In the Old Testament, God has revealed himself and salvation truth in the words, deeds, symbolic actions and events in the history of the Chosen People. The fullness of revelation is in and through the person and mission of Jesus, presented in the Gospel accounts of Matthew, Mark, Luke and John, in the other writings of the New Testament and in the tradition of the Church.

The writings in both Testaments were composed by men under the inspiration of the Holy Spirit. For this reason, the Second Vatican Council reaffirmed: "The books of Scripture must be acknowledged as teaching firmly, faithfully and without error that truth which God wanted put into the sacred writings for the sake of our salvation."

Tradition: Tradition consists of revealed truth handed down by the Apostles and transmitted to the Church along with Scripture. This tradition includes the progressive development of doctrine through the living experience, reflection and teaching of the Church in accord with and in the service of the deposit of revelation.

The contents of Scripture and tradition are complete and definitive. No new public revelation will be forthcoming until the second coming of Christ at the end of time.

TRANSMISSION OF REVELATION

Detailed coverage of the foregoing and related subjects is contained in the *Dogmatic Constitution on Revelation* issued by the Second Vatican Council. Following are several key excerpts.

"God has seen to it that what He had revealed for the salvation of all nations would abide perpetually in its full integrity and be handed on to all generations. Therefore Christ the Lord, in whom the full revelation of the supreme God is brought to completion, commissioned the Apostles to preach to all men that Gospel which is the source of all saving truth and moral teaching, and thus to impart to them divine gifts. This Gospel had been promised in former times through the prophets, and Christ himself fulfilled it and promulgated it with His own lips. This commission was faithfully fulfilled by the Apostles who, by their oral preaching, by example and by ordinances, handed on what they had received from Christ . . . or what they had learned through the prompting of the Holy Spirit. The commission was fulfilled, too, by those Apostles and apostolic men who under the inspiration of the same Holy Spirit committed the message of salvation to writing."

TRADITION

"In order to keep the Gospel forever whole and alive within the Church, the Apostles left bishops as their successors, 'handing over their own teaching role' to them. This sacred tradition, therefore, and sacred Scripture of both the Old and the New Testament are like a mirror in which the pilgrim Church on earth looks at God."

"The apostolic preaching, which is expressed in a special way in the inspired books, was to be preserved by a continuous succession of preachers until the end of time. Therefore the Apostles, handing on what they themselves had received, warn the faithful to hold fast to the traditions which they have learned. . . . Now what was handed on by the Apostles includes everything which contributes to the holiness of life and the increase in faith of the People of God; and so the Church, in her teaching, life and worship, perpetuates and hands on to all generations all that she herself is, all that she believes."

DEVELOPMENT OF DOCTRINE

"This tradition which comes from the Apostles develops in the Church with the help of the Holy Spirit. For there is a growth in the understanding of the realities and the words which have been handed down. This happens through the contemplation and study made by believers . . . through the intimate understanding of spiritual things they experience, and through the preaching of those who have received through episcopal succession the sure gift of truth. For, as the centuries succeed one another, the Church constantly moves forward toward the fullness of divine truth until the words of God reach their complete fulfillment in her."

"The words of the holy Fathers (of the Church) witness to the living presence of this tradition, whose wealth is poured into the practice and life of the believing and praying Church. Through the same tradition the Church's full canon of the sacred books is known, and the sacred writings themselves are more profoundly understood and unceasingly made active in her; . . . and the Holy Spirit, through whom the living voice of the Gospel resounds in the Church and, through her, in the world, leads unto all truth those who believe and makes the word of Christ dwell abundantly in them."

TRADITION AND SCRIPTURE

"Hence there exist a close connection and communication between sacred tradition and sacred Scripture. For both of them, flowing from the same divine wellspring, in a certain way merge into a unity and tend toward the same end. For sacred Scripture is the word of God inasmuch as it is consigned to writing under the inspiration of the Holy Spirit. To the successors of the Apostles, sacred tradition hands on in its full purity God's word, which was entrusted to the Apostles by Christ the Lord and the Holy Spirit. Thus, led by the light of the Spirit of truth, these successors can in their preaching preserve this word of God faithfully, explain it and make it more widely known. Consequently, it is not from sacred Scripture alone that the Church draws her certainty about everything which has been revealed. Therefore, both sacred tradition and sacred Scripture are to be accepted and venerated with the same sense of devotion and reverence."

"Sacred tradition and sacred Scripture form one sacred deposit of the word of God, which is committed to the Church."

CHURCH'S TEACHING AUTHORITY

"The task of authentically interpreting the word of God, whether written or handed on, has been entrusted exclusively to the living teaching office of the Church, whose authority is exercised in the name of Jesus Christ. This teaching office is not above the word of God but serves it, teaching only what has been handed on . . . it draws from this one deposit of faith everything which it presents for belief as divinely revealed."

"It is clear, therefore, that sacred tradition, sacred Scripture and the teaching authority of the Church . . . are so linked and joined together that one cannot stand without the others, and that all together and each in its own way under the action of the one Holy Spirit contribute effectively to the salvation of souls."

The Bible

The Catholic Canon of Scripture (official list) consists of 45 books of the Old Testament and 27 works of the New Testament. This listing, attested to by tradition, was firm by the fifth century and was formally defined by the Council of Trent in 1546.

OLD TESTAMENT

The books of the Old Testament are grouped in four categories: Pentateuch, Historical Books, Wisdom Books and the Prophets.

Pentateuch: This is the collective name of the first five books.

Genesis, the book of origins, covers: religious prehistory, including accounts of creation, the original state of innocence and the Fall, the promise of salvation, patriarchs before and after the Deluge, the Tower of Babel narrative and genealogies; the covenant with Abraham and patriarchal history from Abraham to Joseph.

The other four books are Exodus, Leviticus, Numbers and Deuteronomy. Substantially, they identify the Israelites as God's Chosen People, cover their history from Egypt to the border of the Promised Land, contain the Mosaic Law and Covenant, and disclose the promise of salvation to come.

Three books bridge the gap between Deuteronomy and Samuel 1 and 2: Joshua, recording the fulfillment of Yahweh's promise to the Israelites in their conquest and occupation of Canaan under the leadership of Joshua; Judges, containing accounts of charismatic leaders of the tribes of Israel between the death of Joshua and the time of Samuel; Ruth, named for an ancestress of David, on the themes of filial piety, faith in Yahweh and the universality of salvation.

Historical Books: These contain a great deal of factual material but are unique in their interpretation of it in relation to the Mosaic Covenant on which the nation of Israel was founded and in accordance with which community and personal life were judged.

The books are: Samuel 1 and 2, from the end of Judges (c. 1020 B.C) to the end of the reign of King David (c. 961); Kings 1 and 2, from the last days of David to the start of the Babylonian Exile and destruction of the temple in Jerusalem (587); Chronicles 1 and 2, from the reign of Saul (c. 1020-1000) to the return of the people from exile (538); Ezra and Nehemiah, covering the reorganization of the community of the Chosen People after the Exile (458-394); Maccabees 1 and 2, recounting the struggle against the attempted suppression of Judaism by Syrians (168-142).

Tobit, Judith and Esther, listed with the historical books, are categorized as religious novels.

Wisdom Books: These books contain reflections on human experience in the context of the religious tradition of the Jews, for the purpose of understanding and coping with the problems of life: Job, Proverbs, Ecclesiastes, Wisdom and Sirach; also, Psalms, a collection of religious songs, and Song of Songs, a parable in poetic form about the love of God for His people.

Prophetic Books: These books contain severe judgments on the moral conduct of the Chosen People, religious teaching, historical background and the promise of salvation to come. The period of the canonical prophets extended from the first half of the eighth century B.C. (Amos) to the second half of the fifth century. The careers of earlier prophets — including Samuel, Gad, Nathan, Elijah and Elisha — are recounted in historical books.

The major prophets, so called because of the length of the books bearing their names, are Isaiah, Jeremiah, Ezekiel and Daniel; Lamentations and Baruch are related to Jeremiah. The minor prophets are Hosea, Joel, Amos, Obadiah, Jonah, Micah, Nahum, Habakkuk, Zephaniah, Haggai, Zechariah and Malachi.

Old Testament Dates

Significant dates and events of the pre-Christian era include the following.

The period of the great patriarchs (Abraham, Isaac and Jacob) extended from c. 1800 to c. 1600 B.C. The Israelites were in Egypt by c. 1600 and remained there until the Exodus, c. 1250. After their passage through the desert, they entered Canaan c. 1210 and were under the leadership of Judges until c. 1020.

Saul, the first king (c. 1020 to c. 1000), was succeeded by David (c. 1000 to c. 961) and Solomon (c. 961 to 922). The Temple was built during the reign of Solomon; after his death, the kingdom was divided into Israel (North) and Judah (South). Israel was conquered by Assyrians in 721.

Babylonians conquered Judah, destroyed Jerusalem and the Temple in 587 and drove many of the people into the Exile which lasted until 538. A second Temple was dedicated in 515. Restoration and reform of the Jewish religious and political community took place from 458 to 397.

The period of the Maccabees, who fought against the Syrians for the survival of Judaism, extended from 168 to 142. It was followed by the period of the Hasmonean dynasty from 135 to 37. Roman rule began in 63. Herod the Great, during the time of Roman sovereignty, was the King of Judah from 41 B.C. to 4 A.D.

NEW TESTAMENT

The initial proclamation of the coming of the Kingdom of God was made by Jesus in and through His person, teachings and actions, and especially through His passion, death and resurrection. This proclamation became the center of Christian faith and of the oral tradition with which the Good News of salvation was spread by apostolic preaching for several decades before it was committed to writing in the Gospels and other writings of the New Testament.

The Gospels

In the Gospels, the life and teaching of Jesus were not simply reported in a biographical manner for the purpose of preserving their memory, but were preached so as to motivate people to faith in and commitment to Christ and to offer the Church the basis of doctrine concerning faith and morals. The Evangelists presented the true sayings of Jesus and the events of His life in the light of the understanding they had under the inspiration and enlightenment of the Holy Spirit. They did not transform Christ into a mythical person, nor did they distort His teaching.

The core of all the Gospels consists of accounts of the suffering, death and resurrection of Jesus as central events in bringing about and establishing the New Covenant. Leading up to those accounts are others covering the mission of John the Baptizer and the ministry of Jesus, especially in Galilee and finally in Jerusalem. Infancy narratives are provided in Matthew and Luke.

Matthew, Mark and Luke are called the Synoptic Gospels because of the similarities among them. Mark, addressed to non-Jewish Christians, was written about A.D. 65; Matthew and Luke, for Jewish and non-Jewish Christians respectively, were written in the 70s or 80s. John, the most sublime and theological of the Gospels, was written sometime in the 90s.

Other Writings

Acts of the Apostles: This supplement to his Gospel was written by Luke in the 70s or 80s; it describes the origin and spread of the Christian communities to sometime in the early 60s.

Letters: Several of the Apostles wrote letters in response to the needs of the early Christian communities for doctrinal and moral instruction, disciplinary action, practical advice and exhortation to authentic Christian living. The dates of composition range from the early 50s to sometime in the 90s. Letters bearing the name of Paul are a primary and monumental source of the development of Christian theology: Romans, 1 and 2 Corinthians, Galatians, Ephesians, Philippians, Colossians, 1 and 2 Thessalonians, 1 and 2 Timothy, Titus, Philemon and Hebrews. The so-called Catholic Letters are: James; 1 and 2 Peter; 1, 2 and 3 John, and Jude.

Revelation: Written in the 90s along the lines of Johannine thought, this last book of the Bible is a symbolic and apocalyptic treatment of the struggle between good and evil; it includes a theme of hope and assurance to the Church concerning the eventual coming of the Lord in glory.

INTERPRETATION OF THE BIBLE

Hermeneutics is the science of biblical interpretation and explanation; in practice, this science is called exegesis.

The principles of hermeneutics are derived from various disciplines and many factors which have to be considered in explaining the Bible and its parts. These include: the original languages and languages of translation of the sacred texts, through philology and linguistics; the quality of texts, through textual criticism; literary forms and genres, through literary and form criticism; cultural, historical, geographical and other conditions which influenced the writers, through related studies; facts and truths of salvation history; the truths and analogy of faith.

Distinctive to biblical hermeneutics, which differs in important respects from literary interpretation in general, is the fact that the Bible, although written by human authors, is the work of divine inspiration in which God reveals His plan for the salvation of mankind through historical events and persons, and especially through the person and mission of Christ.

Summarily, in the words of the *Dogmatic Constitution on Revelation* issued by the Second Vatican Council: "The interpreter must investigate what meaning the sacred writer intended to express and actually expressed in particular circumstances as he used contemporary literary forms in accordance with the situation of his own time and culture. For the correct understanding of what the sacred author wanted to assert, due attention must be paid to the customary and characteristic styles of perceiving, speaking and narrating which prevailed at the time of the sacred writer, and to the customs men normally followed at that period in their everyday dealings with one another."

Analogy of Faith

"No less serious attention must be given to the content and unity of the whole of Scripture, if the meaning of the sacred texts is to be correctly brought to light. The living tradition of the whole Church must be taken into account along with the harmony which exists between elements of the faith. . . . All of what has been said about the way of interpreting Scripture is subject finally to the judgment of the Church, which carries out the divine commission and ministry of guarding and interpreting the word of God."

Teaching Authority and Infallibility

Responsibility for teaching doctrine and judging orthodoxy belongs, in the first place, to the magisterium, the official teaching authority of the Church.

This authority is personalized in the pope, the successor of St. Peter as head of the Church on earth, and in the bishops together and in union with the pope, as this authority was originally committed to Peter and to the whole college of Apostles under his leadership. They are the official teachers of the Church.

Others have auxiliary relationships with the magisterium: theologians, in the study and clarification of doctrine; teachers — priests, Religious, lay persons — who cooperate in spreading knowledge of religious truth; the faithful who, by their sense of faith and personal witness, contribute to the development of doctrine and the establishment of its relevance to life in the Church and in the world.

The magisterium, in the words of Pope Paul VI, "is a subordinate and faithful echo and secure interpreter of the divine word." It does not reveal new truths, "nor is it superior to sacred Scripture." Its competence extends to the limits of divine revelation manifested in Scripture and tradition and the living experience of the Church with respect to matters of faith, morals and related subjects.

Official teaching in these areas is infallible when it is formally defined, for belief and acceptance by all members of the Church, by the pope acting as the supreme shepherd of the flock of Christ, and when doctrine is proposed and taught with moral unanimity of bishops with the pope in a solemn collegial manner as in an ecumenical council, and/or in the ordinary course of events. Even when not infallibly defined, official teaching in the areas of faith and morals is authoritative and requires religious assent.

The teachings of the magisterium are documented in creeds, formulas of faith, decrees and enactments of ecumenical and particular councils, various kinds of doctrinal statements and other teaching instruments. They are also incorporated into the liturgy, with the result that the law of prayer is said to be a law of belief.

DOCTRINE ON INFALLIBILITY

The essential points of doctrine concerning infallibility in the Church and the infallibility of the pope were reaffirmed by the Second Vatican Council, in the *Dogmatic Constitution on the Church*, as follows.

"This infallibility with which the divine Redeemer willed His Church to be endowed in defining a doctrine of faith and morals extends as far as extends the deposit of divine revelation, which must be religiously guarded and faithfully expounded. This is the infallibility which the Roman Pontiff, the head of the college of bishops, enjoys in virtue of his office when, as the supreme shepherd and teacher of all the faithful, who confirms his brethren in the faith, he proclaims by a definitive act some doctrine of faith or morals. Therefore his definitions, of themselves, and not from the consent of the Church, are justly styled irreformable, for they are pronounced with the assistance of the Holy Spirit, an assistance promised to him in blessed Peter. Therefore they need no approval of others, nor do they allow an appeal to any other judgment. For then the Roman Pontiff is not pronouncing judgment as a private person. Rather, as the supreme teacher of the universal Church, as one in whom the charism of the infallibility of the Church is individually present, he is expounding or defending a doctrine of Catholic faith.''

"The infallibility promised to the Church resides also in the body of bishops when that body exercises supreme teaching authority with the successor of Peter. To the resultant definitions the assent of the Church can never be wanting, on account of the activity of that same Holy Spirit whereby the flock of Christ is preserved and progresses in unity of faith.''

"But when either the Roman Pontiff or the body of bishops together with him defines a judgment, they pronounce it in accord with revelation itself. All are obliged to maintain and be ruled by this revelation, which, as written or preserved by tradition, is transmitted in its entirety through the legitimate succession of bishops and especially through the care of the Roman Pontiff himself.''

"Under the guiding light of the Spirit of truth, revelation is thus religiously preserved and faithfully expounded in the Church. The Roman Pontiff and the bishops, in view of their office and of the importance of the matter, strive painstakingly and by appropriate means to inquire properly into the revelation and to give apt expression to its contents. But they do not allow that there could be any new public revelation pertaining to the divine deposit of faith.''

AUTHENTIC TEACHING

The pope rarely speaks *ex cathedra* — that is, "from the chair" of St. Peter — for the purpose of making an infallible pronouncement. More often and in various other ways, he states authentic teaching in line with Scripture, tradition, the living experience of the Church and the whole analogy of faith. Of such teaching, the Second Vatican Council declared:

"Religious submission of will and of mind must be shown in a special way to the authentic teaching authority of the Roman Pontiff, even when he is not speaking *ex cathedra*. That is, it must be shown in such a way that his supreme magisterium is acknowledged with reverence, and that the judgments made by him are sincerely adhered to, according to his manifest mind and will. His mind and will in the matter may be known chiefly from the character of the documents, from his frequent repetition of the same doctrine, or from his manner of speaking."

With respect to bishops, the constitution states: "They are authentic teachers, that is, teachers endowed with the authority of Christ, who preach to the people committed to them the faith they must believe and put into practice. By the light of the Holy Spirit, they make that faith clear, bringing forth from the treasury of revelation new things and old, making faith bear fruit and vigilantly warding off any errors which threaten their flock."

"Bishops, teaching in communion with the Roman Pontiff, are to be respected by all as witnesses to divine and Catholic truth. In matters of faith and morals, the bishops speak in the name of Christ, and the faithful are to accept their teaching and adhere to it with a religious assent of soul."

PAPAL ENCYCLICALS

Papal encyclicals, perhaps the best known of the various types of papal documents, are pastoral letters addressed by a pope to the whole Church. In general, they concern matters of doctrine, morals, worship, discipline, devotion and subjects worthy of historical commemoration. A few encyclicals, notably *Pacem in Terris* by John XXIII and *Ecclesiam Suam* by Paul VI, have been addressed to "all men of good will" as well as to bishops and the faithful in communion with the Church.

The authority of encyclicals was stated by Pius XII in the encyclical *Humani Generis* Aug. 12, 1950.

"Nor must it be thought that what is contained in encyclical letters does not of itself demand assent, on the pretext that the popes do not exercise in them the supreme power of their teaching authority. Rather, such teachings belong to the ordinary magisterium, of which it is true to say: 'He who hears you, hears me' (Lk. 10:16); for the most part, too, what is expounded and inculcated in encyclical letters already appertains to Catholic doctrine for other reasons. But if the supreme pontiffs in their official documents purposely pass judgment on a matter debated until then, it is obvious to all that the matter, according to the mind and will of the same pontiffs, cannot be considered any longer a question open for discussion among theologians."

Other documents and acts of a pope include papal bulls, apostolic constitutions, apostolic letters, apostolic exhortations, encyclical epistles, allocutions, and documents on particular subjects issued on the pope's own initiative (*motu proprio*).

THEOLOGY

Theology is knowledge of God and religion, deriving from and based on the data of divine revelation, organized and systematized according to some kind of scientific method. It involves systematic study and presentation of the truths of divine revelation in sacred Scripture, tradition and the teaching of the Church.

The Second Vatican Council, in its *Constitution on Revelation*, made the following declaration about theology and its relation to divine revelation: "Sacred theology rests on the written word of God, together with sacred tradition, as its primary and perpetual foundation. By scrutinizing in the light of faith all truth stored up in the mystery of Christ, theology is most powerfully strengthened and constantly rejuvenated by that word. For the sacred Scriptures contain the word of God and, since they are inspired, really are the word of God; and so the study of the sacred page is, as it were, the soul of sacred theology."

Theology has been divided under various subject headings. Some of the major fields have been: dogma (systematic theology), moral, pastoral, ascetics (the practice of virtue and means of attaining holiness and perfection), mysticism (higher states of religious experience). Other subject headings include ecumenism (Christian unity, interfaith relations), ecclesiology (the nature and constitution of the Church), Mariology (doctrine concerning the Blessed Virgin Mary), the sacraments, etc.

Pope John Paul II, addressing theologians Nov. 1, 1982, at the Pontifical University of Salamanca, noted that theology, which is necessary for "creative as well as faithful" renewal of the Church, must flow from faith because "doing theology is . . . a task exclusively proper to the believer as believer; it is a task vitally aroused and sustained at every moment by faith."

"Christian faith is ecclesial," he added. "One cannot believe in Christ without believing in the Church, 'the body of Christ'; one cannot believe with Catholic faith within the Church without believing in her irrenounceable magisterium as well."

He called theology "ecclesial science at the service of the Church" and said it must be "dynamically integrated into the Church's mission. Thus, the theologian's task has the character of an ecclesial mission, as a participation in the Church's evangelizing mission and as outstanding service to the ecclesial community. This is where the theologian's grave responsibility rests."

Apostles and Evangelists

The Apostles were the men selected, trained and commissioned by Christ to preach the Gospel, to baptize, to establish, direct and care for his Church as servants of God and stewards of his mysteries. They were the first bishops of the Church.

St. Matthew's Gospel lists the Apostles in this order: Peter, Andrew, James the Greater, John, Philip, Bartholomew, Thomas, Matthew, James the Less, Jude, Simon and Judas Iscariot. Matthias was elected to fill the place of Judas. Paul became an Apostle by a special call from Christ. Barnabas was called an Apostle.

Two of the Evangelists, John and Matthew, were Apostles. The other two, Luke and Mark, were closely associated with the apostolic college.

Andrew: Born in Bethsaida, brother of Peter, disciple of John the Baptist, a fisherman, the first Apostle called; according to legend, preached the Gospel in northern Greece, Epirus and Scythia, and was martyred at Patras about 70; in art, is represented with an x-shaped cross, called St. Andrew's Cross; feast, Nov. 30; is honored as the patron of Russia and Scotland.

Barnabas: Originally called Joseph but named Barnabas by the Apostles, among whom he is ranked because of his collaboration with Paul; a Jew of the Diaspora, born in Cyprus; a cousin of Mark and member of the Christian community at Jerusalem; influenced the Apostles to accept Paul, with whom he became a pioneer missionary outside Palestine and Syria, to Antioch, Cyprus and southern Asia Minor; legend says he was martyred in Cyprus during the Neronian persecution; feast, June 11.

Bartholomew (Nathaniel): A friend of Philip; according to various traditions, preached the Gospel in Ethiopia, India, Persia and Armenia, where he was martyred by being flayed and beheaded; in art, is depicted holding a knife, an instrument of his death; feast, Aug. 24 in the Roman Rite, Aug. 25 in the Byzantine Rite.

James the Greater: A Galilean, son of Zebedee, brother of John (with whom he was called a "Son of Thunder"), a fisherman; with Peter and John, witnessed the raising of Jairus' daughter to life, the transfiguration, the agony of Jesus in the Garden of Gethsemani; first of the Apostles to die, by the sword in 44 during the rule of Herod Agrippa; there is doubt about a journey legend says he made to Spain and also about the authenticity of relics said to be his at Santiago de Compostela; in art, is depicted carrying a pilgrim's bell; feast, July 25 in the Roman Rite, Apr. 30 in the Byzantine Rite.

James the Less: Son of Alphaeus, called "Less" because he was younger in age or shorter in stature than James the Greater; one of the Catholic Letters bears his name; was stoned to death in 62 or thrown from the top of the temple in Jerusalem and clubbed to death in 66; in art, is depicted with a club or heavy staff; feast, May 3 in the Roman Rite, Oct. 9 in the Byzantine Rite.

John: A Galilean, son of Zebedee, brother of James the Greater (with whom he was called a "Son of Thunder"), a fisherman, probably a disciple of John the Baptist, one of the Evangelists, called the "Beloved Disciple"; with Peter and James the Greater, witnessed the raising of Jairus' daughter to life, the transfiguration, the agony of Jesus in the Garden of Gethsemani; Mary was commended to his special care by Christ; the fourth Gospel, three Catholic Letters and Revelation bear his name; according to various accounts, lived at Ephesus in Asia Minor for some time and died a natural death about 100; in art, is represented by an eagle, symbolic of the sublimity of the contents of his Gospel; feast, Dec. 27 in the Roman Rite, May 8 in the Byzantine Rite.

Jude Thaddeus: One of the Catholic Letters, the shortest, bears his name; various traditions say he preached the Gospel in Mesopotamia, Persia and elsewhere, and was martyred; in art, is depicted with a halberd, the instrument of his death; feast, Oct. 28 in the Roman Rite, June 19 in the Byzantine Rite.

Luke: A Greek convert to the Christian community, called "our most dear physician" by Paul, of whom he was a missionary companion; author of the third Gospel and Acts of the Apostles; the place — Achaia, Bithynia, Egypt — and circumstances of his death are not certain; in art, is depicted as a man, a writer, or an ox (because his Gospel starts at the scene of temple sacrifice); feast, Oct. 18.

Mark: A cousin of Barnabas and member of the first Christian community at Jerusalem; a missionary companion of Paul and Barnabas, then of Peter; author of the Gospel which bears his name; according to legend, founded the Church at Alexandria, was bishop there and was martyred in the streets of the city; in art, is depicted with his Gospel and a winged lion, symbolic of the voice of John the Baptist crying in the wilderness, at the beginning of his Gospel; feast, Apr. 25.

Matthew: A Galilean, called Levi by Luke and John and the son of Alphaeus by Mark, a tax collector, one of the Evangelists; according to various accounts, preached the Gospel in Judea, Ethiopia, Persia and Parthia, and was martyred; in art, is depicted with a spear, the instrument of his death, and as a winged man in his role as Evangelist; feast, Sept. 21 in the Roman Rite, Nov. 16 in the Byzantine Rite.

Matthias: A disciple of Jesus whom the faithful 11 Apostles chose to replace Judas before the Resurrection; uncertain traditions report that he preached the Gospel in Palestine, Cappadocia or Ethiopia; in art, is represented with a cross and a halberd, the instruments of his death as a martyr; feast, May 14 in the Roman Rite, Aug. 9 in the Byzantine Rite.

Paul: Born at Tarsus, of the tribe of Benjamin, a Roman citizen; participated in the persecution of Christians until the time of his miraculous conversion on the way to Damascus; called by Christ, who revealed himself to him in a special way; became the Apostle of the Gentiles, among whom he did most of his preaching in the course of three major missionary journeys through areas north of Palestine, Cyprus, Asia Minor and Greece; 14 letters bear his name; two years of imprisonment at Rome, following initial arrest in Jerusalem and confinement at Caesarea, ended with martyrdom, by beheading, outside the walls of the city in 64 or 67 during the Neronian persecution; in art, is depicted in various ways with St. Peter, with a sword, in the scene of his conversion; feasts, June 29, Jan. 25 (Roman Rite).

Peter: Simon, son of Jonah, born in Bethsaida, brother of Andrew, a fisherman; called Cephas or Peter by Christ who made him the chief of the Apostles and head of the Church as His vicar; named first in the listings of Apostles in the Synoptic Gospels and the Acts of the Apostles; with James the Greater and John, witnessed the raising of Jairus' daughter to life, the transfiguration, the agony of Jesus in the Garden of Gethsemani; was the first to preach the Gospel in and around Jerusalem and was the leader of the first Christian community there; established a local church in Antioch; presided over the Council of Jerusalem in 51; wrote two Catholic Letters to the Christians in Asia Minor; established his see in Rome where he spent his last years and was martyred by crucifixion in 64 or 67 during the Neronian persecution; in art, is depicted carrying two keys, symbolic of his primacy in the Church; feasts, June 29, Feb. 22 (Roman Rite).

Philip: Born in Bethsaida; according to legend, preached the Gospel in Phrygia where he suffered martyrdom by crucifixion; feast, May 3 in the Roman Rite, Nov. 14 in the Byzantine Rite.

Simon: Called the Cananean or the Zealot; according to legend, preached in various places in the Middle East and suffered martyrdom by being sawed in two; in art, is depicted with a saw, the instrument of his death, or a book, symbolic of his zeal for the law; feast, Oct. 28 in the Roman Rite, May 10 in the Byzantine Rite.

Thomas (Didymus): Notable for his initial incredulity regarding the resurrection and his subsequent forthright confession of the divinity of Christ risen from the dead; according to legend, preached the Gospel in places from the Caspian Sea to the Persian Gulf and eventually reached India where he was martyred near Madras; Thomas Christians trace their origin to him; in art, is depicted kneeling before the risen Christ, or with a carpenter's rule and square; feast, July 3 in the Roman Rite, Oct. 6 in the Byzantine Rite.

Judas: A Judean, from Carioth; keeper of the purse in the apostolic band; called a petty thief by John; betrayed Christ for 30 pieces of silver which, after confessing the betrayal of an innocent man, he cast into the temple; Matthew says he hanged himself; Acts states that he swelled up and burst open; it is thought he betrayed Christ because of disillusionment and unwillingness to accept the concept of a suffering Messiah and personal suffering of his own as an Apostle.

Ecumenical Councils

An ecumenical council is an assembly of the college of bishops, with and under the presidency of the pope, which has supreme authority over the Church in matters pertaining to faith, morals, worship and discipline.

The councils have played a highly significant role in the history of the Church by witnessing to and defining truths of revelation, by shaping forms of worship and discipline, and by promoting measures for the ever-necessary reform and renewal of Catholic life. In general, they have represented attempts of the Church to mobilize itself in times of crisis for self-preservation, self-purification and growth.

The Second Vatican Council stated as follows with respect to these councils: "The supreme authority with which this college (of bishops) is empowered over the whole Church is exercised in a solemn way through an ecumenical council. A council is never ecumenical unless it is confirmed or at least accepted as such by the successor of Peter. It is the prerogative of the Roman Pontiff to convoke these councils, to preside over them, and to confirm them."

The pope is the head of an ecumenical council; he presides over it either personally or through legates. Conciliar decrees and other actions have binding force only when confirmed and promulgated by him. If a pope dies during a council, it is suspended until reconvened by another pope. An ecumenical council is not superior to a pope; hence, there is no appeal from a pope to a council.

Collectively, the bishops with the pope represent the whole Church. They do this not as democratic representatives of the faithful in a kind of church parliament, but as the successors of the Apostles with divinely given authority, care and responsibility over the whole Church.

All and only bishops who are members of the college of bishops have the right and duty to participate in an ecumenical council with a deliberative vote. The pope can call on others to attend and can determine the manner of their participation.

Basic legislation concerning ecumenical councils is contained in the Code of Canon Law. Basic doctrinal considerations were stated by the Second Vatican Council in the *Dogmatic Constitution on the Church*.

BACKGROUND

Ecumenical councils had their prototype in the Council of Jerusalem in 51, at which the Apostles under the leadership of St. Peter decided that converts to the Christian faith were not obliged to observe all the prescriptions of Old Testament law (Acts 15). As early as the second century, bishops got together in regional meetings, synods or councils to take common action for the doctrinal and pastoral good of their communities of faithful. The expansion of such limited assemblies to ecumenical councils was a logical and historical evolution.

Emperors were active in summoning or convoking the first eight councils, especially the first five and the eighth. Among reasons for intervention of this kind were the facts that the emperors regarded themselves as guardians of the faith; that the settlement of religious controversies, which had repercussions in political and social turmoil, served the cause of peace in the state; and that the emperors had at their disposal ways and means of facilitating gatherings of bishops. Imperial actions, however, did not account for the formally ecumenical nature of the councils.

Some councils were attended by relatively few bishops, and the ecumenical character of several was open to question for a time. However, confirmation and de facto recognition of their actions by popes and subsequent councils established them as ecumenical.

The first eight ecumenical councils were held in the East; the other 13, in the West. The majority of separated Eastern Churches — e.g., the Orthodox — recognize the ecumenical character of the first seven councils, which formulated a great deal of basic doctrine. Nestorians, however, acknowledge only the first two councils; the Monophysite Armenians, Syrians, and Copts acknowledge the first three.

THE 21 COUNCILS

The 21 ecumenical councils in the history of the Church are listed below, with indication of their names or titles (taken from the names of the places where they were held); the dates; the reigning and/or approving popes; the most significant actions.

1. Nicaea I, 325; St. Sylvester I. Condemned Arianism, which denied the divinity of Christ; contributed to formulation of the Nicene Creed, fixed the date of Easter; passed regulations concerning clerical discipline; adopted the civil division of the Empire as the model for the organization of the Church.

2. Constantinople I, 381; St. Damasus I. Condemned various brands of Arianism, and Macedonianism which denied the divinity of the Holy Spirit; contributed to formulation of the Nicene Creed; approved a canon which made the bishop of Constantinople the ranking prelate in the East, with primacy next to that of the pope. Doubt about the ecumenical character of this council was resolved by the ratification of its acts by popes and the Council of Chalcedon.

3. Ephesus, 431; St. Celestine I. Condemned Nestorianism, which denied the real unity of the divine and human natures in the Person of Christ; defined *Theotokos* ("Bearer of God") as the title of Mary, Mother of the Son of God made Man; condemned Pelagianism, which reduced the supernatural to the natural order of things.

4. Chalcedon, 451; St. Leo I. Condemned: Monophysitism, also called Eutychianism, which denied the humanity of Christ by holding that He had only one, the divine, nature; and the Monophysite Robber Synod of Ephesus, of 449.

5. Constantinople II, 553; Vigilius. Condemned the Three Chapters, Nestorian-tainted writings of Theodore of Mopsuestia, Theodoret of Cyrus and Ibas of Edessa.

6. Constantinople III, 680-81; St. Agatho, St. Leo II. Condemned Monothelitism, which held that there was only one will, the divine, in Christ; censured Pope Honorius I for a letter to Sergius, bishop of Constantinople, in which he made an ambiguous but not infallible statement about the unity of will and/or operation in Christ. Constantinople III is also called the Trullan Council because its sessions were held in the domed hall, Trullos, of the imperial palace.

7. Nicaea II, 787; Adrian I. Condemned: Iconoclasm, which held that the use of images was idolatry; and Adoptionism, which claimed that Christ was not the Son of God by nature but only by adoption. This was the last council regarded as ecumenical by Orthodox Churches.

8. Constantinople IV, 869-70; Adrian II. Condemned Iconoclasm; condemned and deposed Photius as patriarch of Constantinople, restored Ignatius to the patriarchate. This was the last ecumenical council held in the East. It was first called ecumenical by canonists toward the end of the 11th century.

9. Lateran I, 1123; Callistus II. Endorsed provisions of the Concordat of Worms concerning the investiture of prelates; approved reform measures in 25 canons.

10. Lateran II, 1139; Innocent II. Adopted measures against a schism organized by antipope Anacletus; approved 30 disciplinary measures and canons, one of which stated that holy orders is an invalidating impediment to marriage.

11. Lateran III, 1179; Alexander III. Enacted measures against the Waldenses and Albigensians; approved reform decrees in 17 canons; provided that popes be elected by two-thirds vote of the cardinals.

12. Lateran IV, 1215; Innocent III. Ordered annual confession and Communion; defined and made first official use of the term "transubstantiation" (change of substance of bread and wine into the Body and Blood of Christ); adopted measures to counteract the Cathari and Albigensians; approved 70 canons.

13. Lyons I, 1245; Innocent IV. Confirmed the deposition of Emperor Frederick II; approved 22 canons.

14. Lyons II, 1274; Gregory X. Accomplished a temporary reunion of separated Eastern Churches with the Roman Church; issued regulations concerning conclaves for papal elections; approved 31 canons.

15. Vienne, 1311-12; Clement V. Suppressed the Knights Templar; enacted a number of reform decrees.

16. Constance, 1414-18; Gregory XII, Martin V. Took successful action to end the Western Schism; rejected the teachings of Wycliff; condemned Hus as a heretic. One decree, passed in the earlier stages of the council, asserted the superiority of an ecumenical council over the pope; this was later rejected.

17. Florence, 1438-45; Eugene IV. Preliminary sessions were held at Basel and Ferrara before definitive work was accomplished at Florence. Reaffirmed the primacy of the pope against the claims of conciliarists that an ecumenical council is superior to the pope; formulated and approved decrees of union — with Greeks, Armenians and Jacobites — which failed to gain general or lasting acceptance in the East.

18. Lateran V, 1512-17; Julius II, Leo X. Stated the relation and position of the pope with respect to an ecumenical council; acted to counteract the Pragmatic Sanction of Bourges and exaggerated claims of liberty by the French Church; condemned erroneous teachings concerning the nature of the human soul; stated doctrine concerning indulgences. The council reflected concern for abuses in the Church and the need for reforms but failed to take decisive action in the years immediately preceding the Reformation.

19. Trent, 1545-63; Paul III, Julius III, Pius IV. Issued a great number of decrees concerning doctrinal matters opposed by the Reformers, and mobilized the Counter-Reformation. Definitions covered the rule of faith, the nature of justification, grace, faith, original sin and its effects, the seven sacraments, the sacrificial nature of the Mass, the veneration of saints, use of sacred images, belief in purgatory, the doctrine of indulgences, the jurisdiction of the pope over the whole Church. Initiated many reforms for renewal in the liturgy and general discipline in the Church, the promotion of religious instruction, the education of the clergy through the foundation of seminaries, etc. Trent ranks with Vatican II as the greatest ecumenical council held in the West.

20. Vatican I, 1869-70; Pius IX. Defined papal primacy and infallibility in a dogmatic constitution on the Church; covered natural religion, revelation, faith, and the relations between faith and reason in a dogmatic constitution on the Catholic faith. The council suspended sessions Sept. 1 and was adjourned Oct 20, 1870.

Vatican II

The Second Vatican Council, which was forecast by Pope John XXIII Jan. 25, 1959, was held in four sessions in St. Peter's Basilica.

Pope John convoked it and opened the first session, which ran from Oct. 11 to Dec. 8, 1962. Following John's death June 3, 1963, Pope Paul VI reconvened the council for the other three sessions, which ran from Sept. 29 to Dec. 4, 1963; Sept. 14 to Nov. 21, 1964; Sept. 14 to Dec. 8, 1965.

A total of 2,860 Fathers participated in council proceedings, and attendance at meetings varied between 2,000 and 2,500. For various reasons, including the denial of exit from Communist-dominated countries, 274 Fathers could not attend.

The council formulated and promulgated 16 documents — two dogmatic and two pastoral constitutions, nine decrees and three declarations — all of which reflect its basic pastoral orientation toward renewal and reform in the Church. Given below are the Latin and English titles of the documents and their dates of promulgation.

* *Lumen Gentium* (Dogmatic Constitution on the Church), Nov. 21, 1964.
* *Dei Verbum* (Dogmatic Constitution on Divine Revelation), Nov. 18, 1965.
* *Sacrosanctum Concilium* (Constitution on the Sacred Liturgy), Dec. 4, 1963.
* *Gaudium et Spes* (Pastoral Constitution on the Church in the Modern World), Dec. 7, 1965.
* *Christus Dominus* (Decree on the Bishops' Pastoral Office in the Church), Oct. 28, 1965.
* *Ad Gentes* (Decree on the Church's Missionary Activity), Dec. 7, 1965.
* *Unitatis Redintegratio* (Decree on Ecumenism), Nov. 21, 1964.
* *Orientalium Ecclesiarum* (Decree on Eastern Catholic Churches), Nov. 21, 1964.
* *Presbyterorum Ordinis* (Decree on the Ministry and Life of Priests), Dec. 7, 1965.
* *Optatam Totius* (Decree on Priestly Formation), Oct. 28, 1965.
* *Perfectae Caritatis* (Decree on the Appropriate Renewal of the Religious Life), Oct. 28, 1965.
* *Apostolicam Actuositatem* (Decree on the Apostolate of the Laity), Nov. 18, 1965.
* *Inter Mirifica* (Decree on the Instruments of Social Communication), Dec. 4, 1963.
* *Dignitatis Humanae* (Declaration on Religious Freedom), Dec. 7, 1965.
* *Nostra Aetate* (Declaration on the Relationship of the Church to Non-Christian Religions), Oct. 28, 1965.
* *Gravissimum Educationis* (Declaration on Christian Education), Oct. 28, 1965.

The key documents were the four constitutions, which set the ideological basis for all the others. To date, the documents with the most visible effects are those on the liturgy, the Church, the Church in the world, ecumenism, the renewal of religious life, the life and ministry of priests, the lay apostolate.

The main business of the council was to explore and make explicit dimensions of doctrine and Christian life requiring emphasis for the full development of the Church and the better accomplishment of its mission in the contemporary world.

Fathers and Doctors of the Church

The writers listed below were outstanding and authoritative witnesses to authentic Christian belief and practice, and played significant roles in giving them expression.

APOSTOLIC FATHERS

Apostolic Fathers were Christian writers of the first and second centuries whose writings echo genuine apostolic teaching.

Chief in importance are: St. Clement (d. 97), bishop of Rome and third successor of St. Peter in the papacy; St. Ignatius (50-107), bishop of Antioch and second successor of St. Peter in that see, reputed to be a disciple of St. John; St. Polycarp (69-155), bishop of Smyrna and a disciple of St. John. The authors of the *Didache* and the *Epistle of Barnabas* are also numbered among the Apostolic Fathers.

Other early ecclesiastical writers included: St. Justin, martyr (100-165), of Asia Minor and Rome, a layman and apologist; St. Irenaeus (130-202), bishop of Lyons, who opposed Gnosticism; and St. Cyprian (210-258), bishop of Carthage, who opposed Novatianism.

FATHERS AND DOCTORS

The Fathers of the Church were theologians and writers of the first eight centuries who were outstanding for sanctity and learning. They were such authoritative witnesses to the belief and teaching of the Church that their unanimous acceptance of doctrines as divinely revealed has been regarded as evidence that such doctrines were so received by the Church in line with apostolic tradition and sacred Scripture. Their unanimous rejection of doctrines branded them as heretical. Their writings, however, were not necessarily free of error in all respects.

The greatest of these Fathers were: Sts. Ambrose, Augustine, Jerome and Gregory the Great in the West; Sts. John Chrysostom, Basil the Great, Gregory of Nazianzen and Athanasius in the East.

The Doctors of the Church were ecclesiastical writers of eminent learning and sanctity who have been given this title because of the great advantage the Church has derived from their work. Their writings, however, were not necessarily free of error in all respects.

Albert the Great, St. (1200-1280): Born in Swabia, Germany; Dominican; bishop of Regensburg (1260-1262); wrote extensively on logic, natural sciences, ethics, metaphysics, Scripture, systematic theology; contributed to development of Scholasticism; teacher of St. Thomas Aquinas; canonized and proclaimed doctor, 1931; named patron of natural scientists, 1941; called Doctor Universalis, Doctor Expertus; feast, Nov. 15.

Alphonsus Liguori, St. (1696-1787): Born near Naples, Italy; bishop of Saint Agatha of the Goths (1762-1775); founder of the Redemptorists; in addition to his principal work, *Theologiae Moralis,* wrote on prayer, the spiritual life and doctrinal subjects in response to controversy; canonized, 1839; proclaimed doctor, 1871; named patron of confessors and moralists, 1950; feast, Aug. 1.

Ambrose, St. (340-397): Born in Trier, Germany; bishop of Milan (374-397); one of the strongest opponents of Arianism in the West; his homilies and other writings — on faith, the Holy Spirit, the incarnation, the sacraments and other subjects — were pastoral and practical; influenced the development of a liturgy at Milan which was named for him; Father and Doctor of the Church; feast, Dec. 7.

Anselm, St. (1033-1109): Born in Aosta, Piedmont, Italy; Benedictine; archbishop of Canterbury (1093-1109); in addition to his principal work, *Cur Deus Homo,* on the atonement and reconciliation of man with God through Christ, wrote about the existence and attributes of God and defended the *Filioque* explanation of the procession of the Holy Spirit from the Father and the Son; proclaimed doctor, 1720; called Father of Scholasticism; feast, Apr. 21.

Anthony of Padua, St. (1195-1231): Born in Lisbon, Portugal; first theologian of the Franciscan Order; preacher; canonized, 1232; proclaimed doctor, 1946; called Evangelical Doctor; feast, June 13.

Athanasius, St. (c. 297-373): Born in Alexandria, Egypt; bishop of Alexandria (328-373); participant in the Council of Nicaea I while still a deacon; dominant opponent of Arians whose errors regarding Christ he refuted in *Apology against the Arians, Discourses against the Arians* and other works; Father and Doctor of the Church; called Father of Orthodoxy; feast, May 2.

Augustine, St. (354-430): Born in Tagaste, North Africa; bishop of Hippo (395-430) after conversion from Manichaeism; works include the autobiographical and mystical *Confessions, City of God,* treatises on the Trinity, grace, passages of the Bible and doctrines called into question and denied by Manichaeans, Pelagians and Donatists; had strong and lasting influence on Christian theology and philosophy; Father and Doctor of the Church; called Doctor of Grace; feast, Aug. 28.

Basil the Great, St. (c. 329-379): Born in Caesarea, Cappadocia, Asia Minor; bishop of Caesarea (370-379); wrote three books *Contra Eunomium* in refutation of Arian errors, a treatise on the Holy Spirit, many homilies and several rules for monastic life, on which he had lasting influence; Father and Doctor of the Church; called Father of Monasticism in the East; feast, Jan. 2.

Bede the Venerable, St. (c. 673-735): Born in Northumberland, England; Benedictine; in addition to his principal work, *Ecclesiastical History of the English Nation* (covering the period 597-731), wrote scriptural commentaries; regarded as probably the most learned man in West Europe at time; called Father of English History; feast, May 25.

Bernard of Clairvaux, St. (c. 1090-1153): Born near Dijon, France; abbot; monastic reformer, called the second founder of the Cistercian Order; mystical theologian with great influence on devotional life; opponent of the rationalism brought forward by Abelard and others; canonized, 1174; proclaimed doctor, 1830; called Mellifluous Doctor because of his eloquence; feast, Aug. 20.

Bonaventure, St. (c. 1217-1274): Born near Viterbo, Italy; Franciscan; bishop of Albano (1273-1274); cardinal; wrote *Itinerarium Mentis in Deum, De Reductione Artium ad Theologiam, Breviloquium,* scriptural commentaries, additional mystical works affecting devotional life and a life of St. Francis of Assisi; canonized, 1482; proclaimed doctor, 1588; called Seraphic Doctor; feast, July 15.

Catherine of Siena, St. (c. 1347-1380): Born in Siena, Italy; member of the Third Order of St. Dominic; mystic; authored a long series of letters, mainly concerning spiritual instruction and encouragement, to associates, and *Dialogue,* a spiritual testament in four treatises; was active in support of a crusade against the Turks and efforts to end war between papal forces and the Florentine allies; had great influence in inducing Gregory XI to return himself and the Curia to Rome in 1376, to end the Avignon period of the papacy; canonized, 1461; proclaimed the second woman doctor, Oct. 4, 1970; feast, Apr. 29.

Cyril of Alexandria, St. (c. 376-444): Born in Egypt; bishop of Alexandria (412-444); wrote treatises on the Trinity, the incarnation and other subjects, mostly in refutation of Nestorian errors; made key contributions to the development of Christology; presided at the Council of Ephesus, 431; proclaimed doctor, 1882; feast, June 27.

Cyril of Jerusalem, St. (c.315-387): Bishop of Jerusalem (350-387); a vigorous opponent of Arianism; principal work, *Catecheses,* a pre-baptismal explanation of the creed of Jerusalem; proclaimed doctor, 1882; feast, Mar. 18.

Ephraem, St. (c. 306-373): Born in Nisibis, Mesopotamia; counteracted spread of Gnostic and Arian errors with poems, hymns of his own composition; wrote also on Eucharist, Mary; proclaimed doctor, 1920; called Deacon of Edessa, Harp of the Holy Spirit; feast, June 9.

Francis de Sales, St. (1567-1622): Born in Savoy; bishop of Geneva (1602-1622); spiritual writer with strong influence on devotional life through treatises such as *Introduction to a Devout Life,* and *The Love of God;* canonized, 1665; proclaimed doctor, 1877; patron of Catholic writers and the Catholic press; feast, Jan. 24.

Gregory Nazianzen, St. (c. 330-c. 390): Born in Arianzus, Cappadocia, Asia Minor; bishop of Constantinople (381-390); vigorous opponent of Arianism; in addition to five theological discourses on the Nicene Creed and the Trinity for which he is best known, wrote letters and poetry; Father and Doctor of the Church; called the Christian Demosthenes because of his eloquence and, in the Eastern Church, The Theologian; feast, Jan. 2.

Gregory I, the Great, St. (c. 540-604): Born in Rome; pope (590-604); wrote many scriptural commentaries, a compendium of theology in the *Book of Morals* based on Job, *Dialogues* concerning the lives of saints, the immortality of the soul, death, purgatory, heaven and hell, and 14 books of letters; enforced papal supremacy and established the position of the pope vis-a-vis the emperor; worked for clerical and monastic reform and the observance of clerical celibacy; Father and Doctor of the Church; feast, Sept. 3.

Hilary of Poitiers, St. (c. 315-368): Born in Poitiers, France; bishop of Poitiers (c. 353-368); wrote *De Synodis,* with the Arian controversy in mind, and *De Trinitate,* the first lengthy study of the doctrine in Latin; introduced Eastern theology to the West; contributed to the development of hymnology; proclaimed doctor, 1851; called the Athanasius of the West because of his vigorous defense of the divinity of Christ against Arians; feast, Jan. 13.

Isidore of Seville, St. (c. 560-636): Born in Cartagena, Spain; bishop of Seville (c. 600-636); in addition to his principal work, *Etymologiae,* an encyclopedia of the knowledge of his day, wrote on theological and historical subjects; regarded as the most learned man of his time; proclaimed doctor, 1722; feast, Apr. 4.

Jerome, St. (c. 343-420): Born in Stridon, Dalmatia; translated the Old Testament from Hebrew into Latin and revised the existing Latin translation of the New Testament to produce the Vulgate version of the Bible; wrote scriptural commentaries and treatises on matters of controversy; regarded as Father and Doctor of the Church from the eighth century; called Father of Biblical Science; feast, Sept. 30.

John Chrysostom, St. (c. 347-407): Born in Antioch, Asia Minor; archbishop of Constantinople (398-407); wrote homilies, scriptural commentaries and letters of wide influence in addition to a classical treatise on the priesthood; proclaimed doctor by the Council of Chalcedon, 451; called the greatest of the Greek Fathers; named patron of preachers, 1909; called Golden-Mouthed because of his eloquence; feast, Sept. 13.

John Damascene, St. (c. 675-c. 749): Born in Damascus, Syria; monk; wrote *Fountain of Wisdom,* a three-part work including a history of heresies and an exposition of the Christian faith, three *Discourses against the Iconoclasts,* homilies on Mary, biblical commentaries and treatises on moral subjects; proclaimed doctor, 1890; called Golden Speaker because of his eloquence; feast, Dec. 4.

John of the Cross, St. (1542-1591): Born in Old Castile, Spain; Carmelite; founder of Discalced Carmelites; one of the greatest mystical theologians, wrote *The Ascent of Mt. Carmel — The Dark Night, The Spiritual Canticle, The Living Flame of Love;* canonized, 1726; proclaimed Doctor of Mystical Theology, 1926; feast, Dec. 14.

Lawrence of Brindisi, St. (1559-1619): Born in Brindisi, Italy; Franciscan (Capuchin); vigorous preacher of strong influence in the post-Reformation period; 15 tomes of collected works include scriptural commentaries, sermons, homilies and doctrinal writings; canonized, 1881; proclaimed doctor, 1959; feast, July 21.

Leo I, the Great, St. (c. 400-461): Born in Tuscany, Italy; pope (440-461); wrote the *Tome of Leo,* to explain doctrine concerning the two natures and one Person of Christ, against the background of the Nestorian and Monophysite heresies; other works included sermons, letters and writings against the errors of Manichaeism and Pelagianism; was instrumental in dissuading Attila from sacking Rome in 452; proclaimed doctor, 1574; feast, Nov. 10.

Peter Canisius, St. (1521-1597): Born in Nijmegen, Holland; Jesuit; wrote popular expositions of the Catholic faith in several catechisms which were widely circulated in 20 editions in his lifetime alone; was one of the moving figures in the Counter-Reformation period, especially in south, west Germany; canonized, proclaimed doctor, 1925; feast, Dec. 21.

Peter Chrysologus, St. (c. 400-450): Born in Imola, Italy; served as archbishop of Ravenna (c. 433-450); his sermons and writings, many of which were designed to counteract Monophysitism, were pastoral and practical; proclaimed doctor, 1729; feast, July 30.

Peter Damian, St. (1007-1072): Born in Ravenna, Italy; Benedictine; cardinal; his writings and sermons, many of which concerned ecclesiastical and clerical reform, were pastoral and practical; proclaimed doctor, 1828; feast, Feb. 21.

Robert Bellarmine, St. (1542-1621): Born in Tuscany, Italy; Jesuit; archbishop of Capua (1602-1605); wrote *Controversies,* a three-volume exposition of doctrine under attack during and after the Reformation, two catechisms and the spiritual work *The Art of Dying Well*; was an authority on ecclesiology and Church-state relations; canonized, 1930; proclaimed doctor, 1931; feast, Sept. 17.

Teresa of Jesus, St. (1515-1582): Born in Avila, Spain; entered the Carmelite Order, 1535; in the early 1560s, initiated a primitive Carmelite, discalced-Alcantarine reform which greatly influenced men and women Religious, especially in Spain; wrote extensively on spiritual and mystical subjects; principal works include her *Autobiography, Way of Perfection, The Interior Castle, Meditations on the Canticle, The Foundations, Visitations of the Discalced Nuns*; canonized, 1614; proclaimed first woman doctor, Sept. 27, 1970; feast, Oct. 15.

Thomas Aquinas, St. (1225-1274): Born near Naples, Italy; Dominican teacher and writer on virtually the whole range of philosophy and theology; principal works were *Summa contra Gentiles*, a manual and systematic defense of Christian doctrine, and *Summa Theologiae*, a new (at that time) exposition of theology on philosophical principles; canonized, 1323; proclaimed doctor, 1567; called Doctor Communis, Doctor Angelicus, the Great Synthesizer because of the way in which he related faith and reason, theology and philosophy (especially that of Aristotle), and systematized the presentation of Christian doctrine; named patron of Catholic schools and education, 1880; feast, Jan 28.

Catholic Beliefs

Key points of Catholic doctrine are stated in creeds, which are simplified summaries designed for use in professing the faith, in prayer and instruction.

The **Apostles' Creed** reflects the teaching of the apostles but is not of apostolic origin. It probably originated in the second century as a rudimentary formula of faith professed by catechumens before the reception of baptism. Baptismal creeds in fourth-century use at Rome and elsewhere in the West closely resembled the present text, which was quoted in a handbook of Christian doctrine written between 710 and 724. This text was in wide use throughout the West by the ninth century. The Apostles' Creed is common to all Christian confessional churches in the West. The Creed of Nicaea-Constantinople (Nicene Creed) prevails in Eastern Churches.

The **Nicene Creed** (Creed of Nicaea-Constantinople) consists of elements of doctrine contained in the early baptismal creed of Jerusalem and enactments of the Council of Nicaea (325) and the Council of Constantinople (381). Its strong Trinitarian content reflects the doctrinal errors, especially of Arianism, it served to counteract. Theologically, it is more sophisticated than the Apostles' Creed. Since late in the fifth century, it has been the only creed in liturgical use in the Eastern Churches. The Western Church adopted it for liturgical use by the end of the eighth century.

TEXT OF THE APOSTLES' CREED

I believe in God, the Father Almighty, Creator of heaven and earth; and in Jesus Christ, His only Son, Our Lord, who was conceived by the Holy Spirit, born of the Virgin Mary, suffered under Pontius Pilate, was crucified, died, and was buried. He descended into hell; the third day He arose again from the dead; He ascended into heaven, sits at the right hand of God, the Father Almighty; from thence He shall come to judge the living and the dead. I believe in the Holy Spirit, the Holy Catholic Church, the communion of saints, the forgiveness of sins, the resurrection of the body, and life everlasting. Amen.

DOCTRINAL SUMMARY

This brief summary of Catholic doctrine follows, in general, the sequence of the Apostles' Creed. Additional points of doctrine are contained in other entries.

God: There is one God, pure spirit, transcendent and supreme being, infinite in perfection: eternal, all good, all holy, all loving, omnipotent, omniscient, omnipresent.

Trinity: There are three persons in the one God, of the same divine nature and equal in every respect: the Father; the Son, begotten of the

Father; the Holy Spirit, proceeding eternally from the Father and the Son. The divine works of creation, redemption and sanctification are attributed, respectively, to the Father, the Son, and the Holy Spirit.

Creation and the Fall: God created the angels, pure spiritual beings; some of them fell from grace, were consigned to hell and became devils; their chief is Satan. God created Adam and Eve, the first parents of the human race, and endowed them not only with grace but also with exceptional gifts of nature — all of which were lost to them and their descendants through Adam's sin of disobedience in the Garden of Paradise. Because of the fall of Adam, all human beings (except Mary) have been and are born in the state of original sin (alienation from God); all persons have been and are and in need of redemption through Jesus Christ the Savior.

Jesus Christ, Redeemer: The Savior is the Second Person of the Trinity, Jesus Christ, true God and true man. The divine person of Christ unites His divine and human natures (hypostatic union).

Jesus was conceived of the Virgin Mary by the power of the Holy Spirit, without a human father. He proclaimed the good news of the Kingdom of God by word and work during a two-and-one-half- to three-year public ministry climaxed by His redemptive suffering, death and resurrection. After rising from the dead, He manifested himself to His disciples during a period of 40 days before ascending into heaven, where He continually intercedes for us. He opened the gates of heaven to the just who lived before His time.

The Catholic Church: Jesus instituted the Church by selecting, training and commissioning the Apostles to preach the good news of salvation, to baptize and to form the community of faith in His name. They began to fulfill this mission after receiving the gift of the Holy Spirit at Pentecost, 10 days after the ascension of the Lord. The Catholic Church, the one Church instituted by Christ, is "the initial budding forth" of the Kingdom of God. It is necessary for salvation and is marked by unity, holiness, catholicity and apostolicity. (See separate entry.)

The Church's Rule of Faith: The Catholic rule of faith consists of Scripture and tradition as authentically preserved, interpreted and taught by the teaching authority of the Church. (See separate entries. Revelation, Authentic Teaching.)

Sacraments of the Church: The seven sacraments properly so called are: baptism, confirmation, the Eucharist, penance, anointing of the sick, orders and matrimony. (See separate entry.)

Communion of Saints: In the Church, there is a communion of saints — i.e., a communion of grace and good works embracing the faithful on earth (the Pilgrim Church), in purgatory (the Church Suffering) and in heaven (the Church in Glory). The faithful on earth are in communication with one another through prayer and good works, with the souls in purgatory through prayer for their release from the state of purification, and with the blessed in heaven by imitating their example, by honoring them in prayer and by seeking their intercession with God. The blessed in heaven communicate with the faithful on earth and the souls in purgatory by interceding for them with God.

Forgiveness of Sins: Original sin is remitted by baptism, by which a person is incorporated in Christ in and through the Church. The ordinary means for the forgiveness of grave sins committed after baptism is the sacrament of penance; venial sins are also forgiven in this sacrament. Contrition and purpose of amendment are conditions for the forgiveness of sin in all cases. Grave sin is forgiven with perfect contrition, which includes the intention of receiving the sacrament.

Death, Judgment, Heaven, Hell: Christ judges all persons in a particular manner at the time of death; according to their spiritual condition, they are consigned to heaven, purgatory or hell. At the end of the world, the dead, good and bad, will rise to be judged in a general judgment, according to their works: the good will go to heaven, body and soul, to be happy with God forever; the wicked will be condemned, body and soul, to the everlasting punishment of hell.

Original Sin: The sin of Adam (Gn. 2:8—3:24), personal to him and passed on to all persons as a state of privation of grace. Despite this privation and the related wounding of human nature and weakening of natural powers, original sin leaves unchanged all that man himself is by nature. The scriptural basis of the doctrine was stated especially by Paul in 1 Cor. 15-21, ff., and Rom. 5:12-21. Original sin is remitted by baptism and incorporation in Christ, through whom grace is given to persons.

Justification: The act by which God makes a person just, and the consequent change in the spiritual status of a person, from sin to grace; the remission of sin and the infusion of sanctifying grace through the merits of Christ and the action of the Holy Spirit.

Grace: A free gift of God to man (and angels), grace is a created sharing or participation in the life of God. It is given to men through the merits of Christ and is communicated by the Holy Spirit. It is necessary for salvation. The principal means of grace are the sacraments (especially the Eucharist), prayer and good works.

Sanctifying or habitual grace makes persons holy and pleasing to God, adopted children of God, members of Christ, temples of the Holy Spirit, heirs of heaven capable of supernaturally meritorious acts. With grace, God gives persons the supernatural virtues and gifts of the Holy Spirit. The sacraments of baptism and penance were instituted to give grace to those who do not have it; the other sacraments, to increase it in those already in the state of grace. The means for growth in holiness, or the increase of grace, are prayer, the sacraments, and good works. Sanctifying grace is lost by the commission of serious sin.

Actual grace is a supernatural help of God which enlightens and strengthens a person to do good and to avoid evil. It is not a permanent quality, like sanctifying grace. It is necessary for the performance of supernatural acts. It can be resisted and refused. Persons in the state of sin are given actual grace to lead them to repentance.

Merit: The right to a supernatural reward for good works freely done for a supernatural motive by a person in the state of grace and with the assistance of grace. The right to such a reward is from God, who binds himself to give it. Accordingly, good works as here described are not only meritorious but also necessary for salvation.

Salvation: The liberation of persons from sin and its effects, reconciliation with God in and through Christ, the attainment of union with God forever in the glory of heaven as the supreme purpose of life and as the God-given reward for fulfillment of His will on earth. Salvation-in-process begins and continues in this life through union with Christ in faith professed and in action; its final term is union with God and the whole community of the saved in the ultimate perfection of God's kingdom. The Church teaches that: God wills the salvation of all men; men are saved in and through Christ; membership in the Church instituted by Christ, known and understood as the community of salvation, is necessary for salvation; persons with this knowledge and understanding who deliberately reject this Church cannot be saved. The Catholic Church is the Church founded by Christ.

Salvation History: The facts and the record of God's relations with men, in the past, present and future, for the purpose of leading them to live in accordance with His will for the eventual attainment after death of salvation, or everlasting happiness with Him in heaven.

The essentials of salvation history are: God's love for all men and will for their salvation; His intervention and action in the world to express this love and bring about their salvation; the revelation He made of himself and the covenant He established with the Israelites in the Old Testament; the perfecting of this revelation and the covenant of grace through Christ in the New Testament; the continuing action-for-salvation carried on in and through the Mystical Body of Christ, the Catholic Church; the communication of saving grace to men through the merits of Christ and the operations of the Holy Spirit in the here-and-now circumstances of daily life and with the cooperation of men themselves.

Moral Obligations

The basic norm of Christian morality is life in Christ. This involves, among other things, the observance of the Ten Commandments, their fulfillment in the twofold law of love of God and neighbor, the implications of the Sermon on the Mount and the whole New Testament, and membership in the Church instituted by Christ.

THE TEN COMMANDMENTS

The Ten Commandments (Decalogue) were given by God through Moses to His Chosen People for the guidance of their moral conduct in accord with the demands of the covenant He established with them as a divine gift.

In the traditional Catholic enumeration and according to Dt. 5:6-21, the Commandments are as follows.

1. "I, the Lord, am your God . . . You shall not have other gods besides me. You shall not carve idols. . . ."

2. "You shall not take the name of the Lord, your God, in vain. . . ."

3. "Take care to keep holy the Sabbath day. . . ."

4. "Honor your father and your mother. . . ."

5. "You shall not kill."

6. "You shall not commit adultery."

7. "You shall not steal."

8. "You shall not bear dishonest witness against your neighbor."

9. "You shall not covet your neighbor's wife."

10. "You shall not desire your neighbor's house or field, nor his male or female slave, nor his ox or ass, nor anything that belongs to him" (summarily, his goods).

Another version of the Commandments, substantially the same, is given in Ex. 20:1-17.

The traditional enumeration of the Commandments in Protestant usage differs from the above. Thus: two commandments are made of the first, as above; the third and fourth are equivalent to the second and third, as above, and so on; and the 10th includes the ninth and 10th, as above.

Love of God and Neighbor

The first three commandments deal directly with a person's relations with God, viz: acknowledgment of one true God and the rejection of false gods and idols; honor due to God and His name; observance of the Sabbath (Sunday) as the Lord's Day.

The rest of the commandments cover interpersonal relationships, viz.: the obedience due to parents and, logically, to other persons in legitimate authority, and the obligations of parents to children and of persons in authority to those under their care; respect for life, physical and moral well-being; fidelity in marriage, and chastity; justice and rights; truth; internal respect for chastity, fidelity in marriage; respect for the goods of others.

PRECEPTS OF THE CHURCH

These are moral precepts binding Roman Catholics in conscience. They originated in the Middle Ages; five of them were mentioned in the writings of St. Peter Canisius and St. Robert Bellarmine in the second half of the 16th century.

1. Participate in Mass on Sundays and holy days of obligation, and abstain from work and business concerns that impede divine worship and appropriate mental and physical relaxation.

2. Fast and abstain on the days appointed. (See separate entry, Days of Fast and Abstinence.)

3. Confess one's sins at least once a year (binding if one has committed grave sin).

4. Receive the Eucharist during the Easter Time (in the U.S., from the first Sunday of Lent to Trinity Sunday).

5. Contribute to the support of the Church.

6. Observe the laws of the Church concerning marriage.

BEATITUDES

Beatitudes are blessings promised to persons for various reasons. Those recounted in Mt. 5:3-11 and Lk. 6:20-30 identify blessedness with participation in the Kingdom of God and His righteousness, and describe the qualities of Christian perfection.

In Matthew's account, the Beatitudes are as follows.

"How blest are the poor in spirit; the reign of God is theirs."

"Blest too are the sorrowing; they shall be consoled."

"(Blest are the lowly; they shall inherit the land.)"

"Blest are they who hunger and thirst for holiness; they shall have their fill."

"Blest are they who show mercy; mercy shall be theirs."

"Blest are the single-hearted for they shall see God."

"Blest too are the peacemakers; they shall be called sons of God."

"Blest are those persecuted for holiness' sake; the reign of God is theirs."

"Blest are you when they insult you and persecute you and utter every kind of slander against you because of me."

Luke's account of the Beatitudes is as follows.

"Blest are you poor; the reign of God is yours."

"Blest are you who hunger; you shall be filled."

"Blest are you who are weeping; you shall laugh."

"Blest shall you be when men hate you, when they ostracize you and insult you and proscribe your name as evil because of the Son of

Man. On the day they do so, rejoice and exult, for your reward shall be great in heaven.''

WORKS OF MERCY .

Spiritual Works: These are works of spiritual assistance, motivated by love of God and neighbor, to persons in need: counseling the doubtful, instructing the ignorant, admonishing sinners, comforting the afflicted, forgiving offenses, bearing wrongs patiently, praying for the living and the dead.

Corporal Works: These are works of a physical and material kind for the assistance of persons in need, motivated by love of God and neighbor: feeding the hungry, giving drink to the thirsty, clothing the naked, visiting the imprisoned, sheltering the homeless, visiting the sick, burying the dead.

CONSCIENCE

Conscience is practical judgment concerning the moral goodness or sinfulness of an action done, to be done or to be avoided. In the Catholic view, this judgment is made by reference of an action (thought, desire, word, deed), its attendant circumstances and the intentions of the person to the requirements of moral law as expressed in the Ten Commandments, the summary law of love for God and neighbor, the life and teaching of Christ, and the authoritative teaching and practice of the Church with respect to the total demands of divine revelation.

A person is obliged: (1) to form and obey a certain and correct conscience; (2) to obey a certain conscience even if it is inculpably erroneous; (3) not to obey, but to correct, a conscience known to be erroneous or lax; (4) to rectify a scrupulous conscience by following the advice of a confessor and by other measures; (5) to resolve doubts of conscience before acting.

SIN AND REPENTANCE

Actual sin: Personal or actual sin is any free and deliberate violation of the law of God by thought, desire, word or action. Grave or mortal sin — involving serious matter, sufficient reflection and full consent — results in total alienation from God, depriving a person of sanctifying grace and rendering him (her) incapable of performing meritorious supernatural acts and subject to everlasting punishment. Venial sin — involving less serious matter and/or reflection and/or consent — does not have such serious consequences. The only ordinary means for the forgiveness of grave sins is the sacrament of penance (see Sacraments).

Penance or Penitence: The spiritual change or conversion of mind and heart by which a person turns away from sin, and all that it implies, toward God, through a personal renewal under the influence of the Holy Spirit. Penance involves sorrow and contrition for sin, together with other internal and external acts of atonement. It serves the purposes of reestablishing in one's life the order of God's love and commandments, and of making satisfaction to God for sin. A divine precept states the necessity of penance for salvation: "Unless you do penance, you shall all likewise perish" (Lk. 13:3) . . . "Be converted and believe in the Gospel" (Mk. 1:15).

In the penitential discipline of the Church the various works of penance have been classified under the headings of prayer (interior), fasting and almsgiving (exterior). The Church has established minimum requirements for the common and social observance of the divine precept by Catholics — e.g., by requiring them to fast and/or abstain on certain days of the year. These observances, however, do not exhaust all the demands of the divine precept, whose fulfillment is a matter of personal responsibility; nor do they have any real value unless they proceed from the internal spirit and purpose of penance.

Related to works of penance for sins actually committed are works of mortification. The purpose of the latter is to develop — through prayer, fasting, renunciations and similar actions — self-control and detachment from things which could otherwise become occasions of sin.

Contrition: Sorrow for sin coupled with a purpose of amendment. Contrition arising from a supernatural motive is necessary for the forgiveness of sin.

Perfect contrition is total sorrow for and renunciation of attachment to sin, arising from the motive of pure love of God. Perfect contrition, which implies the intention of doing all God wants done for the forgiveness of sin (including confession in a reasonable period of time), is sufficient for the forgiveness of serious sin and the remission of all temporal punishment due for sin. (The intention to receive the sacrament of penance is implicit — even if unrealized, as in the case of some persons — in perfect contrition.)

Imperfect contrition or attrition is sorrow arising from a quasi-selfish supernatural motive; e.g., the fear of losing heaven, suffering the pains of hell, etc. Imperfect contrition is sufficient for the forgiveness of serious sin when joined with absolution in confession, and sufficient for the forgiveness of venial sin even outside of confession.

Indulgence: A remission before God of temporal punishment due for sins that have already been forgiven, which a member of the faithful — with proper dispositions and under prescribed conditions — acquires through the intervention of the Church. The Church grants indulgences in accordance with doctrine concerning the treasury of satisfactions of Christ and the saints, the Power of the Keys to bind and loose the goods of the Kingdom of God, and the sharing of spiritual goods in the Communion of Saints. Indulgences are plenary (remitting all temporal punishment) or partial; they can be gained for oneself or for the dead by way of suffrage. To gain an indulgence, a person must: be baptized and in good standing in the Church, be in the state of grace, have the intention to gain the indulgence, and properly fulfill conditions required.

Social Doctrine

Since the end of the last century, Catholic social doctrine has been formulated in a progressive manner in a number of authoritative documents. Outstanding examples are the encyclicals: *Rerum Novarum*, issued by Leo XIII in 1891; *Quadragesimo Anno*, by Pius IX in 1931; *Mater et Magistra* ("Christianity and Social Progress") and *Pacem in Terris* ("Peace on Earth"), by John XXIII in 1961 and 1963, respectively; *Populorum Progressio* ("Development of Peoples"), by Paul VI in 1967; and *Laborem Exercens* ("On Human Work"), by John Paul II in 1981. Pius XII, among other accomplishments of ideological importance in the social field, made a distinctive contribution with his formulation of a plan for world peace and order in Christmas messages from 1939 to 1941, and in other documents.

These documents represent the most serious attempts in modern times to systematize the social implications of the Gospel and the rest of divine revelation as well as the socially relevant writings of the Fathers and Doctors of the Church. Their contents are theological penetrations into social life, with particular reference to human rights, the needs of the poor and those in underdeveloped countries, and humane conditions of life, freedom, justice and peace. In some respects, they read like juridical documents; underneath, however, they are Gospel-oriented and pastoral in intention.

Nature of the Doctrine

Pope John XXIII, writing in *Christianity and Social Progress*, made the following statement about the nature and scope of the doctrine stated in the encyclicals in particular and related writings in general.

"What the Catholic Church teaches and declares regarding the social life and relationships of men is beyond question for all time valid."

"The cardinal point of this teaching is that individual men are necessarily the foundation, cause, and end of all social institutions . . . insofar as they are social by nature, and raised to an order of existence that transcends and subdues nature."

"Beginning with this very basic principle whereby the dignity of the human person is affirmed and defended, Holy Church — especially during the last century and with the assistance of learned priests and laymen, specialists in the field — has arrived at clear social teachings whereby the mutual relationships of men are ordered. Taking general norms into account, these principles are in accord with the nature of things and the changed conditions of man's social life, or with the special genius of our day. Moreover, these norms can be approved by all."

THE CHURCH IN THE WORLD

Even more Gospel-oriented and pastoral in a distinctive way is the *Pastoral Constitution on the Church in the Modern World* promulgated by the Second Vatican Council in 1965.

Its purpose is to search out the signs of God's presence and meaning in and through the events of this time in human history. Accordingly, it deals with the situations of men in present circumstances of profound change, challenge and crisis on all levels of life.

The first part of the constitution develops the theme of the Church and man's calling, and focuses attention on the dignity of the human person, the problem of atheism, the community of mankind, man's activity throughout the world, and the serving and saving role of the Church in the world. This portion of the document, it has been said, represents the first presentation by the Church in an official text of an organized Christian view of man and society.

The second part of the document considers several problems of special urgency: fostering the nobility of marriage and the family, the proper development of culture, socio-economic life, the life of the political community, the fostering of peace and the promotion of a community of nations.

In conclusion, the constitution calls for action to implement doctrine regarding the role and work of the Church for the total good of mankind.

Excerpts on General Subjects

Following are key excerpts from the ideological heart of the constitution.

One Human Family and Community: God, who has fatherly concern for everyone, has willed that all men should constitute one family and treat one another in a spirit of brotherhood.

For this reason, love for God and neighbor is the first and greatest commandment. Sacred Scripture . . . teaches us that the love of God cannot be separated from love of neighbor. . . . To men growing daily more dependent on one another, and to a world becoming more unified every day, this truth proves to be of paramount importance.

Human Person Is Central: Man's social nature makes it evident that the progress of the human person and the advance of society itself hinge on each other. For the beginning, the subject and the goal of all social institutions is and must be the human person, which for its part and by its very nature stands completely in need of social life. This social life is not something added on to man. Hence, through his dealings with others, through reciprocal duties and through fraternal dialogue, he develops all his gifts and is able to rise to his destiny.

Influence of Social Circumstances: But if by this social life the human person is greatly aided in responding to his destiny, even in its religious dimensions, it cannot be denied that men are often diverted from doing good and spurred toward evil by the social circumstances in which they live and are immersed from their birth. To be sure, the disturbances which so frequently occur in the social order result in part from the natural tensions of economic, political and social forms. But at a deeper level they flow from man's pride and selfishness, which contaminate even the social sphere. When the structure of affairs is flawed by the consequences of sin, man, already born with a bent toward evil, finds there new inducements to sin which cannot be overcome without strenuous efforts and the assistance of grace.

Human Necessities and Rights: Every social group must take account of the needs and legitimate aspirations of other groups, and even of the general welfare of the entire human family.

At the same time, however, there is a growing awareness of the exalted dignity proper to the human person, since he stands above all things and his rights and duties are universal and inviolable. Therefore, there must be made available to all men everything necessary for leading a life truly human, such as food, clothing, and shelter; the right to choose a state of life freely and to found a family; the right to education, to employment, to a good reputation, to respect, to appropriate information, to activity in accord with the upright norm of one's own conscience, to protection of privacy and to rightful freedom in matters religious too.

Hence, the social order and its development must unceasingly work to the benefit of the human person if the disposition of affairs is to be subordinate to the personal realm and not contrariwise, as the Lord indicated when He said that the Sabbath was made for man, and not man for the Sabbath.

Improvement of Social Order: This social order requires constant improvement. It must be founded on truth, built on justice and animated by love; in freedom it should grow every day toward a more humane balance. An improvement in attitudes and widespread changes in society will have to take place if these objectives are to be gained.

God's Spirit, who with a marvelous providence directs the unfolding of time and renews the face of the earth, is not absent from this development. The ferment of the Gospel, too, has aroused and continues to arouse in man's heart the irresistible requirements of his dignity.

Regard for Neighbor as Another Self: Coming down to practical and particularly urgent consequences, this Council lays stress on reverence for man; everyone must consider his every neighbor without exception as another self, taking into account first of all his life and the means necessary to living it with dignity.

In our times a special obligation binds us to make ourselves the neighbor of absolutely every person and to actively help him when he comes across our path.

Inhuman Evils: Whatever is opposed to life itself, such as any type of murder, genocide, abortion, euthanasia, or willful self-destruction; whatever violates the integrity of the human person, such as mutilation, torments inflicted on body or mind, attempts to coerce the will itself;

whatever insults human dignity, such as subhuman living conditions, arbitrary imprisonment, deportation, slavery, prostitution, the selling of women and children; as well as disgraceful working conditions, where men are treated as mere tools for profit rather than as free and responsible persons: all these things and others of their like are infamies indeed. They poison human society, but they do more harm to those who practice them than those who suffer from the injury. Moreover, they are a supreme dishonor to the Creator.

Respect for Those Who Are Different: Respect and love ought to be extended also to those who think or act differently than we do in social, political and religious matters. In fact, the more deeply we come to understand their ways of thinking through such courtesy and love, the more easily will we be able to enter into dialogue with them.

Distinction between Error and Persons in Error: This love and good will, to be sure, must in no way render us indifferent to truth and goodness. Indeed, love itself impels the disciples of Christ to speak the saving truth to all men. But it is necessary to distinguish between error, which always merits repudiation, and the person in error, who never loses the dignity of being a person, even when he is flawed by false or inadequate religious notions. God alone is the judge and searcher of hearts; for that reason he forbids us to make judgments about the internal guilt of anyone.

The teaching of Christ even requires that we forgive injuries, and extends the law of love to include every enemy.

Men Are Equal but Different: Since all men possess a rational soul and are created in God's likeness; since they have the same nature and origin, have been redeemed by Christ, and enjoy the same divine calling and destiny: the basic equality of all must receive increasingly greater recognition.

True all men are not alike from the point of view of varying physical power and the diversity of intellectual and moral resources. Nevertheless, with respect to the fundamental rights of the person, every type of discrimination, whether social or cultural, whether based on sex, race, color, social condition, language or religion, is to be overcome and eradicated as contrary to God's intent.

Humane Conditions for All: Although rightful differences exist between men, the equal dignity of persons demands that a more humane and just condition of life be brought about. For excessive economic and social differences between the members of the one human family . . . cause scandal and militate against social justice, equity and the dignity of the human person as well as social and international peace.

Human institutions, both private and public, must labor to minister to the dignity and purpose of man. At the same time, let them put up a stubborn fight against any kind of slavery, whether social or political, and safeguard the basic rights of man under every political system. Indeed, human institutions themselves must be accommodated by degrees to the highest of all realities, spiritual ones, even though, meanwhile, a long enough time will be required before they arrive at the desired goal.

Profound and rapid changes make it particularly urgent that no one, ignoring the trend of events or drugged by laziness, content himself with a merely individualistic morality. It grows increasingly true that the obligations of justice and love are fulfilled only if each person, contributing to the common good according to his own abilities and the needs of others, also promotes and assists the public and private institutions dedicated to bettering the conditions of human life.

Social Necessities Are Prime Duties: Let everyone consider it his sacred obligation to count social necessities among the primary duties of modern man and to pay heed to them. For the more unified the world becomes, the more plainly do the offices of men extend beyond particular groups and spread by degrees to the whole world. But this challenge cannot be met unless individual men and their associations cultivate in themselves the moral and social virtues and promote them in society. Thus, with the needed help of divine grace, men who are truly new and artisans of a new humanity can be forthcoming.

In order for individual men to discharge with greater exactness the obligations of their conscience toward themselves and the various groups to which they belong, they must be carefully educated to a higher degree of culture through the use of the immense resources available today to the human race.

Living Conditions and Freedom: A man can scarcely arrive at the needed sense of responsibility unless his living conditions allow him to become conscious of his dignity and to rise to his destiny by spending himself for God and for others. But human freedom is often crippled when a man falls into extreme poverty, just as it withers when he indulges in too many of life's comforts and imprisons himself in a kind of splendid isolation. Freedom acquires new strength, by contrast, when a man consents to the unavoidable requirements of social life, takes on the manifold demands of human partnership and commits himself to the service of the human community.

Hence, the will to play one's role in common endeavors should be everywhere encouraged.

Communitarian Character of Life: God did not create man for life in isolation but for the formation of social unity. So also "it has pleased God to make men holy and save them not merely as individuals, without any mutual bonds, but by making them into a single people, a people which acknowledges Him in truth and serves Him in holiness" (*Dogmatic Constitution on the Church*, No. 9). So from the beginning of salvation history He has chosen men not just as individuals but as members of a certain community. Revealing His mind to them, God called these chosen ones "His people" (Ex. 3:7-12) and, furthermore, made a covenant with them on Sinai.

This communitarian character is developed and consummated in the work of Jesus Christ. For the very Word made flesh willed to share in the human fellowship. He was present at the wedding of Cana, visited the house of Zacchaeus, ate with publicans and sinners. He revealed the love of the Father and the sublime vocation of man in terms of the most common of social realities and by making use of the speech and the imagery of plain everyday life. Willingly obeying the laws of His country, He sanctified those human ties, especially family ones, from which social relationships arise. He chose to lead the life proper to an artisan of His time and place.

In His preaching He clearly taught the sons of God to treat one another as brothers. In His prayers He pleaded that all His disciples might be "one." Indeed, as the Redeemer of all He offered himself for all, even to the point of death. He commanded His Apostles to preach to all peoples the Gospel message so that the human race might become the Family of God, in which the fullness of the law would be love.

The Community Founded by Christ: As the firstborn of many brethren and through the gift of His Spirit, He founded after His death and resurrection a new brotherly community composed of all those who receive Him in faith and in love. This he did through His Body, which is the Church. There everyone, as members one of the other, would render mutual service according to the different gifts bestowed on each.

This solidarity must be constantly increased until that day on which it is brought to perfection. Then, saved by grace, men will offer flawless glory to God as a family beloved of God and of Christ their Brother.

Excerpts on Peace and War

Call to Peace: This Council fervently desires to summon Christians to cooperate with all men in making secure among themselves a peace based on justice and love, and in setting up agencies of peace. This Christians should do with the help of Christ, the Author of peace.

Conditions for Peace: Peace is not merely the absence of war. Nor can it be reduced solely to the maintenance of a balance of power between enemies. Nor is it brought about by dictatorship. Instead, it is rightly and appropriately called "an enterprise of justice" (Is. 32:7). Peace results from that harmony built into human society by its divine Founder and actualized by men as they thirst after ever greater justice.

The common good of men is in its basic sense determined by the eternal law. Still, the concrete demands of this common good are constantly changing as time goes on. Hence, peace is never attained once and for all, but must be built up ceaselessly. Moreover, since the human will is unsteady and wounded by sin, the achievement of peace requires that everyone constantly master his passions and that lawful authority keep vigilant.

But such is not enough. This peace cannot be obtained on earth unless personal values are safeguarded and men freely and trustingly share with one another the riches of their inner spirits and their talents.

A firm determination to respect other men and peoples and their dignity, as well as the studied practice of brotherhood, is absolutely necessary for the establishment of peace. Hence, peace is likewise the fruit of love, which goes beyond what justice can provide.

Renunciation of Violence: We cannot fail to praise those who renounce the use of violence in the vindication of their rights and who resort to methods of defense which are otherwise available to weaker parties too, provided that this can be done without injury to the rights and duties of others or of the community itself.

Mass Extermination: The Council wishes to recall first of all the permanent binding force of universal natural law and its all-embracing principles. Man's conscience itself gives ever more emphatic voice to these principles. Therefore, actions which deliberately conflict with these same principles, as well as orders commanding such actions, are criminal. Blind obedience cannot excuse those who yield to them. Among such must first be counted those actions designed for the methodical extermination of an entire people, nation, or ethnic minority. These actions must be vehemently condemned as horrendous crimes. The courage of those who openly and fearlessly resist men who issue such commands merits supreme commendation.

International Agreements: On the subject of war, quite a large number of nations have subscribed to various international agreements aimed at making military activity and its consequences less inhuman. Such are conventions concerning the handling of wounded or captured soldiers, and various similar agreements. Agreements of this sort must be honored. They should be improved upon.

Conscientious Objectors: It seems right that laws make humane provisions for the case of those who for reasons of conscience refuse to bear arms, provided, however, that they accept some other form of service to the human community.

Legitimate Defense: Certainly, war has not been rooted out of human affairs. As long as the danger of war remains and there is no competent and sufficiently powerful authority at the international level, governments cannot be denied the right to legitimate defense once every means of peaceful settlement has been exhausted. Therefore, government authorities and others who share public responsibility have the duty to protect the welfare of the people entrusted to their care and to conduct such grave matters soberly.

But it is one thing to undertake military action for the just defense of the people, and something else again to seek the subjugation of other nations. Nor does the possession of war potential make every military or political use of it lawful. Neither does the mere fact that war has unhappily begun mean that all is fair between the warring parties.

Nature of Military Service: Those who are pledged to the service of their country as members of its armed forces should regard themselves as agents of security and freedom on behalf of their people. As long as they fulfill this role properly, they are making a genuine contribution to the establishment of peace.

Total War Condemned: This most holy Synod makes its own the condemnations of total war already pronounced by recent popes, and issues the following declaration:

Any act of war aimed indiscriminately at the destruction of entire cities or of extensive areas along with their population is a crime against God and man himself. It merits unequivocal and unhesitating condemnation.

The unique hazard of modern warfare consists in this: it provides those who possess modern scientific weapons with a kind of occasion for perpetrating just such abominations. Moreover, through a certain inexorable chain of events, it can urge men on to the most atrocious decisions. That such in fact may never happen in the future, the bishops of the whole world, in unity assembled, beg all men, especially government officials and military leaders, to give unremitting thought to the awesome responsibility which is theirs before God and the entire human race.

Retaliation and Deterrence: Scientific weapons, to be sure, are not amassed solely for use in war. The defensive strength of any nation is considered to be dependent upon its capacity for immediate retaliation against an adversary. Hence this accumulation of arms, which increases each year, also serves, in a way heretofore unknown, as a deterrent to possible enemy attack. Many regard this state of affairs as the most effective way by which peace of a sort can be maintained between nations at the present time.

(Deterrence was one of the key topics in the pastoral letter — "The Challenge of Peace: God's Promise and Our Response" — issued by the bishops of the U.S. in 1983. They made their own the words of Pope John Paul II on the subject: "In current conditions 'deterrence' based on balance, certainly not as an end in itself but as a step on the way toward a progressive disarmament, may still be judged morally acceptable. Nonetheless, in order to ensure peace, it is indispensable not to be satisfied with this minimum which is always susceptible to the real danger of explosion" [Message to a Special Session of the United Nations on Disarmament, June, 1982].

(The bishops said also: "No use of nuclear weapons which would violate the principles of discrimination or proportionality may be intended in a strategy of deterrence." They added: "Deterrence is not an adequate strategy as a long-term basis for peace; it is a transitional strategy justifiable only in conjunction with resolute determination to pursue arms control and disarmament."

(With respect to the initiation of nuclear war, the bishops stated: "We do not perceive any situation in which the deliberate initiation of nuclear war, on however restricted a scale, can be morally justified."

They were "highly skeptical" about the real meaning and/or legitimacy of limited nuclear war.)

Arms Race: Whatever be the case with this method of deterrence, men should be convinced that the arms race in which so many countries are engaged is not a safe way to preserve a steady peace. Nor is the so-called balance resulting from this race a sure and authentic peace. Rather than being eliminated thereby, the causes of war threaten to grow gradually stronger.

While extravagant sums are being spent for the furnishing of ever new weapons, an adequate remedy cannot be provided for the multiple miseries afflicting the whole modern world. Disagreements between nations are not really and radically healed. On the contrary, other parts of the world are infected with them. New approaches initiated by reformed attitudes must be adopted to remove this trap and to restore genuine peace by emancipating the world from its crushing anxiety.

Therefore, it must be said again: the arms race is an utterly treacherous trap for humanity, and one which injures the poor to an intolerable degree. It is much to be feared that, if this race persists, it will eventually spawn all the lethal ruin whose path it is now making ready.

Outlaw Wars: It is our clear duty, then, to strain every muscle as we work for the time when all war can be completely outlawed by international consent. This goal undoubtedly requires the establishment of some universal public authority acknowledged as such by all, and endowed with effective power to safeguard, on behalf of all, security, regard for justice, and respect for rights.

Multilateral and Controlled Disarmament: But before this hoped-for authority can be set up, the highest existing international centers must devote themselves vigorously to the pursuit of better means for obtaining common security. Peace must be born of mutual trust between nations rather than imposed on them through fear of one another's weapons. Hence, everyone must labor to put an end at last to the arms race, and to make a true beginning of disarmament, but one proceeding at an equal pace according to agreement and backed up by authentic and workable safeguards.

In the meantime, efforts which have already been made and are still under way to eliminate the danger of war are not to be underrated. On the contrary, support should be given to the good will of the very many leaders who work hard to do away with war, which they abominate.

Public Opinion: Men should take heed not to entrust themselves only to the efforts of others, while remaining careless about their own attitudes. For government officials, who must simultaneously guarantee the good of their own people and promote the universal good, depend on public opinion and feeling to the greatest possible extent. It does them no good to work at building peace so long as feelings of hostility, contempt, and distrust, as well as racial hatred and unbending ideologies, continue to divide men and place them in opposing camps.

Hence arises a surpassing need for renewed education of attitudes and for new inspiration in the area of public opinion. Those who are dedicated to the work of education . . . should regard as their most weighty task the effort to instruct all in fresh sentiments of peace.

WORK

The nature of work, its relation to social issues and its significance, along with prayer, as the "way of sanctification," were among key subjects treated in Pope John Paul's third encyclical letter, *Laborem Exercens*. Following are several paragraphs from the encyclical delineating a definition of work together with capsule coverage of a number of salient points in the letter.

"Through work man must earn his daily bread and contribute to the continual advance of science and technology and, above all, to elevating unceasingly the cultural and moral level of the society within which he lives in community with those who belong to the same family."

"And work means any activity by man, whether manual or intellectual, whatever its nature or circumstances; it means any human activity that can and must be recognized as work, in the midst of all the many activities of which man is capable and to which he is predisposed by his very nature, by virtue of humanity itself."

"Man is made to be in the visible universe an image and likeness of God himself, and he is placed in it in order to subdue the earth. From the beginning, therefore, he is called to work."

"Work is one of the characteristics that distinguish man from the rest of creatures, whose activity for sustaining their lives cannot be called work. Only man is capable of work and only man works, at the same time by work occupying his existence on earth. Thus, work bears a particular mark of man and of humanity, the mark of a person operating within a community of persons. And this mark decides its interior characteristics; in a sense, it constitutes its very nature."

Salient Points

Fundamental Criterion of Economics: "Respect for the objective rights of the worker. . . must constitute the adequate and fundamental criterion for shaping the whole economy, both on the level of the individual society and state and within the whole of the world economic policy as well as the systems of international relationships that derive from it."

Work and Family: "Work constitutes a foundation of the formation of family life" by providing the economic means necessary to maintain a family.

Just Wage: "A just wage is the concrete means of verifying the justice of the whole socio-economic system and, in any case, of checking that it is functioning justly."

Family Wage: A "family wage" is needed, "a single salary given to the head of the family for his work, sufficient for the needs of the family without the other spouse having to take up gainful employment outside the home," or without the need of recourse to other social provisions for aid.

Women: Women who work "should be able to fulfill their tasks in accordance with their own nature without being discriminated against and without being excluded from jobs for which they are capable." Respect is due "for their family aspirations and for their specific role in contributing, together with men, to the good of society."

Mothers: Provisions should be made for "measures such as family allowances or grants to mothers devoting themselves exclusively to their families."

Unions: Workers have the right to form a union to protect their vital interests and to be "a mouthpiece for the struggle for social justice."

"Union activity undoubtedly enters the field of politics, understood as prudent concern for the common good." But unions should not engage in partisan politics; otherwise, "they become an instrument used for other purposes."

Strike: Workers should be assured the right to strike without being subject to personal sanctions, but have the responsibility of not striking if a strike "is contrary to requirements of the common good."

Unemployment Benefits: "The obligation to provide unemployment benefits . . . is a duty springing from the fundamental principle of the common use of goods or, to put it in another way, the right to life and subsistence."

Disabled Persons: Society should provide work for disabled persons in keeping with their physical abilities. Failure to do so means "a serious form of discrimination, that of the strong and healthy against the weak and sick."

Health Care: "The expenses involved in health care, especially in the case of accidents at work, demand that medical assistance should be easily available for workers."

Technology: It is meant to be the worker's ally but can become his enemy when mechanization supplants him or takes away "all personal satisfaction and the incentive to creativity and responsibility," thus reducing "man to the status of slave."

Haves and Have-Nots: "A disconcerting fact of immense proportions" occurs on the world scene. "While conspicuous natural resources remain unused, there are huge numbers of people who are unemployed or underemployed, and countless multitudes of people suffering from hunger." This means that there is "something wrong with the organization of work and employment" on national and international levels.

Foreign Workers: People have a right to emigrate in search of work. "The person working away from his native land, whether as a permanent emigrant or as a seasonal worker, should not be placed at a disadvantage in comparison with the workers in that society in the matter of working rights. Emigration in search of work must in no way become an opportunity for financial or social exploitation.''

Marxism: Catholic social teaching ''diverges radically from the program of collectivism proclaimed by Marxism and put into practice in various countries.''

Private Property and Capitalism: ''Christian tradition has never upheld'' the right to private property ''as absolute and untouchable. On the contrary, it has always understood this right common to all to use the goods of the whole creation.''

''Deeply desired reforms'' of capitalism ''cannot be achieved by an *a priori* elimination of private ownership of the means of production.'' This is not sufficient to insure ''satisfactory socialization'' because new managers form another special group ''from the fact of exercising power in society. This group . . . may carry out this task badly by claiming for itself a monopoly of the administration and disposal of the means of production and not refraining even from offending basic human rights.''

Exploitation by Multinationals: ''The highly industrialized countries, and even more so the businesses that direct on a large scale the means of industrial production, fix the highest possible prices for their products while trying at the same time to fix the lowest possible prices for raw materials or semi-manufactured goods.''

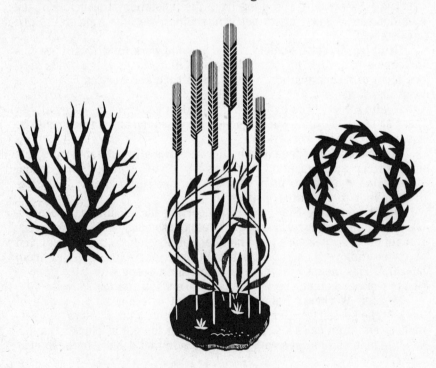

Liturgy

Liturgy, the official worship of the Church, was the subject of the *Constitution on the Sacred Liturgy* issued by the Second Vatican Council. The document describes the nature and purpose of the liturgy as follows.

"It is through the liturgy, especially the divine Eucharistic Sacrifice, that 'the work of our redemption is exercised.' The liturgy is thus the outstanding means by which the faithful can express in their lives, and manifest to others, the mystery of Christ and the real nature of the true Church."

"The liturgy is considered as an exercise of the priestly office of Jesus Christ. In the liturgy the sanctification of man is manifested by signs perceptible to the senses, and is effected in a way which is proper to each of these signs; in the liturgy full public worship is performed by the Mystical Body of Jesus Christ, that is, by the Head and His members."

"From this it follows that every liturgical celebration, because it is an action of Christ the priest and His Body the Church, is a sacred action surpassing all others. No other action of the Church can match its claim to efficacy, nor equal the degree of it."

"The liturgy is the summit toward which the activity of the Church is directed; at the same time it is the fountain from which all her power flows. For the goal of apostolic works is that all who are made sons of God by faith and baptism should come together to praise God in the midst of His Church, to take part in her sacrifice, and to eat the Lord's Supper."

"From the liturgy, therefore, and especially from the Eucharist, as from a fountain, grace is channeled into us; and the sanctification of men in Christ and the glorification of God, to which all other activities of the Church are directed as toward their goal, are most powerfully achieved."

"Mother Church earnestly desires that all the faithful be led to that full, conscious, and active participation in liturgical celebrations which is demanded by the very nature of the liturgy. Such participation by the Christian people as 'a chosen race, a royal priesthood, a holy nation, a purchased people,' is their right and duty by reason of their baptism."

Because of its nature as the official worship of the Church, regulations regarding the substance, forms and conduct of the liturgy — its books and texts, rites and ceremonies — depend on the Apostolic See, regional conferences of bishops and individual bishops, according to provisions of law. No priest has authority to initiate reforms or changes on his own.

MAJOR COMPONENTS
The major components of the liturgy are the Mass and other sacraments (see separate entries), sacramentals, the Liturgy of the Hours (Divine Office), the liturgical year (see Liturgical Year and Calendar), sacred music, sacred art and sacred furnishings.

Sacramentals
Sacramentals "are sacred signs which bear a resemblance to the sacraments; they signify effects, particularly of a spiritual kind, which are obtained through the Church's intercession. By them men are disposed to receive the chief effect of the sacraments, and various occasions in life are rendered holy."

"Thus, for well-disposed members of the faithful, the liturgy of the sacraments and sacramentals sanctifies almost every event in their lives; they are given access to the stream of divine grace which flows from the paschal mystery of the passion, death and resurrection of Christ, the fountain from which all sacraments and sacramentals draw their power. There is hardly any proper use of material things which cannot thus be directed toward the sanctification of men and the praise of God."

Better known sacramentals are priestly blessings (primarily for the faithful and catechumens), and some of the things blessed with the intercession of the Church — e.g., palms, ashes, holy water, medals, rosaries, ceremonies of the Roman Ritual.

Funeral rites for the faithful are ordinarily conducted in their parish church. Catechumens are entitled to ecclesiastical burial. A diocesan bishop can permit ecclesiastical burial for children who die before baptism if their parents intended to have them baptized. Under appropriate conditions, a diocesan bishop can grant ecclesiastical funeral rites to baptized members of a non-Catholic church or ecclesial community. The custom of burying the bodies of the dead is recommended for observance. Cremation is not forbidden unless it is chosen for reasons against church teaching.

Liturgy of the Hours
The Liturgy of the Hours (Divine Office) is the public prayer of the Church for praising God, interceding for the conversion of the world and sanctifying the day. Its daily celebration is required as a sacred obligation of priests, deacons and permanent deacons, and also of members of institutes of consecrated life and of societies of apostolic life, in accord with general and particular directives. Its celebration by others is highly recommended and encouraged in the community of the faithful.

"By tradition going back to early Christian times," declared the Second Vatican Council, "the Divine Office is arranged so that the whole course of the day and night is made holy by the praises of God. Therefore, when this wonderful song of praise is worthily rendered by priests and others who are deputed for this purpose by church ordinance, or by the faithful praying together with the priest in an approved form, then . . . it is the very prayer which Christ himself, together with His Body, addresses to the Father."

"Hence, all who perform this service are not only fulfilling a duty of the Church, but also are sharing in the greatest honor accorded to Christ's spouse, for by offering these praises to God they are standing before God's throne in the name of the Church their Mother."

Following are the principal contents of the Liturgy of the Hours.

Office of Readings, for reflection on the word of God, consisting of a hymn, three psalms, biblical and non-biblical readings.

Morning and Evening Prayer, called the "hinges" of the Office, consisting of a hymn, two psalms, an Old or New Testament canticle, a brief biblical reading, Zechariah's canticle (the *Benedictus*, morning) or Mary's canticle (the *Magnificat*, evening), responsories, intercessions and a concluding prayer.

Daytime Prayer, consisting of a hymn, three psalms, a brief biblical reading and one of three concluding prayers corresponding to the time at which the prayer is offered (midmorning, midday, midafternoon).

Night Prayer, consisting of one or two psalms, a brief biblical reading, Simeon's canticle (*Nunc Dimittis*), a concluding prayer and an antiphon in honor of Mary.

The book used for recitation of the Liturgy of the Hours is the **Breviary**.

Sacred Music

Of sacred music, the Second Vatican Council stated: "The musical tradition of the universal Church is a treasure of immeasurable value, greater even than that of any other art. The main reason for this preeminence is that, as sacred melody united to words, it forms a necessary or integral part of the solemn liturgy."

"Sacred music increases in holiness to the degree that it is intimately linked with liturgical action, winningly expresses prayerfulness, promotes solidarity, and enriches sacred rites with heightened solemnity. The Church indeed approves of all forms of true art, and admits them into divine worship when they show appropriate qualities."

Practically, the Second Vatican Council declared that: participation in sacred song by the whole body of the faithful, and not just by choirs, should be encouraged and brought about; while Gregorian Chant has a unique dignity and relationship to the Latin-Rite liturgy, other kinds of music are acceptable; native musical traditions, especially in mission territories, and various musical instruments compatible with the dignity of divine worship may be used.

Gregorian Chant has been the basis and most highly regarded standard of liturgical music for centuries. It originated probably during the formative period of the Latin liturgy and developed in conjunction with

Gallican and other forms of chant. Pope St. Gregory the Great's connection with it is not clear, although it is known that he had great concern for and interest in church music during his pontificate (590-604).

Sacred Art

The objective of sacred art, according to the Second Vatican Council, is "that all things set apart for use in divine worship should be truly worthy, becoming and beautiful, signs and symbols of heavenly realities. . . . The Church has . . . always reserved to herself the right to pass judgment upon the arts, deciding which of the works of artists are in accordance with faith, piety and cherished traditional laws, and thereby suited to sacred purposes. . . . To the extent that (artistic) works aim exclusively at turning men's thoughts to God persuasively and devoutly. they are dedicated to God and to the cause of His greater honor and glory."

Noble beauty, not sumptuous display, should be sought in art, sacred vestments and ornaments.

"Sacred furnishings should worthily and beautifully serve the dignity of worship."

RITES

Rites are the forms and ceremonial observances of liturgical worship coupled with the total expression of the theological, spiritual and disciplinary heritages of particular churches of the East and the West.

Different rites have evolved in the course of church history, giving to liturgical worship and church life in general forms and usages peculiar and proper to the nature of worship and the culture of the faithful in various circumstances of time and place. Thus, there has been development since apostolic times in the prayers and ceremonies of the Mass, in the celebration of the sacraments, sacramentals and the Liturgy of the Hours, and in observances of the liturgical calendar. The principal sources of rites in present use were practices in the patriarchates of Rome (for the West) and Antioch, Alexandria and Constantinople (for the East). Rites are identified as Eastern or Western on the basis of their geographical area of origin in the Roman Empire.

Eastern Rites are proper to Eastern Catholic Churches (see separate entry). The principal rites are Byzantine, Alexandrian, Antiochene, Armenian and Chaldean.

The Latin or Roman Rite prevails in the Western Church. It was derived from Roman practices and the use of Latin from the third century onward, and has been the rite in general use in the West since the eighth century. Other rites in limited use in the Western Church have been the Ambrosian (in the Archdiocese of Milan), the Mozarabic (in the Archdiocese of Toledo), the Lyonnaise, the Braga, and rites peculiar to some religious orders like the Dominicans, Carmelites and Carthusians.

The purpose of the revision of rites in progress since the Second Vatican Council is to renew them, not to eliminate the rites of particular churches or to reduce all rites to uniformity. The Council reaffirmed the equal dignity and preservation of rites, as follows.

"It is the mind of the Catholic Church that each individual church or rite retain its traditions whole and entire, while adjusting its way of life to various needs of time and place. Such individual churches, whether of the East or the West, although they differ somewhat among themselves in what are called rites (that is, in liturgy, ecclesiastical discipline and spiritual heritage) are, nevertheless, equally entrusted to the pastoral guidance of the Roman Pontiff, the divinely appointed successor of St. Peter in supreme government over the universal Church. They are, consequently, of equal dignity, so that none of them is superior to the others by reason of rite."

Determination of a person's rite is regulated by church law. Through baptism, a child becomes a member of the rite of his or her parents. If the parents are of different rites, the child's rite is decided by mutual consent of the parents; if there is lack of mutual consent, the child is baptized in the rite of the father. A candidate for baptism over the age of 14 can choose to be baptized in any approved rite. Catholics baptized in one rite may receive the sacraments in any of the approved ritual churches; they may transfer to another rite only with the permission of the Holy See and in accordance with other provisions of the Code of Canon Law.

Mass, the Eucharistic Sacrifice

The Second Vatican Council made the following declarations, among others, with respect to the Mass.

"At the Last Supper, on the night when He was betrayed, our Savior instituted the Eucharistic Sacrifice of His Body and Blood. He did this in order to perpetuate the Sacrifice of the Cross throughout the centuries until He should come again, and so to entrust to His beloved spouse, the Church, a memorial of His death and resurrection: a sacrament of love, a sign of unity, a bond of charity, a paschal banquet in which Christ is consumed, the mind is filled with grace, and a pledge of future glory is given to us."

"As often as the Sacrifice of the Cross in which 'Christ, our Passover, has been sacrificed' is celebrated on an altar, the work of our redemption is carried on. At the same time, in the sacrament of the Eucharistic Bread the unity of all believers who form one body in Christ is both expressed and brought about. All men are called to this union with Christ."

"The ministerial priest, . . . acting in the person of Christ, brings about the Eucharistic Sacrifice and offers it to God in the name of all the people. For their part, the faithful join in the offering of the Eucharist by virtue of their royal priesthood."

DECREES OF COUNCIL OF TRENT

The Council of Trent, in its decrees on the Eucharist, stated the following points of doctrine on the Mass.

• There is in the Catholic Church a true Sacrifice, the Mass instituted by Jesus Christ. It is the Sacrifice of His Body and Blood, Soul and Divinity, himself, under the appearances of bread and wine.

• This Sacrifice is identical with the Sacrifice of the Cross, inasmuch as Christ is the Priest and Victim in both. A difference lies in the manner of offering, which was bloody upon the Cross and is bloodless on the altar.

• The Mass is a propitiatory Sacrifice, atoning for sins of the living and dead for whom it is offered.

• The efficacy of the Mass is derived from the Sacrifice of the Cross, whose superabundant merits it applies to men.

• Although the Mass is offered to God alone, it may be celebrated in honor and memory of the saints.

• Christ instituted the Mass at the Last Supper.

• Christ ordained the Apostles priests, giving them power and the command to consecrate His Body and Blood in the Eucharistic Sacrifice.

ORDER OF THE MASS ·

The Mass consists of two principal parts: the Liturgy of the Word features the proclamation of the word of God; the Eucharistic Liturgy focuses on the central act of sacrifice in the Consecration and on the Eucharistic Banquet in Holy Communion. (Formerly, these divisions were called, respectively, the Mass of the Catechumens and the Mass of the Faithful.) In addition to the principal parts of the Mass, there are ancillary introductory and concluding rites.

Following is a description of the Order of the Mass in effect since Nov. 30, 1969.

Introductory Rites

Entrance: The introductory rites begin with the singing or recitation of an entrance song consisting of a hymn or of one or more scriptural verses stating the theme of the mystery, season or feast commemorated in the Mass being celebrated.

Greeting: The priest and people make the Sign of the Cross together. The priest then greets them in one of several alternative ways and they reply in a corresponding manner.

Penitential Rite: The priest and people together acknowledge their sins in a preliminary step toward worthy celebration of the sacred mysteries. This rite includes a brief examination of conscience, a general confession of sin and plea for divine mercy, and a prayer by the priest for forgiveness.

Doxology: A hymn of praise, Glory to God, sung or said on festive occasions.

Opening Prayer: A prayer of petition offered by the priest on behalf of the worshiping community.

I. Liturgy of the Word

Readings: The featured elements of the Liturgy of the Word are readings of passages from the Bible. If three readings are in order, the first is usually from the Old Testament, the second from the New Testament (Letters, Acts, Revelation), and the third from one of the Gospels. Between the readings, psalm verses and a pre-Gospel acclamation are sung or said.

Homily: Sermon on a scriptural or liturgical subject; ideally, it should be related to the liturgical service in progress.

Profession of Faith: The Nicene Creed, by the priest and people on certain occasions.

Prayer of the Faithful: Litany-type prayers of petition, with participation by the people. Called general intercessions, they concern needs of the Church, the salvation of the world, public authorities, persons in need, the local community.

II. Eucharistic Liturgy

Offertory Procession: Presentation to the priest of the gifts of bread and wine, principally, by participating members of the congregation.

Offering and Prayer over the Gifts: Ceremonies and prayers with which the priest offers bread and wine to be consecrated into the Body and Blood of Christ during the Eucharistic Prayer and to be shared by the faithful in Holy Communion.

Washing of Hands: After offering the bread and wine, the priest cleanses his fingers with water in a brief ceremony of purification.

Pray, Brethren: Prayer that the sacrifice to take place will be acceptable to God. The first part of the prayer is said by the priest; the second, by the people.

Prayer over the Gifts: A prayer of petition offered by the priest on behalf of the worshiping community.

Preface: A hymn of praise introducing the Eucharistic Prayer or Canon, said or sung by the priest following responses by the people. The Order of the Mass contains a variety of prefaces, for use on different occasions.

Holy, Holy, Holy; Blessed Is He: Divine praises sung or said by the priest and people.

Eucharistic Prayer

Eucharistic Prayer (Canon): The Eucharistic Prayer focuses on the **Consecration**, when the essential act of sacrificial offering takes place with the changing of bread and wine into the Body and Blood of Christ (transubstantiation). Prayers of the Canon, which are said by the celebrant only, commemorate principal mysteries of salvation history and include petitions for the Church, the living and dead, and remembrances of saints. There are four principal Eucharistic Prayers, for use on various occasions and at the option of the celebrant of the Mass; additional Canons have been authorized for use at Masses with children and for reconciliation.

Doxology: A formula of divine praise sung or said by the priest while he holds aloft the Body and Blood of Christ for adoration by the faithful.

Communion Rite

Lord's Prayer: Sung or said by the priest and people.

Prayer for Deliverance: Related to the final petition of the Our Father, for deliverance from evil, it is said by the priest. It concludes with an allusion to the final return of Christ in glory, to which the people respond: "For the kingdom, the power, and the glory are yours, now and forever."

Prayer for Peace: Said by the priest, with corresponding response by the people. The priest can, in accord with local custom, bid the people to exchange a greeting of peace with one another.

Lamb of God: A prayer for divine mercy sung or said while the priest breaks the consecrated host and places a piece of it into the consecrated wine in the chalice.

Communion: The priest, after saying a preparatory prayer, administers Holy Communion to himself and then to the people, thus completing the Sacrifice-Banquet of the Mass. (This completion is realized even if the celebrant alone receives the Eucharist.) On giving the Eucharist to the people, the priest says to each recipient, "The Body of Christ"; the customary response is "Amen." If the Eucharist is administered under the forms of bread and wine, the priest says, "The Body and Blood of Christ." (In addition to priests, deacons and extraordinary ministers of the Eucharist can give Communion to the faithful.)

Communion Song: Scriptural verses or a suitable hymn said or sung during and/or after the distribution of Holy Communion.

Prayer after Communion: A prayer of petition offered by the priest on behalf of the worshiping community.

Concluding Rite

Announcements: Brief announcements to the people are in order at this time.

Dismissal: Consists of a final greeting by the priest, a blessing and a formula of dismissal. This rite is omitted if another liturgical action immediately follows the Mass; e. g., a procession, the blessing of a body during a funeral rite.

Some parts of the Mass are changeable with the liturgical season or feast, and are called the **Proper of the Mass.** Other parts which remain the same comprise the **Ordinary of the Mass.**

ADDITIONAL NOTES

Catholics are seriously obliged to attend Mass in a worthy manner on Sundays and holy days of obligation. Failure to do so without a proportionately serious reason is gravely wrong.

Priests, according to the Code of Canon Law, are urged to celebrate Mass daily. To satisfy the needs of the faithful on Sundays and holy days of obligation, they are authorized to celebrate Mass twice (bination) or even three times (trination). Bination is permissible on weekdays for pastoral reasons. On Christmas and All Souls' Day, every priest may celebrate three Masses. Mass may be celebrated at any time.

The fruits of the Mass, which in itself is of infinite value, are: general, for all the faithful; special (ministerial), for the intentions of persons specifically intended by the celebrant; most special (personal), for the celebrant himself.

On Sundays and other days specified in church law, a pastor is obliged to offer Mass for his parishioners or to have another priest do so in his place. If a priest accepts a stipend or offering for a Mass, he is obliged in justice to offer the Mass for the designated intention. Mass may be applied for the living and the dead, and for any good intention.

Mass can be celebrated in several ways; e.g., with people present, without their presence, with two or more priests as concelebrants (concelebration), with greater or less solemnity.

Some of the various types of Masses are: for the dead (Funeral Mass or Mass of Christian Burial, Mass for the Dead — formerly called Requiem Mass); nuptial, for married couples in conjunction with or at some time after the wedding ceremony; votive, to honor a Person of the Trinity, a saint, or for some special intention; pontifical, celebrated by a bishop. A Red Mass is a votive Mass of the Holy Spirit celebrated for members of the legal profession that they might exercise prudence and equity in their official capacities. Gregorian Masses are a series of 30 Masses celebrated on consecutive days for a deceased person.

Mass is not celebrated on Good Friday or Holy Saturday. On Good Friday, there is a Celebration of the Lord's Passion consisting of a Liturgy of the Word, Veneration of the Cross and Holy Communion. Mass celebrated before Saturday midnight as part of the Easter Vigil liturgy is considered a Sunday observance.

The ordinary place for celebrating Mass is a church or other sacred place, at a fixed or movable altar that has been dedicated or blessed. Outside of a sacred place, Mass may be celebrated at an appropriate place at a suitable table covered with a linen cloth and corporal.

MASS VESTMENTS

Liturgical vestments are the articles of dress worn by the ministers of divine worship; distinctive in style, they add appropriate decorum to the celebration of the liturgy.

Alb: A body-length tunic of white fabric.

Amice: A rectangular piece of white fabric worn about the neck, tucked into the collar and falling to the shoulders; for use when the alb does not completely cover ordinary clothing at the neck.

Chasuble: Originally, a large mantle or cloak covering the whole body; the outer garment of the celebrant of Mass.

Cincture: A cord which serves the purpose of a belt, holding the alb close to the body.

Dalmatic: The outer garment worn by a deacon in place of a chasuble.

Stole: A long, band-like vestment worn by priests about the neck and falling to about the knees, during Mass and for other functions; worn by deacons over the left shoulder to the right side.

The material, form and ornamentation of these and other vestments are subject to variation and adaptation, according to norms and decisions of the Holy See and concerned conferences of bishops. The overriding norm is that they should be appropriate for use in divine worship. The customary ornamented vestments are the chasuble, stole and dalmatic.

The minimal vestments required for a priest celebrating Mass are an alb, stole and chasuble.

Chasuble-Alb: A vestment combining the features of the chasuble and alb; for use with a stole by concelebrants of Mass and, by way of exception, by celebrants in certain circumstances.

Liturgical Colors

The colors of outer vestments vary with liturgical seasons, feasts and other circumstances.

Green: For the season of Ordinary Time; symbolic of hope and the vitality of the life of faith.

Purple: For Advent and Lent; may also be used in Masses for the dead; symbolic of penance in Lent, preparation for Christmas in Advent.

Red: For the Sunday of the Passion (Palm Sunday), Good Friday, Pentecost; feasts of the Passion of Our Lord, the Apostles and Evangelists, martyrs; symbolic of the supreme sacrifice of life for the love of God.

Rose: May be used in place of purple on the third Sunday of Advent (Gaudete Sunday) and the fourth Sunday of Lent (Laetare Sunday); symbolic of the anticipated joy of Christmas and Easter.

White: For the seasons of Christmas and Easter; feasts and commemorations of Our Lord, except those of the Passion; feasts and commemorations of the Blessed Virgin Mary, angels, saints who are not martyrs, All Saints (Nov. 1), St. John the Baptist (June 24), St. John the Evangelist (Dec. 27), the Chair of St. Peter (Feb. 22), the Conversion of St. Paul (Jan. 25). White, symbolic of purity and integrity of the life of faith, may generally be substituted for other colors and can be used for funerals and other Masses for the dead.

White, purple or black may be used in Masses for the dead in U.S. dioceses.

On solemn occasions, better than ordinary vestments may be used, even though the color (e.g., gold) does not match the ordinary requirements of the day.

Other Vestments

Cassock: A non-liturgical, full-length, close-fitting robe for use by priests and other clerics under liturgical vestments and in ordinary use; usually black for priests, purple for bishops and other prelates, red for cardinals, white for the pope. In place of a cassock, members of male religious institutes wear the habit proper to their institute.

Cope: A mantle-like vestment open in front and fastened across the chest; worn by sacred ministers in processions and other ceremonies as prescribed by appropriate directives.

Habit: The ordinary (non-liturgical) garb of members of religious institutes, analogous to the cassock of diocesan priests; the form of habits varies from institute to institute.

Humeral Veil: A rectangular vestment worn about the shoulders by a deacon or priest in Eucharistic processions and other ceremonies.

Mitre: A headdress worn at some liturgical functions by bishops, abbots and, in certain cases, other ecclesiastics.

Pallium: A circular band of white wool about two inches wide with front and back pendants, marked with six crosses and worn about the neck. A symbol of the fullness of the episcopal office, its use is restricted to the pope and archbishops of metropolitan sees. Pallia are made from the wool of lambs blessed by the pope on the feast of St. Agnes (Jan. 21).

Rochet: A knee-length, white linen-lace garment of prelates worn under outer vestments.

Surplice: A loose, flowing vestment of white fabric with wide sleeves. For some functions, it is interchangeable with an alb.

Zucchetto: A skullcap worn by bishops and other prelates.

SACRED VESSELS

Chalice and Paten: The principal sacred vessels required for the celebration of Mass are the chalice (cup) and paten (plate) in which wine and bread, respectively, are offered, consecrated and consumed. Both should be made of solid and noble material which is not easily breakable or corruptible. Gold coating is required of the interior parts of sacred vessels subject to rust. The cup of a chalice should be of non-absorbent material.

Vessels for containing consecrated hosts can be made of materials other than solid and noble metal, provided the substitute materials are regarded locally as noble or rather precious and are suitable for sacred use. Vessels of this kind are the following.

Ciborium: Used to hold hosts for distribution to the faithful and for the reservation of hosts in the tabernacle.

Luna, Lunula, Lunette: A small receptacle which holds the sacred host in an upright position in the monstrance.

Monstrance, Ostensorium: A portable receptacle so made that the sacred host, when enclosed therein, can be clearly seen, as at Benediction or during extended exposition of the Blessed Sacrament.

Pyx: A watch-shaped vessel used for carrying the Eucharist to the sick.

Sacred vessels should be blessed or consecrated, according to prescribed requirements.

LINENS

Altar Cloth: A cloth covering the table of an altar. One cloth is sufficient.

Burse: A square, stiff, flat case, open at one end, in which the folded corporal can be placed; the outside is covered with material of the same kind and color as the outer vestments of the celebrant.

Corporal: A square piece of white cloth spread on the altar cloth, on

which rest the vessels holding the Sacred Species — the consecrated host(s) and wine — during the Eucharistic Liturgy. The corporal is similarly used whenever the Blessed Sacrament is removed from the tabernacle; e. g., during Exposition the vessel containing the Blessed Sacrament rests on a corporal.

Finger Towel: A white rectangular napkin used by the priest to dry his fingers after cleansing them following the offering of gifts at Mass.

Pall: A cloth-covered square piece of stiff material used to cover the chalice at Mass.

Purificator: A white rectangular napkin used for cleansing sacred vessels after their use at Mass.

Veil: The chalice intended for use at Mass can be covered with a veil made of the same material as the outer vestments of the celebrant.

The Church Building

A church is a building set aside and dedicated for purposes of divine worship, to which the faithful have the right of free access.

A Catholic church is the ordinary place in which the faithful assemble for participation in the Mass and other forms of divine worship.

In the early years of Christianity, the first places of assembly for worship were private homes and, sometimes, catacombs. Church building began in the latter half of the second century during lulls in persecution and became widespread after enactment of the Edict of Milan in 313, when it finally became possible for the Church to emerge completely from the underground. The oldest and basic norms regarding church buildings date from about that time.

The essential principle underlying all norms for church building were formulated by the Second Vatican Council, as follows: "When churches are to be built, let great care be taken that they be suitable for the celebration of liturgical services and for the active participation of the faithful." The Code of Canon Law declares that anything not in accord with the nature of a church as a place of worship is forbidden.

MAIN FEATURES

Sanctuary: The part of the church where the altar of sacrifice is located, the place where the ministers of the liturgy lead the people in prayer, proclaim the word of God and celebrate the Eucharist. It is set off from the body of the church by some kind of distinctive architectural feature — e.g., elevation above the main floor — or by ornamentation. (The traditional communion rail, removed in recent years in many churches, served this purpose of demarcation.) The customary location of the sanctuary is at the front of the church; it may, however, be centrally located.

Altar: The main altar or table of sacrifice is the focal feature of the sanctuary and entire church. It stands by itself, so that the ministers can move about it freely, and is so situated that they face the people during the liturgical action. In addition to the main altar, there may be others also; in new churches, these are ideally situated in side chapels or alcoves removed to some degree from the body of the church. Every church should have a fixed altar; i.e., one attached to the floor of the church. Its table should be of stone or of some other worthy and solid material, and it should be dedicated. The custom of placing relics of martyrs or other saints in a fixed altar should be observed. A movable altar can be made of any solid and suitable material, and it should be blessed or dedicated.

Adornment of the Altar: The altar is covered with an appropriate cloth, preferably of linen. Required candelabra and a crucifix are placed upon or near the altar in plain sight of the people and are so arranged that they do not obscure their view of the liturgical action.

Seats of the Ministers: The seat of the celebrant, corresponding with his role as the presiding minister of the assembly, is best located behind the altar and facing the people; it is raised a bit above the level of the altar but must not have the appearance of a throne. The seats of other ministers are also located in the sanctuary.

Ambo, Pulpit, Lectern: The stand at which scriptural lessons and psalm responses are read, the word of God preached, and the Prayer of the Faithful offered. It is so placed that the ministers can be easily seen and heard by the people.

Places for the People: Seats and kneeling benches (pews) and other accommodations for the people are so arranged that they can participate in the most appropriate way in the liturgical action and have freedom of movement for the reception of Holy Communion. Reserved seats are out of order.

Place for the Choir: Its location depends on the most suitable arrangement for maintaining the unity of the choir with the congregation and for providing its members maximum opportunity for carrying out their proper function and participating fully in the Mass.

Tabernacle: The best place for reserving the Blessed Sacrament is in a chapel suitable for the devotion of the people. If this is not possible, reservation should be at a side altar or other appropriately adorned place. In either case, the Blessed Sacrament should be kept in a tabernacle; i.e., a safe-like, secure receptacle.

Statues: Images of the Lord, the Blessed Virgin Mary and the saints are legitimately proposed for the veneration of the faithful in churches. Their number and arrangement, however, should be ordered in such a way that they do not distract the people from the central celebration of the Mass. There should be only one statue of one and the same saint in a church. The Second Vatican Council declared: "The practice of placing sacred images in churches so that they may be venerated by the faithful is to be firmly maintained. Nevertheless, their number should be moderate and their relative location should reflect right order. Otherwise they may create confusion among the Christian people and promote a faulty sense of devotion."

General Adornment and Arrangement of Churches: Churches should be so adorned and fitted out that they serve the direct requirements of divine worship and the needs and convenience of the people.

Other Items

Ambry: A box-like receptacle containing the holy oils, attached to the wall of the sanctuary in some churches.

Baptistery (Baptistry): The place for administering the sacrament of baptism; practically, in many churches, the baptismal font itself. Some churches have a baptistery adjoining or near the entrance, a position symbolizing the fact that persons are received into the Church and incorporated in Christ through this sacrament. Contemporary liturgical practice favors placement of the baptistery near the sanctuary and altar, or the use of a movable font in the same position, to emphasize the relationship of baptism to the Eucharist, the celebration in sacrifice and banquet of the death and resurrection of Christ.

Candles: Used more for symbolic than illuminative purposes, they represent Christ, the light and life of grace, at liturgical functions. They should be made of beeswax.

Confessional: A booth-like structure for the hearing of confessions, with separate compartments for the priest and penitents and a grating or screen between them. The use of confessionals became general in the Latin Rite after the Council of Trent. Since the Second Vatican Council, there has been a trend in the U.S. to replace or supplement confessionals with small reconciliation rooms so arranged that priest and penitent can converse face-to-face.

Crucifix: A cross bearing the figure of the body of Christ, representative of the Sacrifice of the Cross.

Cruets: Vessels containing the wine and water used at Mass. They are placed on a credence table in the sanctuary.

Holy Water Fonts: Receptacles containing holy water, usually at church entrances, for the use of the faithful.

Sanctuary Lamp: A candle which is kept burning continuously before a tabernacle in which the Blessed Sacrament is reserved, as a sign of the Real Presence of Christ in the Eucharist.

Sacred Places

Oratory: A place set aside for divine worship primarily for the convenience of a particular group or community of people; others may also attend services there. All liturgical services may be held in an oratory.

Chapel, Private: A place set aside for divine worship for the convenience of one or more individuals. Permission of the local bishop is required for the celebration of Mass and other liturgical functions.

Shrine: A church or other sacred place of special devotion frequented by the faithful.

Cathedrals and Basilicas

Cathedrals and basilicas are church buildings with special status.

A cathedral is the principal church in a diocese, the one in which the bishop has his seat (*cathedra*). Because of the dignity of a cathedral, the dates of its dedication and its patronal feast are observed throughout a diocese.

The pope's cathedral, the Basilica of St. John Lateran, is the highest ranking church in the world.

Basilica is a title assigned to certain churches because of their antiquity, dignity, historical importance or significance as centers of worship. Major basilicas have the Holy Door which is opened and closed at the beginning and end of a Holy Year. Minor basilicas have certain ceremonial privileges.

Among the major basilicas are those of St. John Lateran, St. Peter, St. Paul Outside the Walls and St. Mary Major in Rome; St. Francis and St. Mary of the Angels in Assisi.

Minor basilicas in the U.S. are located in the following states: Alabama — Cathedral of the Immaculate Conception (Mobile); California — Mission Dolores (San Francisco), Old Mission of San Carlos (Carmel), St. Joseph (Alameda), Mission San Diego de Alcala (San Diego); Colorado — Cathedral of the Immaculate Conception (Denver); Florida — Cathedral of St. Augustine (St. Augustine); Illinois — Our Lady of Sorrows and Queen of All Saints (Chicago); Indiana — Old Cathedral (Vincennes); Iowa — St. Francis Xavier (Dyersville); Kentucky — Our Lady of Gethsemani (Trappist), Cathedral of the Assumption (Covington); Louisiana — St. Louis King of France (New Orleans);

Maryland — Assumption of the Blessed Virgin Mary (Baltimore); Massachusetts — Perpetual Help "Mission Church" (Roxbury); Michigan — St. Adalbert (Grand Rapids); Minnesota — St. Mary (Minneapolis); Missouri — Basilica of the Immaculate Conception (Conception); St. Louis King of France (St. Louis); New York — Our Lady of Perpetual Help and the Cathedral-Basilica of St. James (Brooklyn), Our Lady of Victory (Lackawanna), Blessed Virgin Mary of the Rosary of Fatima (Youngstown); Ohio — Shrine of Our Lady of Consolation (Carey); Pennsylvania — St. Vincent Basilica (Benedictine Archabbey, Latrobe), Basilica of the Sacred Heart (Conewago), Cathedral of Sts. Peter and Paul (Philadelphia); Texas — St. Mary Cathedral (Galveston); Wisconsin — St. Josaphat (Milwaukee).

National Shrine

The National Shrine of the Immaculate Conception is dedicated to the honor of the Blessed Virgin Mary, who was declared patroness of the United States in 1846. The shrine project was launched in 1914; the site and foundation stone were blessed in 1920; the crypt, an underground church, was completed in 1926; the main church and superstructure were dedicated Nov. 20, 1959; more than 56 chapels and additional interior furnishings have been installed since the dedication. There is a distinctive bell tower housing a 56-bell carillon.

The shrine is the seventh largest religious building in the world and the largest Catholic church in the Western Hemisphere, with normal seating and standing accommodations for 6,000 persons. It contains some of the largest mosaics in the world.

Approximately one million persons visit the shrine each year. It is located adjacent to the Catholic University of America, Michigan Ave. and Fourth St. N.E., Washington, D.C. 20017.

Sacraments

The general concept of sacrament is a means of making someone or something holy.

The Second Vatican Council called Jesus Christ the primordial sacrament of God's presence and action in the world for human redemption and salvation. The *Dogmatic Constitution on the Church* also said that "the Church is a kind of sacrament or sign of intimate union with God and of the unity of all mankind."

The seven sacraments properly so called are actions of Christ and the Church which signify grace, cause it in the act of signifying it, and confer it upon persons properly disposed to receive it. They perpetuate the redemptive activity of Christ, making it present and effective. Sacramental actions consist of the union of sensible signs (matter of the sacraments) with the words of the minister (form of the sacraments).

Christ instituted the seven sacraments of the New Law by determining their essence and the efficacy of their signs to produce the grace they signify. He is the principal priest or minister of every sacrament; human agents are secondary ministers. Sacraments have their efficacy from Christ, not from the personal dispositions of their human ministers.

Each sacrament confers sanctifying grace for the special purpose of the sacrament; this is, accordingly, called sacramental grace. It involves a claim to actual graces corresponding to the purposes of the respective sacraments.

While sacraments infallibly produce the grace they signify, recipients benefit from them in proportion to their personal dispositions of faith and devotion. One of these dispositions is the intention to receive sacraments as sacred signs of God's saving and grace-giving action. The state of grace is necessary for fruitful reception of the Eucharist, confirmation, matrimony, holy orders and anointing of the sick. Baptism is the sacrament of spiritual regeneration; penance is the sacrament by which persons guilty of serious sins after baptism are reconciled with God through the ministry of the Church, and in which persons already in the state of grace are strengthened in that state.

Baptism, confirmation and the Eucharist are sacraments of initiation; penance and anointing of the sick are sacraments of healing; matrimony and holy orders are sacraments of dedication to particular ways of life and service in, to and through the Church.

BAPTISM

Baptism is the sacrament by which persons are freed from original sin (and other sins which may have been committed before baptism), are reborn as children of God, are made like Christ by an indelible character, and are incorporated in the Church. It is necessary for salvation;

by water ordinarily, or at least by desire. It is the primary sacrament of Christian initiation, can be received only once, and makes the recipient eligible for the reception of other sacraments and for participation in the total life and mission of the Church.

The matter of the sacrament is water; the form is, "I baptize you in the name of the Father and of the Son and of the Holy Spirit." In the Latin Rite, baptism can be administered by combining the words of the form with infusion (pouring of water on the forehead) or immersion of the recipient, depending on the decision of the appropriate episcopal conference.

The ordinary minister of baptism is a bishop, priest or deacon. Under certain conditions, a catechist or other designated lay person may lawfully baptize and, in case of necessity, any person with the proper intention (to do what the Church intends) may do so. The Church recognizes the validity of baptisms properly conferred by non-Catholic ministers.

The baptism of infants has always been considered valid, and the general practice of infant baptism was well established by the fifth century. Infants should be baptized within a few weeks of birth. They should be given a name which is not alien to Christian sentiment.

Adults advance from original stages of inquiry and preparation to the reception of baptism and the other sacraments of Christian initiation.

Baptism is administered conditionally when there is reasonable doubt about the validity of a previous baptism. If a person cannot receive baptism of water, it can be supplied by baptism of desire (the implicit intention, at least, of doing whatever God wills persons should do for salvation) or baptism of blood (martyrdom for a Christian motive).

A person being baptized should have a sponsor — a practicing Catholic 16 years of age or older who has received the Eucharist and been confirmed; there may be two sponsors, one of each sex. A non-Catholic Christian can serve as a Christian witness to a baptism but not as a sponsor. Parents may not be baptismal sponsors of their own children.

Parents and sponsors assume appropriate responsibilities with respect to the religious formation and practice of the person baptized.

The ordinary place of baptism is a church, usually in the place where the parents of a child or an adult to be baptized lives.

CONFIRMATION

Confirmation is the sacrament by which a baptized person is enriched with the gift of the Holy Spirit, is joined more closely with the Church, is strengthened and obliged to defend, spread and give witness to the Christian faith. The sacrament carries forward the process of Christian initiation begun with baptism, confers an indelible character and can be received only once.

The sacrament is conferred with the simultaneous anointing of the forehead with chrism, the laying on of hands and recitation by the minister of the formula, "N . . ., be sealed with the Gift of the Holy Spirit."

The ordinary minister is a bishop. Priests may be delegated for the purpose. A pastor can confirm a parishioner in danger of death. Also authorized to confer the sacrament is a priest who baptizes an adult or receives a baptized adult into full communion with the Church.

The recipient of confirmation must be baptized, adequately instructed, properly disposed and capable of renewing the baptismal promises. The general law of the Church sets the age of discretion (about seven years of age) as the time for conferring the sacrament, but leaves to episcopal conferences the option to decide on a later age. The person being confirmed should have a sponsor, preferably the same one as at baptism.

EUCHARIST

The Eucharist is the sacrifice and the sacrament in which Christ the Lord himself is contained, offered and received under the appearances of bread and wine. In the Latin Rite, the matter of the sacrament is unleavened wheat bread and pure grape wine; the form consists of the words of consecration said by the priest at Mass: "This is My Body. . . . This is the cup of My Blood. . . ."

Only a priest can consecrate bread and wine so they become the body and blood of Christ. After consecration, however, the Eucharist can be administered to people by deacons and by extraordinary ministers (designated religious and lay persons). Consecrated hosts are reserved in the tabernacle of a church or oratory primarily for Viaticum and also for adoration by the faithful of Christ really present in the Blessed Sacrament.

Priests celebrating Mass receive the Eucharist under the appearances of bread and wine. In the Latin Rite, others usually receive under the appearances of bread only, i.e., the consecrated host; in some circumstances, however, they may receive under the appearances of both bread and wine. In Eastern-Rite practice, the faithful generally receive a piece of consecrated bread which has been dipped into consecrated wine, i.e., by intinction.

Conditions for receiving the Eucharist, called Holy Communion, are the state of grace (freedom from grave sin), the right intention and observance of the Eucharistic fast (from food and drink, but not water or medicine, for an hour before Communion. The elderly and those suffering from illness, as well as those caring for them, may receive the Eucharist even if they ate or drank something during the preceding hour).

The faithful of the Latin Rite are required by a precept of the Church to receive the Eucharist at least once a year, during the Easter Time (in the U.S. from the first Sunday of Lent to Trinity Sunday, inclusive). Much more frequent reception is urged. Communion can be given outside of Mass to persons unable to receive it during Mass on a given day. A person who has already received the Eucharist may receive it again on the same day only within a Eucharistic celebration in which the person participates. If a person who has received the Eucharist comes into danger of death on the same day, the sacrament should be given to him again as Viaticum (Communion for the dying).

Parents, those who take their place and pastors have the responsibility of seeing that children who have reached the age of discretion are properly prepared for and are given the Eucharist, after sacramental confession. The obligation to receive the Eucharist once a year, during Easter Time, begins with the reception of first Communion.

Forms of Eucharistic devotion outside of Mass are Benediction, exposition of the Blessed Sacrament, processions, holy hours and congresses with appropriate rites.

PENANCE

Penance is the sacrament in which the faithful who confess their sins with sorrow and purpose of amendment receive forgiveness from

God and reconciliation with the Church through the absolution of a priest.

The essential elements of the sacrament are the acts of the penitent — sorrow for sins because of a supernatural motive (love of God, fear of hell), confession (of previously unconfessed grave sins, required; or venial sins also, but not of necessity), purpose of amendment, and reparation (by means of prayer or other means prescribed by the confessor) — and absolution. The minister is an authorized priest, i.e., one who, besides having the power of orders to forgive sins, also has jurisdiction granted by church authority or by church law.

The only ordinary means for the faithful to be reconciled with God and the Church through the forgiveness of grave sins are individual and integral confession and absolution. Private confession and absolution can take place in a simple celebration of the sacrament or in connection with a penitential service for a group of the faithful.

When, in a case of necessity, it is not possible for a person in grave sin to confess before receiving Holy Communion, forgiveness of sin can be achieved through an act of perfect contrition with the intention of confessing as soon as possible.

In extraordinary cases, reconciliation may be attained by general absolution without prior individual confession as, for example, under these circumstances: (1) danger of death, when there is neither time nor priests available for hearing confessions; (2) grave necessity of a number of penitents who, because of a shortage of confessors, would be deprived of sacramental grace and Communion for a lengthy period of time through no fault of their own. Persons receiving general absolution are obliged to be properly disposed and resolved to make an individual confession of the grave sins from which they have been absolved; this confession should be made as soon as the opportunity to confess presents itself and before any second reception of general absolution.

Norms regarding general absolution, issued by the Congregation for the Doctrine of the Faith in 1972, are not intended to provide a basis for convoking large gatherings of the faithful for the purpose of imparting general absolution, in the absence of extraordinary circumstances. Judgment about circumstances that warrant general absolution belongs principally to the bishop of the place, with due regard for related decisions of appropriate episcopal conferences.

The ordinary place for hearing confession is a church or oratory, in the traditional confessional or another appropriate setting.

A precept of the Church obliges the faithful guilty of grave sin to confess at least once a year. The Church favors more frequent reception of the sacrament not only for the reconciliation of persons guilty of serious sins but also for reasons of devotion. Devotional confession — in which venial sins or previously forgiven sins are confessed — serves the purpose of confirming persons in penance and conversion.

ANOINTING OF THE SICK

Anointing of the sick is administered to the faithful who begin to be in danger by reason of illness or old age. By the anointing with blessed oil and the accompanying prayer of a priest, the sacrament confers on the person comforting grace; the remission of venial sins and inculpably unconfessed grave sins, together with at least some of the temporal punishment due for sins; and, sometimes, results in a state of improved health.

The matter of the sacrament is the anointing of the forehead and hands or, in case of necessity, of another part of the body. The form is: "Through this holy anointing and His most loving mercy, may the Lord assist you by the grace of the Holy Spirit so that, when you have been freed from your sins, He may save you and in His goodness raise you up."

Anointing of the sick, formerly called extreme unction, may be received more than once, e.g., in new or continuing stages of serious illness. Ideally, the sacrament should be administered while the recipient is conscious and in conjunction with the sacraments of penance and the Eucharist. In doubt about the person's use of reason or the dangerous nature of the illness or whether the person is dead or not, the sacrament should be administered if there is reason to believe that the recipient, at least implicitly, wanted to receive it.

Anointing of the sick can be administered during a communal celebration in some circumstances, as in a home for the aged, in accord with directives of the appropriate diocesan bishop.

ORDERS

By the sacrament of orders, properly qualified Catholic men are consecrated as sacred ministers — bishops, priests, deacons — for carrying out the offices of teaching, sanctifying and ruling in the service of the People of God. The sacrament, which marks the recipient with an indelible character, is conferred by the laying on of hands and the appropriate prayer by the ordaining bishop.

Bishops: The fullness of the priesthood belongs to those who receive the order of bishop. Bishops, in hierarchical union with the pope and their fellow bishops, are the successors of the Apostles as pastors of the Church; they have individual responsibility for the care of the local churches they serve and collegial responsibility for the care of the universal Church.

Priests: Priests are ordained to celebrate Mass, administer the sacraments, preach and teach the word of God, impart blessings and perform additional pastoral functions according to the mandate of their bishops and/or other ecclesiastical superiors. They "do not possess the highest degree of the priesthood and . . . are dependent on the bishops in the exercise of their power, (but) are nevertheless united with the bishops in sacerdotal dignity. By the power of the sacrament of orders . . .

they are consecrated to preach the Gospel, shepherd the faithful and celebrate divine worship as true priests of the New Testament" (*Dogmatic Constitution on the Church*, Second Vatican Council).

Deacons: "At a lower level of the hierarchy are deacons, upon whom hands are imposed 'not unto the priesthood but unto a ministry of service.' . . . In communion with the bishop and his group of priests, they serve the People of God in the ministry of the liturgy, of the word and of charity. It is the duty of the deacon, to the extent that he has been authorized by competent authority, to administer baptism solemnly, to be custodian and dispenser of the Eucharist, to assist at and bless marriages in the name of the Church, to bring Viaticum to the dying, to read the sacred Scripture to the faithful, to instruct and exhort the people, to preside at the worship and prayer of the faithful, to administer sacramentals, and to officiate at funeral and burial services. (They are) dedicated to duties of charity and administration" (according to the cited constitution).

The order of deacon is conferred on two types of qualified candidates, viz., men who are on the way to the priesthood (transitional deacons) and men who receive the order as a permanent rank. A single candidate for the permanent diaconate, with the public vow of celibacy, can be ordained at the age of 26; he cannot marry after ordination. A married candidate, with the consent of his wife, can be ordained at the age of 36; he cannot marry after the death of his wife.

Steps preliminary to reception of the sacrament of orders are a liturgical rite of admission as a candidate and installation in and practice of the ministries of lector and acolyte.

Celibacy

Celibacy is the unmarried state of life, required in the Roman Church of candidates for holy orders and of men already ordained to holy orders, for the practice of perfect chastity and total dedication to the service of people in the ministry of the Church. Celibacy is enjoined as a condition for ordination by church discipline and law, not by dogmatic necessity.

In the Roman Church, a consensus in favor of celibacy developed in the early centuries while the clergy included both celibates and men who had been married once. The first local legislation on the subject was enacted by a local council held in Elvira, Spain, about 306; it forbade bishops, priests, deacons and other ministers to have wives. Similar enactments were passed by other local councils from that time on, and by the 12th century particular laws regarded marriage by clerics in major orders to be not only unlawful but also null and void. The latter view was translated by the Second Lateran Council in 1139 into what seems to be the first written universal law making holy orders an invalidating impediment to marriage. In 1563 the Council of Trent ruled definitely on the matter and established the discipline in force in the Roman Church.

Some exceptions to this discipline have been made in recent years. Several married Protestant and Episcopalian (Anglican) clergymen who became converts and were subsequently ordained to the priesthood have been permitted to continue in marriage. Married men over the age of 35 can be ordained to the permanent diaconate.

Eastern Church discipline on celibacy differs from that of the Roman Church. In line with legislation enacted by the Synod of Trullo in 692 and still in force, candidates for holy orders may marry before becoming deacons and may continue in marriage thereafter, but marriage after ordination is forbidden. Eastern-Rite bishops in the U.S., however, do not ordain married candidates for the priesthood. Eastern-Rite bishops are unmarried.

MARRIAGE

The matrimonial covenant — by which a baptized man and a baptized woman establish the partnership of their whole lives, and which by its nature is ordered to the good of the spouses and the generation and rearing of children — is a sacrament. There cannot be a valid matrimonial contract between baptized persons which is not a sacrament.

The essential properties of marriage are unity and indissolubility; it is an exclusive one-man, one-woman relationship for life.

Matrimonial consent must be free, mutual, unaffected by impediments, informed and committed to the essential rights and obligations of marriage, and manifested in a lawful manner.

The ministers of the sacrament are the man and woman as they express their mutual giving and acceptance of each other in the rite of marriage. The grace of the sacrament consecrates and dedicates them to the purposes of their covenanted life as husband and wife, father and mother (God willing).

Marriage Laws of the Church

Marriage laws of the Church, which provide juridical norms in support of the sacrament, are binding on all Catholics. Non-Catholics, whether baptized or not, are not considered bound by these laws except in cases of marriage with a Catholic. Certain natural laws, in the Catholic view, bind all men and women, irrespective of their religious beliefs; accordingly, marriage is prohibited before the time of puberty, without knowledge or full consent, in the case of an already existing valid marriage bond, in the case of antecedent and perpetual impotence.

Preparations for marriage, in addition to arrangements for the time and place of the ceremony, include doctrinal and moral instruction concerning marriage and the recording of data which verify in documentary form the eligibility and freedom of the persons to marry. Records of this kind — along with attestations that marriage has taken place — are preserved in a confidential manner in the archives of the church and/or diocese where the marriage takes place. Banns are public announcements made in their parish churches of the names of persons who intend to marry. Persons who know of reasons in church law why a proposed marriage should not take place are obliged to make them known to the appropriate pastor.

Consent and Form of Marriage

The exchange of consent to the marriage covenant must be rational, free, true and mutual. Consent can be invalidated by an essential defect, substantial error, the strong influence of force or fear, the presence of an intention or condition against the nature of marriage.

For validity and lawfulness, a Catholic is required to contract marriage with a Catholic or non-Catholic in the required form — i.e., in the presence of a competent bishop, priest or deacon (or designated lay person in an unusual case of necessity and under certain conditions) and two witnesses. (For dispensation from this form, see item under Mixed Marriages.)

Special regulations are in effect for marriages between Latin-Rite or Eastern-Rite Catholics and members of separated Eastern Churches (e.g., Orthodox). They can contract marriage validly in the presence of a priest of a separated Eastern Church, provided other requirements of law are complied with; with permission of the competent Latin-Rite or Eastern-Rite bishop, this form of marriage is lawful as well as valid.

Church law regarding the form of marriage does not affect the marriage of non-Catholics with each other; neither does it affect the marriage of Catholics who have defected from the Church by a formal act. The Church recognizes as valid the marriages of non-Catholics before ministers of religion and civil officials, unless they are rendered null and void on other grounds.

The ordinary place of marriage is the parish church of either Catholic party or of the Catholic party to a mixed marriage. The local bishop can grant permission for a mixed marriage to take place in an other-than-Catholic church or in another suitable place.

Special Cases

Diriment impediments are factors which render a person incapable of contracting marriage in a valid manner. The most common ones are an existing valid marriage bond and disparity of cult. The latter obtains when one party is a Catholic and the other party is unbaptized. Diocesan bishops can dispense from the impediment of disparity of cult. No dispensation is possible from the impediment of a valid bond. Some dispensations are reserved to the Holy See.

The express permission of competent church authority is required for the marriage of a Catholic with a baptized, non-Catholic Christian. This difference of religion was a prohibitory (but not invalidating) impediment prior to church law in effect since November 27, 1983.

A valid and consummated marriage of baptized persons cannot be dissolved by any human authority or any cause other than the death of one of the persons.

In other circumstances, for serious reasons connected with the spiritual welfare of the concerned persons and under strict conditions: (1) A valid but unconsummated marriage of baptized persons or of a baptized and an unbaptized person can be dissolved by dispensation of the pope. (2) A legitimate marriage, even consummated, of unbaptized persons can be dissolved in favor of one of them who subsequently receives the sacrament of baptism (Pauline Privilege), if the unbaptized person refuses to live in peace with the husband or wife who has been baptized. (3) A legitimate and consummated marriage of a baptized and an unbaptized person can be dissolved by the pope in virtue of the Privilege of Faith (Petrine Privilege).

Because of the unity and indissolubility of marriage, the Church denies that civil divorce can dissolve the bond of a valid marriage, whether the marriage involves two Catholics, a Catholic and a non-Catholic, or non-Catholics with each other.

In view of serious circumstances of marital distress, however, the Church permits an innocent and aggrieved wife or husband to separate and/or to seek and obtain a civil divorce for the purpose of acquiring title and right to the civil effects. Under other circumstances — as would obtain if a marriage was invalid — civil divorce is permitted for civil effects and as the civil ratification of the fact that the marriage bond does not exist.

A decree of annulment is a decision by competent church authority that an apparently valid marriage was actually invalid from the beginning because of the unknown or concealed existence, from the beginning, of a diriment impediment, an essential defect in consent, radical incapability for marriage, or a condition placed by one or both of the parties against the very nature of marriage.

MIXED MARRIAGES

Pastoral experience, which the Catholic Church shares with other religious bodies, confirms the fact that marriages of persons of different beliefs involve special problems related to the continuing religious practice of the concerned persons and to the religious education and formation of their children. Pastoral measures to minimize these problems include instruction of a non-Catholic party in essentials of the Catholic faith for purposes of understanding. Some instruction should also be given to the Catholic party regarding his or her partner's beliefs.

The Catholic party to a mixed marriage is required to declare his (her) intention of continuing practice of the Catholic faith and to promise to do all in his (her) power to share his (her) faith with children born of the marriage by having them baptized and raised as Catholics. No declarations or promises are required of the non-Catholic partner, but he (she) must be informed of the declaration and promise made by the Catholic party. Notice of the Catholic's declaration and promise is an essential part of the application made to a bishop for dispensation from the impediment of mixed religion or of disparity of cult.

Church law requires that the marriage ordinarily take place according to the usual form before a competent bishop, priest or deacon and two witnesses. The ordinary place of the marriage is the parish church of the Catholic party, although a bishop can permit the celebration in another church or suitable place. A non-Catholic minister may not only attend the ceremony but may also address, pray with and bless the couple.

For appropriate pastoral reasons, a bishop can grant a dispensation from the Catholic form of marriage and permit a non-Catholic minister to officiate, with a Catholic priest in attendance to address, pray with and bless the couple.

It is not permitted to have two religious services or to have a single service in which both the Catholic marriage ritual and a non-Catholic marriage ritual are celebrated jointly or successively.

Liturgical Year and Calendar

The liturgical year is the arrangement throughout the year of a series of seasons and feasts (Proper of Seasons) which focus attention on the principal mysteries of the redemption for purposes of divine worship and strengthening Christian life. An annual cycle also honors Mary, the Mother of God, and commemorates a representative number of martyrs and other saints of universal significance who are proposed as intercessors and examples of Christian life to the faithful (Proper of the Saints).

In the Latin Rite, the arrangement of the year is governed by a general calendar in effect since Jan. 1, 1970, in line with the revision of the liturgical year decreed by the Second Vatican Council. The liturgical year begins on the first Sunday of Advent and ends on the Saturday following the solemnity of Christ the King.

PROPER OF SEASONS

Advent, a season of four weeks or slightly less duration with four Sundays, is a time of preparation and joyful expectation of the coming of Christ. During the first two weeks, the second coming of Christ at the end of time is the focus of attention. From December 17 to 24, the emphasis shifts to anticipation of the celebration of His birth on the solemnity of Christmas. Since the 10th century, the first Sunday has marked the beginning of the liturgical year in the Western (Latin) Church.

The **Christmas season** begins on the evening before Christmas (Vigil of Christmas) and lasts until the Sunday after January 6. It commemorates Christ's birth and early manifestations of His divinity. Major celebrations include Christmas and its octave, the Solemnity of Mary, the Epiphany, and the feasts of the Holy Family and Baptism of the Lord.

The season of **Lent** begins on Ash Wednesday, which occurs between February 4 and March 11, depending on the date of Easter, and lasts until the Mass of the Lord's Supper (Holy Thursday). It has six Sundays. The sixth Sunday marks the beginning of Holy Week and is known as Passion (formerly called Palm) Sunday. Lent is a time of preparation for Easter, with a baptismal and penitential character. The origin of lenten observances dates back to the fourth century or earlier.

The **Easter (Paschal) Triduum** begins with evening Mass of the Lord's Supper (Holy Thursday) and ends with Evening Prayer on Easter Sunday. It is the yearly celebration of the Paschal Mystery and takes precedence over all other liturgical days. The Mass of the Lord's Supper commemorates the institution of the sacraments of the Eucharist and holy orders; Good Friday observances commemorate the passion and death of Christ; Easter Vigil ceremonies are all related to the resurrection and renewal-in-grace theme of Easter.

The **Easter season** lasts for 50 days, from Easter to Pentecost; the theme is resurrection from sin to life. The terminal phase of the season, between the Ascension and Pentecost, stresses anticipation of the coming and action of the Holy Spirit.

Ordinary Time: The season of Ordinary Time begins at the conclusion of the Christmas season (Monday after the Sunday following January 6) and continues until the day before Ash Wednesday, inclusive; it resumes on the Monday after Pentecost and ends on the Saturday before the first Sunday of Advent. It consists of 33 or 34 weeks which, unlike Lent and other seasons, celebrate no particular aspect of the mystery of Christ. The purpose of the season is to elaborate the themes of salvation. The last Sunday is celebrated as the solemnity of Christ the King. Other movable solemnities of the Lord observed during Ordinary Time are of the Holy Trinity, Corpus Christi and the Sacred Heart.

PROPER OF THE SAINTS

Celebrated concurrently with the Proper of Seasons but subordinate to it is the Proper of the Saints. The commemoration of a saint, as a general rule, is observed on the day of death (*dies natalis*, day of birth to glory). Exceptions are those of John the Baptist, who is honored on the day of his birth, and several who are honored in joint feasts (e.g., Sts. Cyril and Methodius).

SUNDAYS, OTHER HOLY DAYS

Sunday, the Lord's Day, is the weekly celebration of the resurrection. It is the original Christian feast day and primary holy day of obligation. From apostolic times, Christians gathered on the first day of the week, the day of the resurrection, to celebrate the Eucharist.

Other holy days of obligation prescribed for the universal Church are: Christmas, the Nativity of the Lord, Dec. 25; Epiphany, Jan. 6; Ascension; Corpus Christi; Solemnity of Mary, Jan. 1; Immaculate Conception, Dec. 8; Assumption, Aug. 15; St. Joseph, Mar. 19; Sts. Peter and Paul, June 29; All Saints, Nov. 1. Episcopal conferences have the option of suppressing or transferring the observance of certain holy days of obligation. In the United States, Epiphany and Corpus Christi are transferred to Sundays; the solemnities of St. Joseph and Sts. Peter and Paul are not prescribed for observance.

On Sundays and other holy days of obligation, Catholics are seriously obliged, unless excused for sound reasons, to assist at Mass and to avoid work and involvement in business which impede participation in divine worship and enjoyment of rest and relaxation.

Scriptural readings at Mass on Sundays and holy days are arranged in a three-year cycle (designated Year A, B, or C) so that widely representative portions of Scripture may be read to the faithful as decreed by the Second Vatican Council. There is also a two-phased cycle of readings for the weekdays of Ordinary Time.

FEAST DAYS, WEEKDAYS, DAYS OF PRAYER

Feast days in the general calendar are ranked according to dignity and manner of observance: solemnity (the highest), feast, memorial and optional memorial. Observances of the first three categories are universal in the Latin Rite; optional memorials are observable by choice. Fixed celebrations are those which are celebrated on the same calendar day each year. Movable observances are Easter and feasts which depend on Easter (e.g., Ascension, Pentecost) and are held on different dates each year. When two celebrations of equal rank fall on the same day, observance is held of the one listed first in the table of precedence in the norms of the general calendar; the other is not celebrated that year unless it is a solemnity or a feast which is transferred to another date.

Weekdays are days on which no proper feast is celebrated in the Mass or Liturgy of the Hours. On such days, the Mass may be that of the preceding Sunday, which expresses the liturgical spirit of the season, an optional memorial, a votive Mass or a Mass for the dead. The weekdays of Advent and Lent are in a special category.

Days of prayer (for the fruits of the earth, human rights and equality, world justice and peace, penitential observance outside of Lent) are not in the general calendar but are recommended to local bishops for insertion in particular calendars according to local needs and customs. They are contemporary equivalents of what were formerly called ember days and rogation days.

DAYS OF FAST AND ABSTINENCE

The Code of Canon Law declares that the faithful are obliged by divine law to do penance and designates Fridays throughout the year and the season of Lent as times for the common practice of penance by prayer, works of charity and self-denial, and careful fulfillment of the duties of one's state in life. Ash Wednesday and Good Friday are days of fast and abstinence. Abstinence on Fridays (except solemnities) throughout the year is subject to directives of appropriate conferences of bishops. In the U.S., the National Conference of Catholic Bishops has set the Fridays of Lent as days of abstinence and has urged the faithful to perform works of penance of their choice on other Fridays of the year. The obligation to fast (limiting oneself to one full meal and two lighter ones) binds persons from the age of majority (18) until their 59th birthday. The law of abstinence binds all from the age of 14.

Feasts

This list includes solemnities and many feasts and memorials celebrated throughout the year in the universal Church, along with observances proper to the United States and several optional memorials which enjoy great popularity. Saints not included in this listing (Apostles, Evangelists, Fathers and Doctors of the Church) are covered in other articles.

January

Solemnity of Mary, Mother of God, Jan. 1, holy day of obligation. The Marian character of the solemnity, formerly the feast of the Circumcision of Jesus, was reinstated with the calendar reform in effect since 1970.

St. Elizabeth Ann Bayley Seton (1774-1821), Jan. 4, memorial in the U.S. Converted in 1805 after the death of her husband; foundress of the Sisters of Charity in the U.S.; canonized in 1975, the first saint born in the U.S.

St. John Neumann (1811-1860), Jan. 5, memorial in the U.S. Born in Bohemia; ordained to the priesthood in 1836 in New York; joined the Redemptorists in 1840; ordained bishop of Philadelphia in 1852; canonized in 1977.

Blessed André Bessette (1845-1937), Jan. 6, optional memorial in the U.S. Canadian brother of the Congregation of the Holy Cross; prime mover in the building of St. Joseph's Oratory, Montreal; beatified in 1982.

Epiphany, on a Sunday between Jan. 2 and 8 in the U.S. (Jan. 6 in the general calendar), solemnity. Celebrates the manifestation of the divinity of Christ; of Eastern origin and one of the oldest Christian feasts, was adopted by the Western Church in the middle of the fourth century.

Baptism of the Lord, on the Sunday after Jan. 6, feast. Celebrates the manifestation of Christ as Son of Man and Son of God.

St. Anthony, Abbot (c. 251-c. 354), Jan. 17, memorial. Egyptian hermit; patriarch of all monks; established communities for hermits which became models for monastic life, especially in the East.

St. Agnes (d. c. 304), Jan. 21, memorial. Roman virgin-martyr; patroness of young girls.

Conversion of St. Paul, Jan. 25, feast. Commemorates the conversion and vocation of St. Paul.

St. John Bosco (1815-1888), Jan. 31, memorial. Italian priest; founded the Society of St. Francis de Sales (Salesians) for education of boys.

February

Presentation of the Lord, Feb. 2, feast. Restored as a feast of the Lord in the calendar reform in effect since 1970; formerly entitled

Purification of Mary; also called Candlemas because of the blessing of candles on this day.

St. Blase (d.c. 316), Feb. 3, optional memorial. Armenian bishop, martyr; the blessing of throats on his feast day derives from tradition that his intercession was instrumental in saving the life of a boy who had half-swallowed a fish bone.

St. Agatha (d. c. 250), Feb. 5, memorial. Sicilian virgin-martyr; her intercession credited in Sicily with stopping eruptions of Mt. Etna.

Sts. Paul Miki and Companions (d. 1597), Feb. 6, memorial. Paul Miki, Japanese Jesuit, and 25 other priests and laymen were martyred at Nagasaki, Japan; the first canonized martyrs (1862) of the Far East.

St. Scholastica (d.c. 559), Feb. 10, memorial. Sister of St. Benedict; the first nun of the Benedictine Order.

Sts. Cyril (d. 869) and Methodius (d. 885), Feb. 14, memorial. Brothers; missionaries to Slavs; developed a Slavonic alphabet; patrons of Europe with St. Benedict.

Chair of St. Peter, Feb. 22, feast. A liturgical expression of belief in the episcopacy and hierarchy of the Church; observed since the fourth century.

St. Polycarp (2nd century), Feb. 23, memorial. Bishop-martyr; ecclesiastical writer.

Ash Wednesday, between Feb. 4 and Mar. 11, depending on the date of Easter, fast and abstinence. Established as the first day of Lent by Pope St. Gregory the Great (590-604); ashes, symbolic of penance, are blessed and distributed to the faithful.

March

St. Patrick (389-461), Mar. 17, optional memorial. Missionary to Ireland; organized and established the Church there on a lasting foundation.

St. Joseph, Mar. 19, solemnity. Joseph is honored as the husband of Mary and patron of the universal Church.

Annunciation of the Lord, Mar. 25, solemnity. Commemoration of the Incarnation of Jesus as the Son of Mary; formerly entitled the Annunciation of Mary.

April

St. John Baptist de la Salle (1651-1719), Apr. 7, memorial. French priest; founder of the Brothers of the Christian Schools.

St. Stanislaus (1030-1079), Apr. 11, memorial. Polish bishop; martyr; one of the patrons of Poland.

Movable Celebrations

Passion Sunday (Palm Sunday), the Sunday before Easter. Marks the start of Holy Week, with the blessing of palm, a procession before the principal Mass of the day, and reading of the Passion Narrative of Matthew, Mark or Luke.

Holy Thursday, the Thursday before Easter. Commemoration of the institution of the Eucharist and holy orders, and the washing of the feet of the Apostles at the Last Supper. The Mass of the Lord's Supper in the evening marks the start of the Easter Triduum. Following the Mass, the Blessed Sacrament is carried in procession to a place of reposition for adoration by the faithful. At an earlier Mass of Chrism, bishops bless oils (of catechumens, chrism, the sick) for use during the year.

Good Friday, the Friday before Easter, fast and abstinence. Commemoration of the passion and death of Christ. Mass is not celebrated. Liturgical elements of the observance are reading of the Passion (according to John), special prayers for the Church and people of all ranks, veneration of the Cross and a Communion service.

Holy Saturday, the day before Easter. Mass is not celebrated, and Holy Communion may be given only as Viaticum.

Easter Vigil, called by St. Augustine the "Mother of All Vigils," the night before Easter. Ceremonies: blessing of new fire, procession with the Easter Candle, singing of the Easter Proclamation (*Exsultet*), Liturgy of the Word with at least three Old Testament readings, the Litany of Saints, blessing of water, baptism of converts and infants, renewal of baptismal promises, Liturgy of the Eucharist.

Easter, on the first Sunday after the full moon following the vernal equinox (between Mar. 22 and Apr. 25), solemnity with an octave. Commemorates the resurrection of Christ from the dead. Observance of this mystery, kept since the first days of the Church, extends from Easter to Pentecost, a period of 50 days, as one great feast.

Ascension, 40 days after Easter, holy day of obligation, solemnity. Commemorates the ascension of Christ into heaven, recalling the completion of His mission on earth for the salvation of all peoples and His entry into heaven with glorified human nature.

Pentecost, on Sunday, 50 days after Easter, solemnity. The last day of the Easter season, commemorating the coming of the Holy Spirit upon the Apostles and the beginning of their preaching the good news of salvation.

Holy Trinity, the Sunday after Pentecost, solemnity. Commemorates the sublime mystery of Three Divine Persons — Father, Son and Holy Spirit — in one God; observed from the seventh century.

Corpus Christi, the Sunday after Trinity Sunday in the U.S. (Thursday after Trinity Sunday in the general calendar), solemnity. Commemorates the institution of the Holy Eucharist; the observance dates from the 13th century.

Sacred Heart of Jesus, the Friday after Corpus Christi in the U.S. (Friday after the Second Sunday after Pentecost in the general calendar), solemnity. Devotion to the Sacred Heart, commemorating the love of Christ; the commemoration was introduced in the liturgy in the 17th century.

Immaculate Heart of Mary, the Saturday after the Solemnity of the Sacred Heart, optional memorial. Devotion to Mary under the title Most Pure Heart originated in the Middle Ages; Pius XII consecrated the world to Mary under this title in 1942.

May

St. Isidore the Farmer (d. 1170), May 15, optional memorial in the U.S.; Spanish layman; farmer.

St. Philip Neri (1515-1595), May 26, memorial. Italian priest; founded the Congregation of the Oratory.

Visitation, May 31, feast. Commemorates Mary's visit to her cousin Elizabeth after the annunciation.

June

St. Justin (100-165), June 1, memorial. Early ecclesiastical writer; martyr.

Sts. Charles Lwanga and Companions (d. 1886 and 1887), June 3, memorial. Ugandan martyrs; canonized 1964; the first martyrs of Black Africa.

St. Boniface (Winfrid) (d. 754), June 5, memorial. English Benedictine missionary in Germany; archbishop of Mainz; martyred near Dukkum in Holland; apostle of Germany.

St. Aloysius Gonzaga (1568-1591), June 21, memorial. Italian Jesuit; died while nursing plague-stricken; patron of youth.

Birth of St. John the Baptist, June 24, solemnity. Observed universally in the liturgy by the fourth century.

St. Irenaeus (130-202), June 28, memorial. Early ecclesiastical writer; bishop of Lyons; traditionally regarded as a martyr.

Sts. Peter and Paul, June 29, solemnity. The joint commemoration of the martyrdom of the chief Apostles dates from about 258.

July

St. Benedict (c. 480-547), July 11, memorial. Abbot; father of monasticism in the West; established monastery at Monte Cassino; patron of Europe.

Blessed Kateri Tekakwitha (1656-1680), July 14, memorial in the U.S. Indian maiden, "Lily of the Mohawks"; baptized a Christian in 1676; beatified in 1980.

Our Lady of Mt. Carmel, July 16, optional memorial.

St. Mary Magdalene (first century), July 22, memorial. Gospels record her as a devoted follower of Christ to whom He appeared after the resurrection.

Sts. Joachim and Ann, July 26, memorial. Commemorates the parents of Mary, known by these names from an ancient tradition.

St. Martha (first century), July 29, memorial. Sister of Lazarus and Mary of Bethany.

St. Ignatius of Loyola (1491-1556), July 31, memorial. Born in Spain; founded the Society of Jesus (Jesuits) in 1534, in Paris.

August

St. John Vianney (Curé of Ars) (1786-1859), Aug. 4, memorial. French priest; noted confessor; patron of parish priests.

Transfiguration of the Lord, Aug. 6, feast. Commemorates the manifestation of His divinity by Christ to Peter, James and John.

St. Dominic (1170-1221), Aug. 8, memorial. Spanish priest; founder of the Dominican Order (Friars Preachers).

St. Lawrence (d. 258), Aug. 10, feast. Deacon of the Church of Rome; a martyr.

St. Clare (1194-1253), Aug. 11, memorial. Born at Assisi; foundress of the Poor Clares.

St. Maximilian Kolbe (1894-1941), Aug. 14, memorial. Polish Conventual Franciscan; offered his life in place of a fellow prisoner at Auschwitz; canonized in 1982.

Assumption, Aug. 15, holy day of obligation, solemnity. Commemorates the taking into heaven of Mary, soul and body, at the end of her life on earth, a truth of faith proclaimed a dogma by Pius XII in 1950; one of the oldest and most solemn feasts of Mary.

Queenship of Mary, Aug. 22, memorial. Commemorates the high dignity of Mary as Queen of heaven, angels and men.

St. Monica (332-387), Aug. 27, memorial. Mother of St. Augustine; model of a patient, prayerful mother.

Beheading of St. John the Baptist, Aug. 29, memorial. Commemorates death of John the Baptist at the order of Herod.

September

Birth of Mary, Sept. 8, feast. A very old feast which originated in the East.

St. Peter Claver (1581-1654), Sept. 9, memorial in the U.S.; Spanish Jesuit; missionary in South America and West Indies; patron of Catholic missions among black peoples.

Triumph of the Cross, Sept. 14, feast. Celebrates the finding in 326 of the true cross on which Christ was crucified and the consecration of the Basilica of the Holy Sepulchre nearly 10 years later.

Our Lady of Sorrows, Sept. 15, memorial. Recalls the sorrows experienced by Mary.

Sts. Cornelius (d. 253) and Cyprian (d. 258), Sept. 16, memorial. Cornelius, pope-martyr, and Cyprian, ecclesiastical writer and bishop of Carthage, have been honored in a joint feast from at least the fourth century.

St. Vincent de Paul (1581?-1660), Sept. 27, memorial. French priest; founder of the Congregation of the Mission (Vincentians, Lazarists) and co-founder of the Sisters of Charity; patron of all charitable organizations and works.

Michael, Gabriel and Raphael, Archangels, Sept. 29, feast. This joint feast in honor of the three angels named in Scripture was instituted in the calendar reform in effect since 1970, replacing separate feasts.

October

St. Thérèse of Lisieux (Little Flower) (1873-1897), Oct. 1, memorial. French Carmelite nun; her "little way" of spiritual perfection became widely known through her spiritual autobiography; patroness of foreign missions.

Guardian Angels, Oct. 2, memorial. Commemorates angels as protectors from spiritual and physical danger; the observance dates from the early 17th century.

St. Francis of Assisi (1182-1226), Oct. 4, memorial. Founder of the Franciscans in 1209; one of best known and best loved saints; patron of Italy, Catholic Action and ecologists.

Blessed Marie-Rose Durocher (1811-1849), Oct. 6, optional memorial in the U.S.; Canadian Religious; foundress of the Sisters of the Most Holy Names of Jesus and Mary; beatified in 1982.

Our Lady of the Rosary, Oct. 7, memorial. Commemorates the Virgin Mary as revealed in the mysteries of the Rosary; the observance was established to commemorate a Christian victory over invading Mohammedan forces at Lepanto in 1571.

St. Ignatius of Antioch (d.c. 107), Oct. 17, memorial. Bishop of Antioch in Syria for 40 years; early ecclesiastical writer; martyr.

Sts. Isaac Jogues, John de Brébeuf and Companions (d. between 1642 and 1649), Oct. 19, memorial in the U.S. Six French Jesuit and two lay missionaries who were martyred in North America; canonized in 1930.

November

All Saints, Nov. 1, holy day of obligation, solemnity. Honors all saints of every time and place.

All Souls, Nov. 2. Commemoration of all the faithful departed on the day after All Saints was common by the tenth century; priests may say three Masses on this day.

St. Charles Borromeo (1538-1584), Nov. 4, memorial. Italian cardinal, bishop of Milan; influential figure in church reform in Italy.

Dedication of St. John Lateran, Nov. 9, feast. Commemorates the consecration in 324 of the Archbasilica of the Most Holy Savior (known since the 12th century as St. John Lateran), the pope's patriarchal basilica, regarded as the church of highest dignity in the Latin Rite.

St. Martin of Tours (316-397), Nov. 11, memorial. Bishop of Tours; pioneer of Western monasticism, before St. Benedict.

St. Josaphat Kuncevyc (1584-1623), Nov. 12, memorial. Born in Poland; Basilian monk; archbishop of Polotsk, Lithuania; worked for the reunion of separated Easterners; martyr.

St. Frances Xavier Cabrini (1850-1917), Nov. 13, memorial in the U.S. Born in Italy; founded the Missionary Sisters of the Sacred Heart in 1877; missionary among Italian immigrants in the U.S. from 1889; became an American citizen in 1909; canonized in 1946, the first American citizen so honored.

St. Elizabeth of Hungary (1207-1231), Nov. 17, memorial. Queen; became secular Franciscan after the death of her husband in 1227.

Presentation of Mary, Nov. 21, memorial. Commemorates the dedication in 543 of a church of St. Mary near the Temple of Jerusalem.

St. Cecilia (second or third century), Nov. 22, memorial. Roman virgin-martyr; traditional patroness of musicians.

Christ the King, the last Sunday of the liturgical year, solemnity.

December

St. Francis Xavier (1506-1552), Dec. 3, memorial. Spanish Jesuit; missionary to the Far East; one of the greatest Christian missionaries; patron of foreign missions.

St. Nicholas (fourth century), Dec. 6, optional memorial. Bishop of Myra in Asia Minor; popular saint in both East and West.

Immaculate Conception, Dec. 8, holy day of obligation, solemnity. Commemorates Mary's freedom from original sin from the first moment of her conception; defined as a dogma of faith in 1854. Mary was proclaimed patroness of the U.S. under this title in 1846.

Our Lady of Guadalupe, Dec. 12, memorial in the U.S. Commemorates appearances of Mary in Guadalupe, Mexico, to Juan Diego in 1531. Mary is patroness of the Americas under this title.

St. Lucy (d. 304), Dec. 13, memorial. Sicilian maiden; martyred during the Diocletian persecution.

Christmas, Birth of Our Lord Jesus Christ, Dec. 25, holy day of obligation, solemnity with an octave. Observed on this date from at least 354. There are texts for three Christmas Masses — at midnight, dawn and during the day

Holy Family, Sunday within the octave of Christmas, feast. The observance proposes the Holy Family of Jesus, Mary and Joseph as the model of domestic society, holiness and virtue.

St. Stephen (d. c. 33), Dec. 26, feast. Chosen by the Apostles as the first of the seven deacons; first Christian martyr.

Holy Innocents, Dec. 28, feast. Commemorates the infants who suffered death at the hands of Herod's soldiers seeking the Child Jesus.

Mary, Mother of Jesus

Mary has a special place in Catholic doctrine and devotion because of her unique role as the Mother of Jesus and His closest human cooperator in the work of redemption. She was conceived without original sin (her Immaculate Conception) through the application to her of the merits of her Son before His redemptive death and resurrection. She was full of grace and sinless throughout her life. She was a virgin before, in and after the birth of Jesus. She cared for Him in infancy, childhood and adolescence. She witnessed the preaching and work of His ministry. At His crucifixion, Jesus bequeathed her to all peoples as their spiritual mother. She was with the Apostles in prayer as they awaited the coming of the Holy Spirit at Pentecost and the beginning of their mission to preach and to baptize. Pope Pius XII, in proclaiming the dogma of the Assumption, declared: "The Immaculate Mother of God, the ever Virgin Mary, having completed the course of her earthly life, was assumed body and soul into heavenly glory." There, according to the Second Vatican Council's *Dogmatic Constitution on the Church,* her maternity in the order of grace "will last until the eternal fulfillment of all the elect. For, taken up to heaven, she did not lay aside this saving role, but by her manifold acts of intercession continues to win for us gifts of eternal salvation."

SPECIAL STATUS

The Council also said the following about Mary.

"Mary was involved in the mysteries of Christ. As the most holy Mother of God she was, after her Son, exalted by divine grace above all angels and men. Hence the Church appropriately honors her with special reverence. Indeed, from most ancient times the Blessed Virgin has been venerated under the title of 'God-bearer' (*Theotokos*). In all perils and needs, the faithful have fled prayerfully to her protection. Especially after the Council of Ephesus (431) the cult of the People of God toward Mary wonderfully increased in veneration and love, in invocation and imitation, according to her own prophetic words (of the *Magnificat*): 'All generations shall call me blessed; because He who is mighty has done great things for me.' "

"As it has always existed in the Church, this cult (of Mary) is altogether special. Still, it differs essentially from the cult of adoration which is offered to the Incarnate Word, as well as to the Father and the Holy Spirit. Yet devotion to Mary is most favorable to this supreme cult. The Church has endorsed many forms of piety toward the Mother of God, provided that they were within the limits of sound and orthodox doctrine. . . . While honoring Christ's Mother, these devotions cause her Son to be rightly known, loved and glorified, and all His commands observed."

AUTHENTIC CULT AND DEVOTION

"This most holy Synod . . . admonishes all the sons of the Church that the cult, especially the liturgical cult, of the Blessed Virgin, be generously fostered. It charges that the practices and exercises of devotion toward her be treasured as recommended by the teaching authority of the Church in the course of centuries, and that those decrees issued in earlier times regarding the veneration of images of Christ, the Blessed Virgin and the saints be religiously observed."

"Under the guidance of the Church's teaching authority, let them (the theologians and preachers) rightly explain the offices and privileges of the Blessed Virgin which are always related to Christ, the Source of all truth, sanctity and piety."

"Let them painstakingly guard against any word or deed which could lead separated brethren or anyone else into error regarding the true doctrine of the Church. Let the faithful remember, moreover, that true devotion consists neither in fruitless and passing emotion, nor in a certain vain credulity. Rather, it proceeds from true faith, by which we are led to know the excellence of the Mother of God and are moved to a filial love toward our Mother and to the imitation of her virtues."

While noting that "the Catholic Church honors her with filial affection and piety as a most beloved Mother," the Council also said in its *Constitution on the Liturgy:* "In celebrating the annual cycle of Christ's mysteries, holy Church honors with special love blessed Mary, Mother of God, who is joined by an inseparable bond to the saving work of her Son. In her the Church holds up and admires the most excellent fruit of the redemption, and joyfully contemplates, as in a faultless manner, that which she herself wholly desires and hopes to be."

Mary is honored with many titles, among them: Mother of God, *Theotokos* ("God-bearer"), because she bore and gave human birth to the Son of God; Ever Virgin, Highly Favored Daughter, Our Lady of the Immaculate Conception, Our Lady of the Rosary, Blessed Mother, Mother of the Church. She is venerated with liturgical observances such as the solemnities of her Maternity, Assumption and Immaculate Conception, along with other commemorations. The popular Marian devotion with the longest history is the Rosary. (See also entries under Devotions, Feasts.)

Saints

Saints are all those in glory with God in heaven. Liturgical veneration (in Mass and the Liturgy of the Hours, with feast or memorial commemoration in the calendar) is given to those recognized by the Church through actual or equivalent canonization. Limited liturgical veneration is permitted for servants of God who have been declared blessed.

Veneration accorded the saints is called *dulia*. It is essentially different in nature and degree from the adoration (*latria*) given to God alone; by its very nature, however, it terminates in the worship of God.

The Second Vatican Council, in its *Dogmatic Constitution on the Church*, declared: "It is supremely fitting . . . that we love those friends and fellow heirs of Jesus Christ, who are also our brothers and extraordinary benefactors, that we render due thanks to God for them and 'suppliantly invoke them and have recourse to their prayers, their power and help in obtaining benefits from God through His Son, Jesus Christ, our Lord, who is our sole Redeemer and Savior.' For by its very nature every genuine testimony of love which we show to those in heaven tends toward and terminates in Christ, who is the 'crown of all saints.' Through Him it tends toward and terminates in God, who is wonderful in His saints and is magnified in them."

The purpose of this devotion was outlined as follows by the Council.

"The authentic cult of saints consists not so much in the multiplying of external acts but rather in the intensity of our active love. By such love, for our own greater good and that of the Church, we seek from the saints example in their way of life, fellowship in their communion, and aid by their intercession. . . . Our communion with those in heaven, provided that it is understood in the more adequate light of faith, in no way weakens but, conversely, more thoroughly enriches the supreme worship we give to God the Father through Christ in the Spirit."

CANONIZATION

Canonization is the infallible declaration by the pope that a person who died as a martyr and/or practiced Christian virtue to a heroic degree is in heaven and is worthy of honor and imitation by all the faithful. Such a declaration is preceded by the process of beatification and subsequent detailed investigation concerning the person's reputation for holiness, writings and (except in the case of martyrs) miracles ascribed to his or her intercession after death. The pope, in a case of equivalent canonization, can by way of exception declare a person a saint without requiring execution of all of the usual formalities of the canonization process.

The first official canonization by a pope for the universal Church of which there is record is that of St. Ulrich of Augsburg (d. 973) by John XV in 993. In 1171, Alexander III reserved the process of canonization to the Holy See. The Sacred Congregation of Rites was established by Sixtus V in 1588 to handle causes for beatification and canonization; this function is now carried out by the Congregation for the Causes of Saints established by Paul VI in 1969. Basic procedures in canonization causes were established by Urban VIII in 1634. Norms issued in 1983 stressed the use of scientific and historical method in investigating causes.

The essential portion of a canonization decree states: "For the honor and glory of the holy and undivided Trinity; for the exaltation of the Catholic faith and the increase of Christian life; with the authority of Our Lord Jesus Christ, of the blessed Apostles Peter and Paul, and with our own authority; after mature deliberation and with divine assistance, often implored; with the counsel of many of our brothers: We decree and define (name) is a saint and inscribe him (her) in the Catalogue of Saints, stating that he (she) shall be venerated in the universal Church with pious devotion. In the name of the Father and of the Son and of the Holy Spirit. Amen."

BEATIFICATION

Beatification is a preliminary step toward canonization of a saint. It begins with an investigation of the candidate's life, writings and heroic practice of virtue, and certification of miracles worked by God through the candidate's intercession. If the findings of the investigation so indicate, the pope decrees that the servant of God may be called blessed and may be honored locally or in a limited way in the liturgy. Additional procedures lead to canonization. The pope can dispense with all or some of these procedures and issue a decree of equivalent beatification; Fra Angelico was beatified in this manner by John Paul II in 1983.

Beatification and canonization causes are initiated under the jurisdiction of the diocesan bishop of the place where the candidate lived and/or worked. A priest, religious or lay person, called the postulator, is appointed by the bishop to gather information to be forwarded to the Holy See for consideration as the basis for the formal introduction of a cause. Once a cause has been formally introduced, jurisdiction is transferred to the Congregation for the Causes of Saints which conducts its own investigations and evaluations. The promoter of the faith, an official of the congregation, acts as an expert in evaluating evidence for and against the cause. The role of this official in challenging the validity of evidence regarding the holiness of candidates for beatification and canonization earned him the popular title of "Devil's Advocate."

The official listing of saints and blessed according to feast or memorial day is continued in the *Roman Martyrology* and related decrees issued since its last publication in 1956. This official liturgical book, which evolved from early lists of martyrs of particular churches, is under revision in accordance with directives of the Second Vatican Council. The martyrology, along with other historical records, is an important source of writings on the saints (hagiography).

PATRONS

A patron is a saint or blessed who is venerated as a model to be imitated and as a special intercessor before God. Liturgical celebration may be accorded only to those officially designated or approved by the Church. The Sacred Congregation for the Sacraments and Divine Worship handles procedures for the choice and approval of liturgical veneration for patrons. Popular devotions to patrons are lawful if they accord with the laws and norms of the Holy See and are subordinate to and in harmony with the liturgy.

Patrons may be designated for places (nations, regions, dioceses, etc.), religious families and moral persons (societies, organizations, etc.). Some examples of officially designated patrons are, with date given in parentheses: St. Benedict (1964), Sts. Cyril and Methodius (1980), patron and co-patrons, respectively, of Europe; St. Francis of Assisi, Catholic Action (1916) and Ecologists (1979); St. Francis Xavier (1904) and St. Thérèse of Lisieux (1927), foreign missions; St. Francis de Sales (1923), journalists and writers.

Many saints have become popular as patrons of occupational and professional groups and intercessors for special needs through longstanding devotion rather than official designation. There is historical obscurity regarding the origin of patronage. The attitude of the Church has been to allow traditional, non-liturgical devotions if they do not conflict with Christian truth and the mind of the Church.

RELICS

Relics of the saints are their physical remains and instruments of their penance, suffering or death (first class), and objects that had some contact with their bodies or graves (second class). The Church recognizes the lawfulness of the veneration of relics since they are representative of persons in glory with God. Discipline concerning relics — e.g., prohibition against their sale — is subject to control by the Holy See, in line with norms laid down by the Council of Trent and later enactments. The ancient practice of enclosing relics, generally of martyrs, within an altar remains in force for fixed altars, according to the Code of Canon Law. A vessel for the keeping and display of relics is called a reliquary.

Devotions

Pious practices of members of the Church include not only participation in various acts of the liturgy but also in other acts of worship generally called popular or private devotions. Concerning these, the Second Vatican Council said in the *Constitution on the Sacred Liturgy*: "Popular devotions of the Christian people are warmly commended, provided they accord with the laws and norms of the Church. Such is especially the case with devotions called for by the Apostolic See. Devotions proper to the individual churches also have a special dignity. . . . These devotions should be so drawn up that they harmonize with the liturgical seasons, accord with the sacred liturgy, are in some fashion derived from it, and lead the people to it, since the liturgy by its very nature far surpasses any of them."

Devotions of a liturgical type are exposition of the Blessed Sacrament and recitation of portions of the Liturgy of the Hours. Examples of paraliturgical devotions are a Bible service, the Angelus, the Rosary and Stations of the Cross, which have a strong scriptural basis.

EUCHARISTIC DEVOTIONS

Exposition of the Blessed Sacrament: "In churches where the Eucharist is regularly reserved, it is recommended that solemn exposition of the Blessed Sacrament for an extended period of time should take place once a year, even though the period is not strictly continuous. . . . Shorter expositions of the Eucharist (**Benediction**) are to be arranged in such a way that the blessing with the Eucharist is preceded by a reasonable time for readings of the word of God, songs, prayers and a period for silent prayer." So stated Vatican directives issued in 1973.

Forty Hours is a Eucharistic observance consisting of solemn exposition of the Blessed Sacrament coupled with special Masses and forms of prayer for the purpose of making reparation for sin and praying for the blessings of grace and peace. The devotion was instituted in 1534 in Milan; it was authorized and promoted in the churches of Rome by Pope Clement VIII (d. 1605). St. John Neumann of Philadelphia was the first bishop in the U.S. to prescribe its observance in his diocese. For many years in this country, the observance was held annually on a rotating basis in all parishes of a diocese. Simplified and abbreviated observances have taken the place of this devotion in some places.

Eucharistic Congresses: Public demonstrations of faith in the Holy Eucharist. Combining liturgical services, other public ceremonies, subsidiary meetings, different kinds of instructional and inspirational elements, they are unified by central themes and serve to increase understanding of and devotion to Christ in the Eucharist, and to relate this liturgy of worship and witness to life.

The first international congress developed from a proposal by Marie

Marthe Tamisier of Touraine, organizing efforts of Msgr. Louis Gaston de Segur, and backing by industrialist Philibert Vrau. It was held with the approval of Pope Leo XIII at the University of Lille, France, and was attended by some 800 persons from France, Belgium, Holland, England, Spain and Switzerland.

International congresses are planned and held under the auspices of a permanent committee for international Eucharistic congresses. Participants include clergy, Religious and lay persons from many countries, and representatives of national and international Catholic organizations. Popes have usually been represented by legates, but Paul VI attended two congresses personally, the 38th at Bombay and the 39th at Bogota.

Forty-two international congresses were held from 1881 to 1981.

Lille (1881), Avignon (1882), Liege (1883), Freiburg (1885), Toulouse (1886), Paris (1888), Antwerp (1890), Jerusalem (1893), Rheims (1894), Paray-le-Monial (1897), Brussels (1898), Lourdes (1899), Angers (1901), Namur (1902), Angouleme (1904), Rome (1905), Tournai (1906), Metz (1907), London (1908), Cologne (1909), Montreal (1910), Madrid (1911), Vienna (1912), Malta (1913), Lourdes (1914), Rome (1922), Amsterdam (1924), Chicago (1926), Sydney (1928), Carthage (1930), Dublin (1932), Buenos Aires (1934), Manila (1937), Budapest (1938), Barcelona (1952), Rio de Janeiro (1955), Munich (1960), Bombay (1964), Bogota (1968), Melbourne (1973), Philadelphia (1976), Lourdes (1981).

The 43rd international congress was scheduled to be held in 1985 in Nairobi, Kenya.

OTHER DEVOTIONS

Stations of the Cross: A series of meditations on the sufferings of Christ: His condemnation to death and taking up of the Cross; the first fall on the way to Calvary; meeting His Mother; being assisted by Simon of Cyrene, and by Veronica, who wiped His face; the second fall; meeting the women of Jerusalem; the third fall; being stripped and nailed to the Cross; His death; the removal of His body from the Cross and His burial. Depictions of these scenes are mounted in most churches, chapels and in some other places, beneath small crosses.

A person making the Way of the Cross passes before these Stations, or stopping points, pausing at each for meditation. If the Stations are made by a group of people, only the leader has to pass from Station to Station. Prayer for the intentions of the pope is one of the conditions required for gaining the indulgence granted for the Stations.

Those unable to make the Stations in the ordinary manner, because they are impeded from visiting a church or other place where the Stations are, can still practice the devotion by meditating on the sufferings of Christ; praying the Our Father, Hail Mary and Glory for each Station and five times in commemoration of the wounds of Christ; and praying for the intentions of the pope. This practice has involved the use of a Stations Crucifix.

The Stations originated, remotely, from the practice of Holy Land pilgrims who visited the actual scenes of incidents in the passion of Christ. Representations elsewhere of at least some of these scenes were known as early as the fifth century. Later, the Stations evolved in connection with and as a consequence of strong devotion to the passion in the 12th and 13th centuries. Franciscans, who were given custody of the Holy Places in 1342, promoted the devotion widely; one of them, St. Leonard of Port Maurice, became known as the greatest preacher of the Way of the Cross in the 18th century. The general features of the devotion were fixed by Clement XII in 1731.

Sacred Heart: The object of this devotion is Christ himself, whose human heart is the symbol of His love for mankind, for whom He accomplished the work of redemption. The devotion called the Enthronement of the Sacred Heart is an acknowledgment of the sovereignty of Christ over the Christian family, expressed by the installation of an image or picture of the Sacred Heart in a place of honor in the home, accompanied by an act of consecration.

Rosary: A form of mental and vocal prayer centered on mysteries or events in the lives of Jesus and Mary. Its essential elements are meditation on the mysteries and the recitation of a number of decades of Hail Marys, each beginning with the Lord's Prayer. Introductory prayers are the Apostles' Creed, an initial Our Father, three Hail Marys and a Glory Be to the Father; each decade is customarily concluded with a Glory Be to the Father; at the end, it is customary to say the Hail, Holy Queen and a prayer from the liturgy for the feast of the Blessed Virgin Mary of the Rosary.

The Mysteries of the Rosary, which are the subject of meditation, are: (1) Joyful — the annunciation to Mary that she was to be the mother of Christ, her visit to Elizabeth, the birth of Jesus, the presentation of Jesus in the Temple, and finding of Jesus in the Temple. (2) Sorrowful — Christ's agony in the Garden of Gethsemani, scourging at the pillar, crowning with thorns, carrying of the cross to Calvary, and crucifixion. (3) Glorious — the resurrection and ascension of Christ, the descent of the Holy Spirit upon the Apostles, Mary's assumption into heaven and her crowning as Queen of angels and men.

The complete Rosary, called the Dominican Rosary, consists of 15 decades. In customary practice, only five decades are usually said at one time. Rosary beads are used to aid in counting the prayers without distraction.

The Rosary originated through the coalescence of popular devotions to Jesus and Mary from the 12th century onward. Its present form dates from about the 15th century. Carthusians contributed greatly toward its development; Dominicans have been its greatest promoters.

Angelus: A devotion commemorating the incarnation. It consists of three versicles, three Hail Marys and a special prayer; it recalls the announcement to Mary by the Archangel Gabriel that she was chosen to be the Mother of Christ and her acceptance of the divine will (Lk 1:26-38). The Angelus is recited in the morning, at noon and in the evening. The practice of reciting the Hail Mary in honor of the incarnation was introduced by the Franciscans in 1263. The *Regina Caeli,* commemorating the joy of Mary at Christ's resurrection, replaces the Angelus during the Easter season.

First Friday: A devotion consisting of the reception of Holy Communion on the first Friday of nine consecutive months in honor of the Sacred Heart of Jesus and in reparation for sin.

First Saturday: A devotion tracing its origin to the apparitions of the Blessed Virgin Mary at Fatima in 1917. Those practicing the devotion go to confession and, on the first Saturday of five consecutive months, receive Holy Communion, recite five decades of the Rosary, and meditate on the mysteries for 15 minutes. Prayer intentions are for the conversion of sinners and in reparation for sin.

Bible Service: A devotion consisting of common prayer of a biblical-liturgical character, readings from Scripture, possibly discussion and a homily.

Litany: Prayer in the form of responsive petition; e.g., St. Joseph, pray for us, etc. Examples are the litanies of Loreto (Litany of the Blessed Mother), the Holy Name, All Saints, the Sacred Heart, the Precious Blood, St. Anthony, Litany for the Dying.

Novena: A term designating public or private devotional practices over a period of nine consecutive days; or, by extension, over a period of nine weeks, in which one day a week is set aside for the devotions.

Triduum: A three-day period of devotional practices.

Holy Year: One during which the pope grants a plenary jubilee indulgence to the faithful who fulfill certain conditions. For those who make a pilgrimage to Rome, the conditions are reception of the sacraments of penance and the Eucharist, visits and prayer for the intentions of the pope in the major basilicas of St. Peter, St. John Lateran, St. Paul Outside the Walls and St. Mary Major. For those who do not make a pilgrimage to Rome, the conditions are reception of the sacraments and prayer for the intentions of the pope during a visit or community celebration in a church designated by the bishop of the locality. The first Holy Years we e observed in 1300, 1350 and 1390. Pope Paul II (1464-1471) set the 25-yea timetable. In 1500, Pope Alexander VI prescribed that a Holy Year would begin and end with the opening and closing of the Holy Doors in the major basilicas on successive Christmas Eves. All but a few of the earlier Holy Years were classified as ordinary. Several — like those of 1933 and 1983-1984, commemorating the 1900th and 1950th anniversaries of the redemptive death and resurrection of Christ — were in the extraordinary category.

Eastern Catholic Churches

Eastern Catholic Churches are those whose liturgy, tradition and discipline are derived from the Antiochene, Alexandrian, Byzantine, Chaldean or Armenian Rites. They are called Eastern because they originated in centers located in the Eastern portion of the Roman Empire and its borders; their members are now spread throughout the world. With the Church of the West, whose rite is predominantly Latin, they form one Church under the supreme authority of the pope.

VATICAN II DECREE

The Second Vatican Council, in its *Decree on Eastern Catholic Churches*, stated the following points regarding Eastern heritage, patriarchs, sacraments and worship.

"The Catholic Church holds in high esteem the institutions of the Eastern Churches, their liturgical rites, ecclesiastical traditions, and Christian way of life. For, distinguished as they are by their venerable antiquity, they are bright with that tradition which was handed down from the Apostles through the Fathers, and which forms part of the divinely revealed and undivided heritage of the universal Church."

"That Church, Holy and Catholic, which is the Mystical Body of Christ, is made up of the faithful who are organically united in the Holy Spirit through the same faith, the same sacraments, and the same government and who, combining into various groups held together by a hierarchy, form separate Churches or rites. . . . It is the mind of the Catholic Church that each individual Church or rite retain its traditions whole and entire, while adjusting its way of life to the various needs of time and place."

"Such individual Churches, whether of the East or of the West, although they differ somewhat among themselves in what are called rites (that is, in liturgy, ecclesiastical discipline, and spiritual heritage) are, nevertheless, equally entrusted to the pastoral guidance of the Roman Pontiff, the divinely appointed successor of St. Peter in supreme government over the universal Church. They are consequently of equal dignity, so that none of them is superior to the others by reason of rite."

Eastern Heritage

"Each and every Catholic, as also the baptized . . . of every non-Catholic Church or community who enters into the fullness of Catholic communion, should everywhere retain his proper rite, cherish it, and observe it to the best of his ability."

"The Churches of the East, as much as those of the West, fully enjoy the right, and are in duty bound, to rule themselves. Each should do so according to its proper and individual procedures."

All Eastern-Rite members should know and be convinced that they can and should always preserve their lawful liturgical rites and their established way of life, and that these should not be altered except by way of an appropriate and organic development."

Patriarchs

"The institution of the patriarchate has existed in the Church from the earliest times and was recognized by the first ecumenical Synods."

"By the name Eastern Patriarch is meant the bishop who has jurisdiction over all bishops (including metropolitans), clergy, and people of his own territory or rite, in accordance with the norms of law and without prejudice to the primacy of the Roman Pontiff."

"Though some of the patriarchates of the Eastern Churches are of later origin than others, all are equal in patriarchal dignity. Still the honorary and lawfully established order of precedence among them is to be preserved."

"In keeping with the most ancient tradition of the Church, the patriarchs of the Eastern Churches are to be accorded exceptional respect, since each presides over his patriarchate as father and head."

"This sacred Synod, therefore, decrees that their rights and privileges should be re-established in accord with the ancient traditions of each Church and the decrees of the ecumenical Synods."

"The rights and privileges in question are those which flourished when East and West were in union, though they should be somewhat adapted to modern conditions."

"The patriarchs with their synods constitute the superior authority for all affairs of the patriarchate, including the right to establish new eparchies and to nominate bishops of their rite within the territorial bounds of the patriarchate, without prejudice to the inalienable right of the Roman Pontiff to intervene in individual cases."

"What has been said of patriarchs applies as well, under the norm of law, to major archbishops, who preside over the whole of some individual Church or rite."

Sacraments

"This sacred Ecumenical Synod endorses and lauds the ancient discipline of the sacraments existing in the Eastern Churches, as also the practices connected with their celebration and administration."

"With respect to the minister of holy chrism (confirmation), let that practice be fully restored which existed among Easterners in most ancient times. Priests, therefore, can validly confer this sacrament, provided they use chrism blessed by a patriarch or bishop."

"In conjunction with baptism or otherwise, all Eastern-Rite priests can confer this sacrament validly on all the faithful of any rite, including the Latin; licitly, however, only if the regulations of both common and particular law are observed. Priests of the Latin Rite, to the extent of the faculties they enjoy for administering this sacrament, can confer it also on the faithful of Eastern Churches, without prejudice to rite. They do so licitly if the regulations of both common and particular law are observed."

"The faithful are bound on Sundays and feast days to attend the Divine Liturgy or, according to the regulations or custom of their own rite, the celebration of the Divine Praises. That the faithful may be able to satisfy their obligation more easily, it is decreed that this obligation can be fulfilled from the Vespers (Evening Prayer) of the vigil to the end of the Sunday or the feast day."

"Because of the everyday intermingling of the communicants of diverse Eastern Churches in the same Eastern region or territory, the faculty for hearing confessions, duly and unrestrictedly granted by his proper bishop to a priest of any rite, is applicable to the entire territory of the grantor, also to the places and the faithful belonging to any other rite in the same territory, unless an Ordinary of the place explicitly decides otherwise with respect to the places pertaining to his rite."

"This sacred Synod ardently desires that where it has fallen into disuse the office of the permanent diaconate be restored. The legislative authority of each individual church should decide about the subdiaconate and the minor orders."

"By way of preventing invalid marriages between Eastern Catholics and baptized Eastern non-Catholics, and in the interests of the permanence and sanctity of marriage and of domestic harmony, this sacred Synod decrees that the canonical 'form' for the celebration of such marriages obliges only for lawfulness. For their validity, the presence of a sacred minister suffices, as long as the other requirements of law are honored."

Worship

"Henceforth, it will be the exclusive right of an ecumenical Synod or the Apostolic See to establish, transfer, or suppress feast days common to all the Eastern Churches. To establish, transfer, or suppress feast days for any of the individual Churches is within the competence not only of the Apostolic See but also of a patriarchal or archiepiscopal synod, provided due consideration is given to the entire region and to other individual Churches."

"Until such time as all Christians desirably concur on a fixed day for the celebration of Easter, and with a view meantime to promoting unity among the Christians of a given area or nation, it is left to the patriarchs or supreme authorities of a place to reach a unanimous agreement, after ascertaining the views of all concerned, on a single Sunday for the observance of Easter."

"With respect to rules concerning sacred seasons, individual faithful dwelling outside the area or territory of their own rite may conform completely to the established custom of the place where they live. When members of a family belong to different rites, they are all permitted to observe sacred seasons according to the rules of any one of these rites."

"From ancient times the Divine Praises have been held in high esteem among all Eastern Churches. Eastern clerics and religious should celebrate these Praises as the laws and customs of their own traditions require. To the extent they can, the faithful too should follow the example of their forebears by assisting devoutly at the Divine Praises."

"It is the right of a patriarch with his synod, or of the supreme authority of each Church with its council of Ordinaries, to regulate the use of languages in sacred liturgical functions and, after making a report to the Apostolic See, to approve translations of texts into the vernacular."

Patriarchates, Other Jurisdictions

There are presently six Eastern patriarchates in the Church: Alexandria for the Copts; three of Antioch (for the Melkites, Syrians and Maronites); Babylonia for the Chaldeans; and Cilicia for the Armenians. Lvov (Lwow) of the Ukrainians is a major archbishopric. Other jurisdictions are: metropolitan sees, archeparchies (archdioceses), eparchies (dioceses), apostolic exarchates and ordinariates. In some places where Eastern-Rite Catholics do not have their own bishop, they are under the jurisdiction of an apostolic visitor of their own rite or of the local (Latin-Rite, ordinarily) bishop.

RITES OF EASTERN CATHOLIC CHURCHES

The Byzantine, Alexandrian, Antiochene, Armenian and Chaldean are the five principal rites used in their entirety or modified form by the various Eastern Churches. They evolved from the forms of worship, traditions and liturgical customs of the ancient Eastern patriarchates of Alexandria and Antioch (recognized as such by the Council of Nicaea in 325), and of Jerusalem and Constantinople (given similar recognition by the Council of Chalcedon in 451). The major break in East-West unity in 1054 resulted eventually in the separation of all the Eastern patriarchates from union with Rome. From time to time, some of the Churches, usually identifiable with ethnic groups, returned to full communion with the Holy See while retaining their rites and hierarchy. Most of these rites have counterparts in the Orthodox and other separated Eastern Churches.

Byzantine Rite: The rite of the majority of Eastern Catholics (and of the Eastern Orthodox Church), derived from the Rite of Antioch with some elements and customs from Jerusalem. The rite was proper to the Church of Constantinople (Byzantium, modern Istanbul). Groups using this rite, according to their own traditions, are: Albanians, Bulgarians, Byelorussians (White Russians), Georgians (Southern Russians), Greeks, Hungarians, Italo-Albanians, Melkites (Greek Catholic-Melkites), Romanians, Russians, Ruthenians (Carpatho-Russians), Slovaks, Ukrainians (Galician Ruthenians), Yugoslavs, Serbs and Croatians.

Antiochene Rite: The source of more derived rites than any of the other parent rites, believed to be the oldest and most apostolic of the rites. Groups using the rite are Syrians, Maronites and Malankarese (located in India).

Alexandrian Rite: Called the Liturgy of St. Mark, with branches for Copts and Ethiopians.

Armenian Rite: Used by Armenians exclusively.

Chaldean Rite, also called East Syrian: Derived from the Antiochene Rite, used by the Chaldeans and also the Syro-Malabarese of India who are descended from the St. Thomas Christians.

Eastern Catholics in the U.S.: The majority of Eastern Catholics in the United States belong to the Byzantine Rite (Ruthenians, Ukrainians, Melkites, Romanians, Byelorussians, Russians). The other rites are Antiochene, (Maronite), Armenian and Chaldean.

Eastern
Rites

SEPARATED EASTERN CHURCHES

The *Decree on Ecumenism* and related documents emphasize the special position of separated Eastern Churches which, despite differences, have much in common with the Roman Catholic Church. The decree stated:

"Although these churches are separated from us, they possess true sacraments, above all — by apostolic succession — the priesthood and the Eucharist, whereby they are still joined to us in a very close relationship. Therefore, given suitable circumstances and the approval of church authority, some worship in common is not merely possible but is recommended."

Separated
Eastern
Churches

There are two main groups of separated Eastern churches: the Oriental Orthodox (Armenian, Coptic, Ethiopian, Indian Malabar and Syrian Orthodox) and the Eastern Orthodox. The Oriental Orthodox broke away from unity in the fifth century when they refused to accept doctrine on Christ proclaimed by the Council of Chalcedon in 451. The Eastern Orthodox, the largest and most widespread of the separated Eastern Churches, accept only the first seven ecumenical councils and do not acknowledge and hold communion with the pope as the supreme head of the Church on earth. The definitive break from Rome dates from 1054. Mutual excommunications decreed at that time were nullified by Pope Paul VI and Orthodox Ecumenical Patriarch Athenagoras I in 1965, in an action which helped to establish a climate for dialogue between the churches.

Organization, Government of the Church

The Catholic Church, as a structured society, is organized and governed along hierarchical lines corresponding mainly to the jurisdiction of the pope and bishops over the People of God.

The pope is the supreme pastor of the Church on earth.

Bishops, in communion with the pope as their head and with one another, are the successors of the Apostles for the care of the Church and for the continuation of the saving mission of Christ in the world. They serve the people of their particular churches (dioceses) with authority stemming from ordination and canonical mission. With the pope and one another, they also share in common concern and effort for the general welfare of the entire Church.

Acting in the manner of diocesan bishops are prelates and abbots entrusted with the care of territorial prelatures and territorial abbacies. Vicars apostolic and prefects apostolic, acting in the name of the pope, are the heads of jurisdictions, vicariates apostolic and prefectures apostolic, which are not yet established as dioceses. Also acting in the name of the pope are apostolic administrators, in charge of apostolic administrations. A personal prelate has ordinary power over his prelacy.

THE HIERARCHY

The ministerial hierarchy is the orderly arrangement of the ranks and orders of the clergy to provide for the spiritual care of the faithful, the government of the Church and the accomplishment of the Church's total mission in the world. The term hierarchy is also used to designate an entire body or group of bishops; for example, the hierarchy of the Church, the hierarchy of the United States.

Hierarchy of Order: By divine institution, it consists of the pope, bishops, priests and deacons ordained to sacred orders for the purpose of carrying out the sacramental and pastoral ministry of the Church.

Hierarchy of Jurisdiction: It consists of the pope and bishops by divine institution, and of other ordained church officials by ecclesiastical institution and mandate, who have authority to govern and direct the faithful for spiritual purposes. Those who have the authority of office and jurisdiction in the external forum are Ordinaries; e.g., a metropolitan archbishop, a diocesan bishop.

The Pope

The pope is the Bishop of Rome in succession to St. Peter, head of the College of Bishops, Vicar of Christ, Pastor of the Church on earth, Sovereign Pontiff, Patriarch of the West, Primate of Italy, Sovereign of the State of Vatican City, Servant of the Servants of God. He is called Holy Father and His Holiness.

The pope is elected by the College of Cardinals by a two-thirds, plus-one majority vote in secret balloting. The elected candidate becomes pope from the moment of acceptance of the office if he is already a bishop; if he is not a bishop at the time of election, he becomes pope after episcopal ordination and acceptance of the office. A pope can resign. During an interregnum, the period between the death of one pope and the election of his successor: "The government of the Church is entrusted to the Sacred College of Cardinals for the sole dispatch of ordinary business and of matters which cannot be postponed, and for the preparation of everything necessary for the election of the new pope" (*Romano Pontifici Eligendo,* apostolic constitution, Oct. 1, 1975). The conclave for the election of a new pope begins no sooner than 15 and no later than 20 days after the death of his predecessor.

The pope has full, universal and immediate jurisdiction over the entire Church. He can act on his own initiative as well as in a collegial manner with the College of Bishops. There is no appeal or recourse from decrees of a pope.

Cardinals are high-ranking advisers to the pope and his assistants as key officials in the central administration of the universal Church in and through agencies of the Roman Curia (see separate entries).

The terms Apostolic See and Holy See designate the pope, the Vatican Secretariat of State, the Council for the Public Affairs of the Church, the various congregations and other agencies of the Roman Curia.

Patriarchs

Eastern-Rite patriarchs are bishops of patriarchal sees — Alexandria, Antioch, Babylonia of the Chaldeans, Cilicia of the Armenians — who have jurisdiction over the faithful of their respective rites throughout the world. They are elected by bishops of their rites, and receive approval and the pallium, symbolic of their office, from the pope. Their sees are distinctive because of their status and dignity in the history of the Church.

Patriarchal sees of the Latin Rite are Rome and Jerusalem; others, established during the Crusades, have been abolished. Latin-Rite titular patriarchates (in name only) are those of Lisbon, Venice, the East Indies and the West Indies.

Archbishops

Metropolitan Archbishop: An archbishop in charge of the principal see, an archdiocese, in an ecclesiastical territory called a province and consisting of several dioceses. He has the full powers of a bishop in his own archdiocese. With respect to the other dioceses (suffragans) in the province, he has visitation rights and supervisory responsibility regarding matters of faith and church discipline.

Coadjutor Archbishop: An assistant archbishop to a metropolitan archbishop, with the right of succession to the see.

Non-Metropolitan Archbishop: One in charge of an archdiocese without suffragan sees.

Titular Archbishop: One with the title of an archdiocese which formerly existed in fact but now exists in name only. He does not have ordinary jurisdiction over an archdiocese.

Archbishop ad personam: A title of personal honor and distinction which does not involve ordinary jurisdiction over an archdiocese.

Primate: A title of honor given to the ranking prelate of some countries and regions.

Bishops

Diocesan Bishop: A bishop in charge of a diocese.

Coadjutor Bishop: An assistant bishop to a diocesan bishop, with the right of succession to the see.

Titular Bishop: One who has the title of a diocese which formerly existed in fact but now exists in name only. He has authority of jurisdiction which is delegated in a special or ordinary manner, in line with his assignment, rather than the ordinary jurisdiction of office which belongs to a diocesan bishop.

Episcopal Vicar: An assistant, who may or may not be a bishop, appointed by a diocesan bishop as his deputy for a certain part of a diocese, a particular type of pastoral ministry or apostolic work, or the faithful of a certain rite.

Eparch, Exarch: Titles of bishops of Eastern-Rite churches.

Nomination of Bishops: Nominees for episcopal ordination are selected in several ways, but final appointment and/or approval in all cases is subject to decision by the pope.

In the U.S., bishops periodically submit the names of candidates to the archbishop of their province. The names are then considered at a meeting of the bishops of the province, and those receiving a favorable vote are forwarded to the papal representative in this country for review and transmission to the Holy See. Bishops are free to seek the counsel of priests, religious and lay persons with respect to nominees.

Eastern-Rite churches have their own procedures and synodal regulations for nominating and making final selection of candidates for episcopal ordination.

Former rights and privileges of some civil authorities with respect to the election, nomination, presentation or designation of candidates for the episcopate were rescinded by the Code of Canon Law in effect since Nov. 27, 1983.

Ad Limina Visit: Residential bishops and military vicars are obliged to make a periodic, five-year *ad limina* visit ("to the threshold" of the Apostles) to the tombs of Sts. Peter and Paul, meet with the pope, consult with appropriate Vatican officials and present a written report on conditions in their jurisdictions.

Other Prelates

Prelates and Abbots: Some prelates and abbots, acting in the manner of diocesan bishops, are pastors of the People of God in territories (prelatures and abbacies) not under the jurisdiction of diocesan bishops.

Vicars and Prefects Apostolic: Acting in the name of the pope, they are pastors of the People of God in territories (vicariates and prefectures apostolic) not yet established as dioceses.

Apostolic Administrator: He governs, in the name of the pope, the People of God in a jurisdiction called an apostolic administration which has not been established as a diocese.

Vicar General: A diocesan bishop's deputy for the administration of his diocese; he does not have to be a bishop.

Honorary Prelates aggregated to the Pontifical Household are: Protonotaries Apostolic, Honorary Prelates of His Holiness, and Chaplains of His Holiness. Their title is Reverend Monsignor.

SYNOD OF BISHOPS

The Synod of Bishops was chartered by Pope Paul VI on Sept. 15, 1965, in a document issued on his own initiative under the title *Apostolica Sollicitudo*, major portions of which are contained in Canons 342 to 348 of the Code of Canon Law.

The purposes of the Synod, according to the charter, are: "to encourage close union and valued assistance between the Sovereign Pontiff and the bishops of the entire world; to insure that direct and real information is provided on questions and situations touching upon the internal action of the Church and its necessary activity in the world of today; to facilitate agreement on essential points of doctrine and on methods of procedure in the life of the Church."

The Synod of Bishops is a central ecclesiastical institution, permanent by nature.

The Synod is directly and immediately subject to its president, the pope, who has authority to assign its agenda, call it into session and give it whatever degree of authority he wishes. The Synod is consultative in character but can, by papal action, be given deliberative or decision-making authority.

In addition to a limited number of ex officio members and a few heads of male religious institutes, the majority of the members are elected by and representative of national or regional conferences of bishops throughout the world. The pope has the reserved right to appoint the secretary general, special secretaries and no more than 15 percent of the total membership. The numbers of participants in ordinary assemblies between 1967 and 1983 varied between 197 and 210.

The Synod has a permanent general secretariat with an assistant council of bishops elected by the Synod and appointed by the pope.

The principal subjects on the agenda of six general assemblies and one extraordinary assembly were as follows: the preservation and strengthening of the Catholic faith (1967); collegiality, pope-bishops relations (1969; extraordinary assembly); the ministerial priesthood and justice in the world (1971); evangelization of the modern world (1974); catechetics (1977); the role of the Christian family in the modern world (1980); reconciliation and penance in the mission of the Church (1983).

COLLEGE OF CARDINALS

Cardinals are the principal advisers and assistants to the pope in the central administration of affairs of the universal Church and, together as the Sacred College of Cardinals, have the responsibility of electing the successor to a deceased pope. Provisions regarding their selection, rank, roles and prerogatives are detailed in particular law and in Canons 349 to 359 of the Code of Canon Law.

The college evolved gradually from synods of the Roman clergy with whose assistance popes directed church affairs in the first 11 centuries. The first cardinals, in about the sixth century, were priests of the leading churches of Rome, who were assigned liturgical, advisory and administrative duties with the Holy See, and the regional deacons of Rome. The college was given definite form in 1150, and the selection of its members was reserved exclusively to the pope in 1179. Sixtus V fixed the number at 70 in 1586; John XXIII increased the membership in 1959, and the number reached an all-time high of 145 under Paul VI in 1973. The number of cardinals entitled to participate in papal elections is limited to 120.

In 1567, the title of cardinal was reserved to members of the college; previously, it had been used by priests attached to parish churches of Rome and by the leading clergy of some other churches. The 1918 Code of Canon Law decreed that cardinals must be priests. Previously, there had been lay cardinals (e.g., Cardinal Giacomo Antonelli, secretary of state to Pius IX, who died in 1876). John XXIII provided in 1962 that cardinals would be bishops from that time on; accordingly, priests named to the cardinalate have to be ordained bishops, except in unusual cases.

On the completion of their 75th year, cardinals serving as heads of departments and other permanent sections of the Roman Curia are requested to submit resignations from office which the pope is free to accept or reject. Cardinals over the age of 80 are not eligible to vote in the election of a pope. Cardinals retain membership in the college, with relevant rights and privileges, until death.

Categories

The categories of membership in the college are cardinal bishop, cardinal priest and cardinal deacon.

Cardinal bishops: First in rank are the bishops with the titles of sees neighboring Rome: Ostia, Palestrina, Porto and Santa Rufina, Albano, Velletri, Frascati, Sabina and Poggio Mirteto. The dean of the college has the title of Ostia as well as that of his other suburban see. Cardinal bishops are engaged in full-time service in the Roman Curia.

Eastern patriarchs are in a class by themselves as the heads of sees of apostolic origin with ancient liturgies. Because of their patriarchal dignity and titles, which antedate the dignity and titles of cardinals, they are not aggregated to the Roman clergy and are not, like other cardinals, given title to Roman churches. They are assigned rank among the cardinals in order of seniority, following the suburban titleholders.

Cardinal priests, who were formerly in charge of leading churches in Rome, are bishops whose dioceses are outside of Rome. They have title to churches in Rome, to which they have obligations of counsel and patronage but not of pastoral service. They serve as members and/or consultors of various agencies of the Roman Curia.

Cardinal deacons, who were formerly chosen according to regional divisions of Rome, are titular bishops assigned to full-time service in the Roman Curia.

A **cardinal in petto** is one whose selection has been made by the pope but whose name has not been disclosed; he has no title, rights or duties until such disclosure is made, at which time he takes precedence from the time of the secret selection.

The officers of the college are the dean and subdean (elected by the suburban cardinal bishops), a chamberlain and a secretary.

Cardinals are created by the pope on publication of the appropriate decree in the presence of the Sacred College; in subsequent ceremonies, they receive the cardinalatial red biretta and ring, and concelebrate Mass with the pope and other members of the college. For the conduct of business, cardinals meet with the pope in extraordinary (cardinals only) or ordinary (others admitted) consistories. Cardinals enjoy a number of special rights and privileges; their title, however, while symbolic of high honor, does not signify any extension of the power of sacred orders. They are called princes of the Church.

ROMAN CURIA

The Roman Curia is the complex of agencies which, in the name and with the authority of the pope, administers affairs of the universal Church at the highest level. It consists of the Secretariat of State, the Council for the Public Affairs of the Church, congregations, tribunals, offices, commissions and councils. Its international membership includes cardinals, bishops, priests and lay persons.

The Curia evolved gradually from early advisory assemblies of the Roman clergy (first 11 centuries) and commissions of cardinals (from the 12th century). Its original office was the Apostolic Chancery, established in the fourth century to transmit documents. It was given a structured form by Sixtus V in 1588, reorganized by Pius X in 1908 and, in accordance with directives of the Second Vatican Council, reformed by Paul VI in 1968. The Curia is subject to revision and reorganization for greater effectiveness in dealing with the changing needs of the Church.

Departments

The Secretariat of State provides the pope with the closest possible assistance in the care of the universal Church. The cardinal secretary of state is the key coordinator of curial operations, with authority to call meetings of the heads of all departments for expediting business, consultation and intercommunication. He handles all matters entrusted to him by the pope. The secretariat has offices for preparing and writing letters for the pope, as well as the Central Statistics Office.

The Council for the Public Affairs of the Church, headed by the secretary of state, handles diplomatic and other relations with civil governments and some matters concerned with nunciatures. It has supervision of the Pontifical Commission for Russia.

Congregations

Congregations are administrative bodies with defined spheres of competency. Membership, once limited to cardinals, includes a number of diocesan bishops; all members are appointed by the pope. Congregations and their responsibilities are as follows.

Doctrine of the Faith (safeguarding the doctrine of faith and morals); Oriental Churches (persons, discipline and rites of Eastern Churches); Bishops (matters related to bishops and ecclesiastical jurisdictions); Sacraments and Divine Worship (discipline of the sacraments, ritual and pastoral aspects of divine worship in Latin and other Western rites); Causes of Saints (beatification and canonization causes and the preservation of relics); Clergy (the person, work and pastoral ministry of priests and deacons working in dioceses); Religious and Secular Institutes (men and women religious, secular institutes and societies of apostolic life); Catholic Education (supervision of seminaries, Catholic universities, faculties of studies and other institutes of higher learning dependent on the authority of the Church; Catholic education on other levels); Evangelization of Peoples or Propagation of the Faith (direction and coordination of missionary work throughout the world).

Tribunals and Secretariats

Tribunals are the courts of the Holy See. The Sacred Apostolic Penitentiary has jurisdiction in the internal forum with respect to the private spiritual good of individuals; it issues decisions on cases of conscience, grants absolutions and dispensations, and also has charge of non-doctrinal matters pertaining to indulgences. The Apostolic Signatura, the highest court of the Church, resolves questions concerning juridical procedure, decides the competence of lower courts and has jurisdiction in cases involving personnel and decisions of the Rota. The Sacred Roman Rota is the ordinary court of appeal for cases appealed to the Holy See; it is known for its competency and decisions in cases involving the validity of marriage.

Secretariats deal with interreligious affairs: the Secretariat for Promoting Christian Unity, with the attached Commission for Catholic-Jewish Relations; the Secretariat for Non-Christians, with the attached Commission for Catholic-Moslem Relations; and the Secretariat for Non-Believers.

Offices and Commissions

Offices include: the Prefecture of Economic Affairs, which coordinates and supervises temporalities of the Holy See; the Apostolic Chamber, which administers temporal goods and rights of the Holy See between the death of one pope and election of another; the Administration of the Patrimony of the Holy See, which handles the estate of the Apostolic See; the Prefecture of the Apostolic See, which oversees the papal chapel and household, arranges papal audiences, handles details for papal trips outside the Vatican and settles matters of protocol; the Central Statistics Office, which compiles, systematizes and analyzes information on the status and needs of the Church throughout the world.

Commissions and councils are permanent or temporary special-purpose agencies, some of which are attached to major departments of the Curia. The Pontifical Biblical Commission, linked since 1971 with the Congregation for the Doctrine of the Faith, promotes biblical studies and safeguards the correct interpretation of Scripture. The Theological Commission, an adjunct to the Congregation for the Doctrine of the Faith, provides that body with the consultative and advisory services of theologians and scriptural and liturgical experts representative of various schools of thought. Among other commissions are those for: Justice and Peace, Social Communications, Latin America, Russia, Migration and Tourism, and the Institute for Works of Religion (Vatican Bank).

Councils include: Cor Unum, to provide information and coordinating services to Catholic aid organizations; the Pontifical Council for Culture, to facilitate contacts between the saving message of the Gospel and the plurality of cultures; the Pontifical Council for the Laity, and the Pontifical Council for the Family.

Particular Churches

Particular churches in and from which the one and only Catholic Church exists are dioceses, in the first instance, and also territorial prelatures and abbacies, vicariates and prefectures apostolic, and stable apostolic administrations.

A diocese is a portion of the People of God under the pastoral care of a diocesan bishop and his body of priests. Other portions of the People of

God, as noted above, have their own duly authorized prelates and priests.

Dioceses and other particular churches usually have territorial limits; some, however, are defined by the rite of their members or by other norms.

Parts of dioceses and other particular churches are divided into parishes; neighboring parishes are grouped in vicariates.

Neighboring particular churches comprise an ecclesiastical province (e.g., an archdiocese and its suffragan dioceses). The provinces of a country or territory comprise an ecclesiastical region. Bishops of a region are members of an episcopal conference whose purpose is pastoral for the entire region (e.g., the National Conference of Catholic Bishops in the United States).

The National Conference of Catholic Bishops, established by action of the U.S. hierarchy Nov. 14, 1966, is a strictly ecclesiastical body with defined juridical authority over the Church in this country. It was set up with the approval of the Holy See and in line with directives from the Second Vatican Council. Its constitution was formally ratified during the November, 1967, meeting of the U.S. hierarchy.

The conference, one of many similar territorial conferences envisioned in the Second Vatican Council's *Decree on the Pastoral Office of Bishops in the Church,* is "a council in which the bishops of a given nation or territory (in this case, the United States) jointly exercise their pastoral office to promote the greater good which the Church offers mankind, especially through the forms and methods of the apostolate fittingly adapted to the circumstances of the age."

Its decisions, "provided they have been approved legitimately and by the votes of at least two-thirds of the prelates who have a deliberative vote in the conference, and have been recognized by the Apostolic See, are to have juridically binding force only in those cases prescribed by the common law or determined by a special mandate of the Apostolic See, given either spontaneously or in response to a petition of the conference itself."

The NCCB is the sponsoring organization of the United States Catholic Conference, a civil corporation and operational secretariat in and through which the bishops, together with other members of the Church, act on a wider scale for the good of the Church and society.

Papal Representatives

Papal representatives (legates) and their functions are the subjects of Canons 362 to 367 of the Code of Canon Law. These canons summarize in brief form the contents of a document entitled *Sollicitudo Omnium Ecclesiarum* issued by Paul VI on his own initiative June 24, 1969.

Papal representatives receive from the Roman pontiff the charge of representing him in a stable manner in particular churches or also in states and to public authorities to whom they are sent.

APOSTOLIC DELEGATES AND NUNCIOS

"When their legation is only to local (particular) churches, they are known as apostolic delegates. When to this legation, of a religious and ecclesial nature, there is added diplomatic legation to states and governments, they receive the title of nuncio, pro-nuncio and internuncio."

Other representatives are clerics and lay persons "who form . . . part of a pontifical mission attached to international organizations or take part in conferences and congresses"; they are variously called delegates or observers.

"The primary and specific purpose of the mission of a papal representative is to render ever closer and more operative the ties that bind the Apostolic See and the local churches."

"The ordinary function of a pontifical representative is to keep the Holy See regularly and objectively informed about the conditions of the ecclesial community to which he is sent, and about what may affect the life of the Church and the good of souls."

"On the one hand, he makes known to the Holy See the thinking of the clergy, religious and faithful of the territory where he carries out his mandate, and forwards to Rome their proposals and their requests; on the other hand, he makes himself the interpreter, with those concerned, of the acts, documents, information and instructions emanating from the Holy See."

An apostolic nuncio, who combines diplomatic functions with those of an apostolic delegate, has the diplomatic rank of ambassador extraordinary and plenipotentiary. Traditionally, because the Vatican diplomatic service has the longest uninterrupted history in the world, a nuncio has precedence among diplomats in the country to which he is accredited and serves as dean of the diplomatic corps on occasions of state. Since 1965, pro-nuncios, also of ambassadorial rank, have been assigned to countries in which this prerogative is not recognized.

The mission of a papal representative begins with appointment and assignment by the pope and continues until termination of his mandate. He acts "under the guidance and according to the instructions of the cardinal secretary of state and prefect of the Council for the Public Affairs of the Church, to whom he is directly responsible for the execution of the mandate entrusted to him by the Supreme Pontiff.'' The normal retirement age is 75.

Service and Liaison

Representatives, while carrying out their general and special duties, are bound to respect the autonomy of particular churches and local bishops. Following are their service and liaison responsibilities.

Nomination of Bishops: To play a key role in compiling, with the advice of clergy and lay persons, and submitting lists of names of likely candidates to the Holy See with their own recommendations.

Bishops: To aid and counsel local bishops without interfering in the affairs of their jurisdictions.

Episcopal Conferences: To maintain close relations with them and to assist them in every possible way. (Papal representatives do not belong to these conferences.)

Religious Institutes of Pontifical Rank: To advise and assist major superiors for the purpose of promoting and consolidating conferences of men and women Religious and to coordinate their apostolic activities.

Church-State Relations: The thrust in this area is toward the development of sound relations with civil governments and collaboration in work for the peace and total good of the human family.

Vatican City

The State of Vatican City (*Stato della Città del Vaticano*) is the territorial seat of the papacy. The smallest sovereign state in the world, it is situated within the City of Rome, embraces an area of 108.7 acres, and includes within its limits the Vatican Palace, museums, art galleries, gardens, libraries, radio station, post office, bank, astronomical observatory, offices, apartments, service facilities, St. Peter's Basilica, and neighboring buildings between the Basilica and Viale Vaticano.

The extraterritorial rights of Vatican City extend to more than 10 buildings in Rome, including the major basilicas and office bulidings of various congregations of the Roman Curia, and to the Villa of Castelgandolfo 15 miles southeast of the City of Rome. Castelgandolfo is the summer residence of the Holy Father.

The government of Vatican City is in the hands of the reigning pope, who has full executive, legislative and judicial power. The administration of affairs, however, is handled by the Pontifical Commission for the State of Vatican City. The legal system is based on Canon Law; in cases where this Code does not obtain, the laws of the City of Rome apply. The Vatican is an absolutely neutral state and enjoys all the rights and privileges of a sovereign power. The Papal Secretariat of State handles diplomatic relations with other nations. The citizens of Vatican City, and they alone, owe allegiance to the pope as a temporal head of state.

Cardinals of the Roman Curia residing outside Vatican City enjoy the privileges of extraterritoriality.

The normal population is approximately 1,000. While the greater percentage is made up of priests and Religious, there are several hundred lay persons living in Vatican City. They are housed in their own apartments in the City and are engaged in secretarial, domestic, trade and service occupations. About 4,000 persons are employed by the Vatican.

Services of honor and order are performed by the Swiss Guards, who have been charged with responsibility for the personal safety of popes since 1506. Additional police and ceremonial functions are under the supervision of a special office. These functions were formerly handled by the Papal Gendarmes, the Palatine Guard of Honor, and the Guard of Honor of the Pope (Pontifical Noble Guard) which Pope Paul VI disbanded Sept. 14, 1970.

The **Basilica of St. Peter**, built between 1506 and 1626, is the largest church in Christendom and the site of most papal ceremonies. The pope's own patriarchal basilica, however, is **St. John Lateran**, whose origins date back to 324.

St. Ann's is the parish church of Vatican City.

The **Vatican Library**, one of five in the City, has among its holdings 70,000 manuscripts, 770,000 printed books and 7,500 incunabula.

The independent temporal power of the pope, which is limited to the confines of Vatican City and small areas outside, was for many centuries more extensive than it is now. As late as the nineteenth century, the pope ruled 16,000 square miles of Papal States across the middle of Italy, with a population of over 3,000,000. In 1870 forces of the Kingdom of Italy occupied these lands which, with the exception of the small areas surrounding the Vatican and Lateran in Rome and the Villa of Castelgandolfo, became part of the Kingdom by the Italian law of May 13, 1871.

The **Roman Question**, occasioned by this seizure and the voluntary confinement of the pope to the limited papal lands, was finally settled with ratification of the Lateran Agreement on June 7, 1929, by the Italian government and the Holy See; the treaty provided for a financial indemnity for the former Papal States, which became recognized as part of Italy. The Lateran Agreement became Article 7 of the Italian Constitution May 26, 1947. Current relations between the Vatican and the government of Italy are governed by a concordat ratified in 1984.

The **Papal Flag** consists of two equal vertical stripes of yellow and white, charged with the insignia of the papacy on the white stripe — a triple crown or tiara over two crossed keys, one of gold and one of silver, tied with a red cord and two tassels. The divisions of the crown represent the teaching, sanctifying and ruling offices of the pope. The keys symbolize his jurisdictional authority.

The papal flag is a national flag inasmuch as it is the standard of the supreme pontiff as the sovereign of the State of Vatican City. It is also universally accepted by the faithful as a symbol of the supreme spiritual authority of the Holy Father.

In U.S. Catholic churches, the papal flag is displayed on a staff on the left side of the sanctuary (facing the congregation), and the American flag is displayed on the right.

Vatican Radio: The declared purpose of Vatican Radio Station HVJ is "that the voice of the Supreme Pastor may be heard throughout the world by means of the ether waves, for the glory of Christ and the salvation of souls." Designed by Guglielmo Marconi, the inventor of radio, and supervised by him until his death, the station was inaugurated by Pope Pius XI in 1931. The original purpose has been extended to a wide variety of programming. Vatican Radio operates on international wave lengths, transmits programs in nearly 40 languages, and serves as a channel of communication between the Vatican, church officials and listeners in general in many parts of the world.

Stamps and Coins in several series are issued each year, respectively, by the Vatican Philatelic Office and the Vatican Numismatic Office.

Papal Audiences: General audiences are scheduled weekly, on Wednesday. In Vatican City, they are held in the Audience Hall or, weather permitting, in St. Peter's Square. Audiences are also held at Castelgandolfo during the summer when the pope is there on a working vacation. Arrangements for papal audiences are handled by an office of the Prefecture of the Apostolic Household. American visitors can obtain passes for general audiences by applying to the Bishops' Office for United States Visitors to the Vatican, Casa Santa Maria, Via dell'Umiltà, 30, 00187 Rome. Private and group audiences are reserved for dignitaries of various categories and for special occasions.

PUBLICATIONS

Acta Apostolicae Sedis: The only official commentary of the Holy See, established in 1908 for the publication — mostly in Latin and Italian — of acts of the pope, laws, decrees and other acts of agencies of the Roman Curia. The first edition was published in January, 1909. Laws promulgated for the Church generally take effect three months after publication in this commentary. The immediate predecessor of this publication was *Acta Sanctae Sedis*, founded in 1865 and given official status by the Congregation for the Propagation of the Faith in 1904.

Annuario Pontificio: The yearbook of the Holy See, edited by the Central Statistics Office of the Church and printed in Italian, with some portions in other languages. It covers the worldwide organization of the Church, lists members of the hierarchy and includes a wide range of statistical information. Its antecedents date back to 1716.

L'Osservatore Romano: The daily newspaper of the Holy See. Publication began July 1, 1861, as an independent enterprise under the ownership and direction of four laymen headed by Marcantonio Pacelli, vice minister of the interior under Pope Pius IX. Leo XIII bought the publication in 1890, making it the "Pope's Own Newspaper." Official material in the paper is indicated under the heading, *Nostre Informazione*. Additional material includes news and comment on developments in the Church and world. Italian is the language most used. Weekly roundup editions are published in English and several other languages.

Activities of the Holy See: An annual documentary volume covering the activities of the pope — his daily work, general and special audiences, discourses and messages on special occasions, visits outside the Vatican, missionary and charitable endeavors, meetings with diplomats, heads of state and others — and activities of agencies of the Roman Curia.

Statistical Yearbook of the Church: Issued by the Central Statistics Office of the Church, containing data on the presence and work of the Church in the world. The first issue was published in 1972 under the title, *Collection of Statistical Tables, 1969*. It is printed in corresponding columns in Italian and Latin. Some of the introductory material is printed in other languages.

Vatican Press Office: The establishment of a single press office was announced Feb. 29, 1968, to replace service agencies formerly operated by *L'Osservatore Romano* and an office created for press coverage of the Second Vatican Council.

U.S.-VATICAN RELATIONS

Official relations for trade and diplomatic purposes were maintained by the United States and the Papal States while the latter had the character of and acted like other sovereign powers in the international community.

Consular relations developed in the wake of an announcement, made by the papal nuncio in Paris to the American mission there Dec. 15, 1784, that the Papal States had agreed to open several Mediterranean ports to U.S. shipping.

U.S. consular representation in the Papal States began with the appointment of John B. Sartori, a native of Rome, in June, 1797. Sartori's successors as consuls were: Felix Cicognani, also a Roman, and Americans George W. Greene, Nicholas Browne, William C. Sanders, Daniel LeRoy, Horatio V. Glentworth, W.J. Stillman, Edwin C. Cushman, David M. Armstrong.

Consular officials of the Papal States who served in the U.S. were: Count Ferdinand Lucchesi, 1826 to 1829, who resided in Washington; John B. Sartori, 1829 to 1841, who resided in Trenton, N.J.; Daniel J. Desmond, 1841 to 1850, who resided in Philadelphia; Louis B. Binsse, 1850 to 1895, who resided in New York.

U.S. recognition of the consul of the Papal States did not cease when the States were absorbed into the Kingdom of Italy in 1871, despite pressure from Baron Blanc, the Italian minister. Binsse held the title until his death Mar. 28, 1895. No one was appointed to succeed him.

Diplomatic Relations

The U.S. Senate approved a recommendation, made by President James K. Polk in December 1847, for the establishment of a diplomatic post in the Papal States. Jacob L. Martin, the first charge d'affaires, arrived in Rome Aug. 2, 1848, and presented his credentials to Pius IX Aug. 19. Martin, who died within a month, was succeeded by Lewis Cass, Jr. Cass became minister resident in 1854 and served in that capacity until his retirement in 1858.

John P. Stockton, who later became a U.S. Senator from New Jersey, was minister resident from 1858 to 1861. Rufus King was named to succeed him but, instead, accepted a commission as a brigadier general in the Army. Alexander W. Randall of Wisconsin took the appointment. He was succeeded in August, 1862, by Richard M. Blatchford, who served until the following year. King was again nominated minister resident and served in that capacity until 1867, when the ministry was ended because of objections from some quarters in the U.S. and failure to appropriate funds for its continuation. J.C. Hooker, a secretary, remained in the Papal States until the end of March, 1868, closing the ministry and performing functions of courtesy.

Nearly 120 years later, congressional approval for an end to the ban on funding for a diplomatic mission to the Holy See cleared the way for the mutual announcement Jan. 10, 1984, of the establishment of U.S.-Vatican relations. President Ronald Reagan nominated William A. Wilson to be the U.S. Ambassador. Archbishop Pio Laghi was named Pro-Nuncio to the United States.

Personal Envoys

Myron C. Taylor was appointed by President Franklin D. Roosevelt in 1939 to serve as his personal representative to Pope Pius XII and continued serving in that capacity during the presidency of Harry S. Truman until 1951. None of Truman's three successors — Dwight D. Eisenhower, John F. Kennedy or Lyndon B. Johnson — had a personal representative to the pope. Henry Cabot Lodge was named a personal representative by President Richard M. Nixon in 1970, served also during the presidency of Gerald Ford, and represented President Carter at the canonization of St. John Neumann in 1977.

Miami attorney David Walters, a Catholic, served as the personal envoy of President Jimmy Carter to the pope from July, 1977, until his resignation Aug. 16, 1978. He was succeeded by Robert F. Wagner, also a Catholic and former mayor of New York, who served from October, 1978, to the end of the Carter presidency in January, 1981. William A. Wilson, a California businessman and Catholic, was appointed by President Ronald Reagan in February, 1981, to serve as his personal envoy to the pope.

None of the personal envoys had diplomatic status.

President Harry S. Truman nominated Gen. Mark Clark to be ambassador to the Vatican in 1951, but withdrew the nomination at Clark's request because of controversy over the appointment.

Initiatives for the establishment of diplomatic relations with the Holy See are undertaken by concerned civil governments, not by the Vatican.

Code of Canon Law

Pope John Paul II promulgated a revised Code of Canon Law for the Latin Rite Jan. 25, 1983, with the apostolic constitution *Sacrae Disciplinae Legis* ("Of the Sacred Discipline of Law") and ordered it into effect as of the following Nov. 27. Promulgation of the Code marked the completion of the last major reform in the Church stemming from the Second Vatican Council.

The revised Code has replaced the one which had been in effect since 1918. Framed in the context of valid contents of the former Code, pastoral concern, enactments of the Council, and reforms introduced by Pope Paul VI and related developments, its 1,752 canons are grouped in seven books covering general norms, the People of God, the teaching office of the Church, the sanctifying office of the Church, temporal goods of the Church, sanctions and juridical procedures.

GUIDING PRINCIPLES

When Pope John XXIII announced Jan. 25, 1959, that he was going to convoke the Second Vatican Council, he also called for a revision of the existing Code of Canon Law. His successor, Paul VI, appointed a commission for this purpose in 1963 and subsequently enlarged it. The commission, which began its work after the conclusion of the Council in 1965, was directed by the 1967 assembly of the Synod of Bishops to direct its efforts in line with 10 guiding principles. The bishops said the revised Code should:

- be juridical in character, not just a set of broad moral principles;
- be intended primarily for the external forum (regarding determinable fact, as opposed to the internal forum of conscience);
- be clearly pastoral in spirit;
- incorporate most of the faculties bishops need in their ministry;
- provide for subsidiarity or decentralization;
- be sensitive to human rights;
- state clear procedures for administrative processes and tribunals;
- be based on the principle of territoriality;
- reduce the number of penalties for infractions of law;
- have a new structure.

The commission carried out its mandate with the collegial collaboration of bishops all over the world and in consultation and correspondence with individuals and bodies of experts in canon law, theology and related disciplines. The group finished its work in 1981 and turned its final draft over to Pope John Paul II at its final plenary meeting in October of that year.

FEATURES
The revised Code is shorter (1,752 canons) than the one it has replaced (2,414 canons).

It is more pastoral and flexible, as well as more theologically oriented than the former Code.

It gives greater emphasis than its predecessor to a number of significant facets and concepts in church life.

In the apostolic constitution with which he promulgated the Code, Pope John Paul II called attention to its nature and some of its features, as follows.

"This Code has arisen from a single intention, that of restoring Christian living. All the work of the (Second Vatican) Council actually drew its norms and its orientation from such an intention."

"A . . . question . . .arises about the very nature of the Code of Canon Law. In order to answer this question well, it is necessary to recall the distant heritage of law contained in the books of the Old and New Testaments, from which, as from its first spring, the whole juridical legislation of the Church derives."

"Christ the Lord did not in fact will to destroy the very rich heritage of the law and the prophets which had been forming over the course of the history and experience of the People of God in the Old Testament. On the contrary, He gave fulfillment to it (cf. Mt 5:17). Thus, in a new and more lofty way, it became part of the inheritance of the New Testament."

"Therefore although, when expounding the paschal mystery, St. Paul teaches that justification is not obtained through the works of the law but through faith (cf. Rom. 3:28; Gal 2:16), he does not thereby exclude the obligatory force of the Decalogue (cf. Rom. 13:28; Gal. 5:13-25 and 6:2), nor does he deny the importance of discipline in the Church of God (cf. 1 Cor. 5 and 6). The writings of the New Testament, therefore, allow us to understand the importance of discipline even better and to understand better how discipline is more closely connected with the salvific character of the Gospel message itself."

Prime Legislative Document
"Since this is so, it seems clear enough that the Code in no way has as its scope to substitute for faith, grace, the charisms, and especially charity in the life of the Church or the faithful. On the contrary, its end is rather to create such order in ecclesial society that, assigning primacy to love, grace and charisms, it at the same time renders more active their organic development in the life both of the ecclesial society and of the individuals belonging to it."

"Inasmuch as it is the Church's prime legislative document, based on the juridical and legislative heritage of revelation and tradition, the Code must be regarded as the necessary instrument whereby due order is preserved in both individual and social life and in the Church's activity. Therefore, besides containing the fundamental elements of the hierarchical and organic structure of the Church, laid down by her divine Founder or founded on apostolic or at any rate most ancient tradition, and besides outstanding norms concerning the carrying out of the task mandated to the Church herself, the Code must also define a certain number of rules and norms of action.''

Suits the Nature of the Church

''The instrument the Code is fully suits the Church's nature, for the Church is presented, especially through the magisterium of the Second Vatican Council, in her universal scope, and especially through the Council's ecclesiological teaching. In a certain sense, indeed, this new Code may be considered as a great effort to transfer that same ecclesiological or conciliar doctrine into canonical language. And, if it is impossible for the image of the Church described by the Council's teaching to be perfectly converted into canonical language, the Code nonetheless must always be referred to that very image, as the primary pattern whose outline the Code ought to express as well as it can by its own nature.''

''From this derive a number of fundamental norms by which the whole of the new Code is ruled, of course within the limits proper to it as well as the limits of the very language befitting the material.''

''It may rather be rightly affirmed that from this comes that note whereby the Code is regarded as a complement to the magisterium expounded by the Second Vatican Council.''

''The following elements are most especially to be noted among those expressing a true and genuine image of the Church: the doctrine whereby the Church is proposed as the People of God and the hierarchical authority is propounded as service; in addition, the doctrine which shows the Church to be a 'communion' and from that lays down the mutual relationships which ought to exist between the particular and universal Church and between collegiality and primacy; likewise, the doctrine whereby all members of the People of God, each in the manner proper to him, share in Christ's threefold office of priest, prophet and king; to this doctrine is also connected that regarding the duties and rights of the Christian faithful, particularly the laity; then there is the effort which the Church has to make for ecumenism.''

Code Necessary for the Church

''Indeed, the Code of Canon Law is extremely necessary for the Church. . . . The Church needs it for her hierarchical and organic structure to be visible: so that exercise of the offices and tasks divinely entrusted to her, especially her sacred power and administration of the sacraments, should be rightly ordered; so that mutual relations of the Christian faithful may be carried out according to justice based on charity, with the rights of all being safeguarded and defined; so that we may then prepare and perform our common tasks, and that these, undertaken in order to live a Christian life more perfectly, may be fortified by means of the canonical laws."

"Thus, canonical laws need to be observed because of their very nature. Hence it is of the greatest importance that the norms be carefully expounded on the basis of solid juridical, canonical and theological foundations."

BOOKS OF THE CODE

Book I, General Norms (Canons 1-203): Canons in this book cover: church laws in general, custom and law, general decrees and instructions, administrative acts, statutes, physical and juridical persons, juridical acts, the power of governing, ecclesiastical offices, prescription (rights having the force of law), the reckoning of time.

Book II, The People of God (Canons 204-746): Canons in Part I cover: the obligations and rights of all the faithful, the obligations and rights of lay persons, sacred ministers and clerics, personal prelatures and associations of the faithful.

Canons in Part II cover the hierarchic constitution of the Church under the headings: the supreme authority of the Church and the college of bishops, particular churches and the authority constituted in them, councils of particular churches and the internal order of particular churches.

Canons in Part III cover institutes of consecrated life and societies of apostolic life.

Book III: The Teaching Office of the Church (Canons 747-833): Canons under this heading cover: the ministry of the divine word, the missionary action of the Church, Catholic education, the instruments of social communication and books in particular, and the profession of faith.

Book IV, The Sanctifying Office of the Church (Canons 834-1253): Canons under this heading cover: each of the seven sacraments — baptism, confirmation, the Eucharist, penance, anointing of the sick, holy orders and matrimony; other acts of divine worship including sacramentals, the Liturgy of the Hours, ecclesiastical burial; the veneration of saints, sacred images and relics, vows and oaths.

Book V, Temporal Goods of the Church (Canons 1254-1310): Canons under this heading cover: the acquisition and administration of goods, contracts, the alienation of goods, wills and pious foundations.

Book VI, Sanctions in the Church (Canons 1311-1399): Canons in Part I cover crimes and penalties in general: the punishment of crimes in general, penal law and penal precept, persons subject to penal sanctions, penalties and other punishments, the application and cessation of penalties.

Canons in Part II cover penalties for particular crimes: crimes against religion and the unity of the Church; crimes against the authorities of the Church and the liberty of the Church; the usurpation of church offices and crimes in exercising office; false accusation of a confessor; crimes against special obligations; crimes against human life and liberty; a general norm regarding the punishment of external violations of divine and canon law not specificially covered in the Code.

Book VII, Procedures (Canons 1400-1752): Judicial proceedings are the principal subjects of canons under this heading: tribunals and their personnel, parties to proceedings, details regarding litigation and the manner in which it is conducted, special proceedings — with emphasis on matrimonial cases.

RIGHTS AND OBLIGATIONS OF ALL THE FAITHFUL

The following rights are listed in Canons 208-223 of the Code of Canon Law; additional rights are specified in other canons.

Because of their baptism and regeneration in Christ, they are equal with respect to dignity and to cooperative activity for building up the Body of Christ.

They are bound always to preserve communion with the Church.

According to their condition and circumstances, they must strive to lead a holy life and promote the growth and holiness of the Church.

They have the right and duty to work for the spread of the divine message of salvation to all peoples of all times and places.

They are bound to obey declarations and orders given by their pastors in their capacity as representatives of Christ, teachers of the faith and rectors of the Church.

They have the right to make known their needs, especially their spiritual needs and desires, to pastors of the Church.

They have the right, and sometimes the duty, of making known to pastors and others of the faithful their opinions about things pertaining to the good of the Church.

They have the right to receive help from their pastors, from the spiritual goods of the Church and especially from the word of God and the sacraments.

They have the right to divine worship performed according to prescribed rules of their rite, and to follow their own form of spiritual life in line with the doctrine of the Church.

They have the right to freely establish and control associations for good and charitable purposes, to foster the Christian vocation in the world, and to hold meetings related to the accomplishment of these purposes.

They have the right to promote and support apostolic action but may not call it "Catholic" unless they have the consent of competent authority.

They have a right to a Christian education.

Those in sacred studies have a right to lawful freedom of inquiry and to the prudent expression of opinions in the fields of their expertise, in accordance with the teaching authority of the Church.

They have a right to freedom from coercion in the choice of their state of life.

No one has the right to harm the good name of another person or to violate his or her right to maintain personal privacy.

They have the right to vindicate the rights they enjoy in the Church, and to defend themselves in a competent ecclesiastical forum.

They have the obligation to provide for the needs of the Church, with respect to things pertaining to divine worship, apostolic and charitable works, and the reasonable support of ministers of the Church.

They have the obligation to promote social justice and to help the poor from their own resources.

In exercising their rights, the faithful must have regard for the common good of the Church and for the rights and duties of others.

Church authority has the right to monitor the exercise of rights proper to the faithful, with the common good in view.

RIGHTS AND OBLIGATIONS OF LAY PERSONS

In addition to rights and obligations common to all the faithful and those stated in other canons, lay persons are bound by the obligations and enjoy the rights specified in these canons (224-231).

Lay persons, like all the faithful, are called by God to the apostolate in virtue of their baptism and confirmation. They have the obligation and right, individually or together in associations, to work for the spread and acceptance of the divine message of salvation among people everywhere; this obligation is more urgent in those circumstances in which people can hear the Gospel and get to know Christ only through them (lay persons).

They are bound to bring an evangelical spirit to bear on the order of temporal things and to give Christian witness in carrying out their secular pursuits.

Married couples are obliged to work for the building up of the People of God through their marital and family life.

Parents have the most serious obligation to provide for the Christian education of their children according to the doctrine handed down by the Church.

Lay persons have the same civil liberty as other citizens. In the use of this liberty, they should take care that their actions be imbued with an evangelical spirit. They should attend to the doctrine proposed by the magisterium of the Church but should take care that, in questions of opinion, they do not propose their own opinion as the doctrine of the Church.

Qualified lay persons are eligible to hold and perform the duties of ecclesiastical offices open to them in accord with the provisions of law.

Properly qualified lay persons can assist pastors of the Church as experts and counselors.

Lay persons have the obligation and enjoy the right to acquire knowledge of doctrine commensurate with their capacity and condition.

They have the right to pursue studies in the sacred sciences in pontifical universities or faculties and in institutes of religious sciences, and to obtain academic degrees.

If qualified, they are eligible to receive from ecclesiastical authority a mandate to teach sacred sciences.

Laymen can be invested by liturgical rite and in a stable manner in the ministries of lector and acolyte.

Lay persons, by temporary assignment, can fulfill the office of lector in liturgical actions; likewise, all lay persons can perform the duties of commentator or cantor or other functions, according to the prescriptions of law.

In cases of necessity and in the absence of the usual ministers, lay persons — even if not lectors or acolytes — can exercise the ministry of the word, lead liturgical prayers, confer baptism and distribute Communion, according to the prescripts of law.

Lay persons who devote themselves permanently or temporarily to the service of the Church are obliged to acquire the formation necessary for carrying out their duties in a proper manner.

They have a right to a remuneration for their service which is just and adequate to provide for their own needs and those of their families; they also have a right to insurance, social security and health insurance.

Apostolate of Lay Persons

Lay persons and their apostolate in the world were among subjects of the Second Vatican Council's *Dogmatic Constitution on the Church.*

"The term laity is here understood to mean all the faithful except those in holy orders and those in the state of religious life."

"What specifically characterizes the laity is their secular nature. . . . The laity, by their very vocation, seek the kingdom of God by engaging in temporal affairs and by ordering them according to the plan of God. They live in the world, that is, in each and all of the secular professions and occupations. They live in the ordinary circumstances of family and social life, from which the very web of their existence is woven. They are called there by God in order that, by exercising their proper function and led by the spirit of the Gospel, they may make Christ known to others, especially by the testimony of a life resplendent in faith, hope and charity. Therefore, since they are tightly bound up in all types of temporal affairs, it is their special task to order and to throw light upon these affairs in such a way that they may come into being and then continually increase according to Christ, to the praise of the Creator and Redeemer.

Call to Apostolate

In its *Decree on the Apostolate of the Laity,* the Council developed these concepts and outlined the principal features of this apostolate.

The laity, made sharers in the priestly, prophetic and royal office of Christ, discharge their own roles in the mission of the whole People of God in the Church and in the world.

Lay persons, "incorporated into Christ's Mystical Body by baptism and strengthened by the power of the Holy Spirit in Confirmation . . . are assigned to the apostolate by the Lord himself . . . that they may offer spiritual sacrifices in everything and bear witness to Christ throughout the world."

"By the precept of charity . . . all the faithful are impelled to promote the glory of God through the coming of His kingdom and to obtain eternal life for all men. . . . On all Christians, therefore, is placed the noble duty of collaborating to make the divine message of salvation known and accepted by all men throughout the world."

"For the exercise of this apostolate, the Holy Spirit . . . gives the faithful special gifts (1 Cor. 12:7) . . . for the building up of the whole Body in charity (Eph. 4:16). From the receiving of these charisms . . . there arises for each believer the right and duty to use them in the Church and in the world for the good of men and building up of the Church."

The spiritual life of the laity "should take its specific character from their married and family state, their single or widowed state, from their state of health, and from their professional and social activity. They should not cease to develop continually the qualities and talents bestowed on them in accord with these conditions of life, and to make use of the gifts which they have received from the Holy Spirit."

Goals and Methods

"The mission of the Church is not only to bring the message and grace of Christ to men but also to permeate and perfect the temporal order with the spirit of the Gospel."

"The temporal order must be renewed in such a way that, without detriment to its own proper laws, it may be brought into conformity with the higher principles of the Christian life. . . . Pre-eminent among the works of this type of apostolate is that of Christian social action which the holy Council desires to see extended to the whole temporal sphere, including culture."

"The apostolate in the social milieu, that is, the effort to infuse a Christian spirit into the mentality, customs, laws and structures of the community in which one lives, is so much the duty and responsibility of the laity that it can never be performed properly by others."

"The individual apostolate . . . admits of no substitutes."

"The group apostolate . . . happily corresponds to both the human and the Christian need of the faithful and at the same time signifies the communion and unity of the Church in Christ."

"Deserving of special honor and commendation . . . are those lay people . . . who devote themselves with professional skill, either permanently or temporarily, to the service of associations and their activities."

SECULAR ORDERS

Third Orders or Secular Orders are societies of the faithful living in the world who seek to deepen their Christian life and apostolic commitment in the spirit and under the overall direction of various religious institutes. The orders have their own rules and constitutions approved by the Apostolic See. They are called "third" because their foundation followed the establishment of the first (for men) and second (for women) religious orders with which they are associated. Third Orders became popular in the Church in the 13th century, especially with the institution of the Third Order of St. Francis and the approval of its rule in 1221.

Religious: Men and Women

Religious orders and congregations are institutes of consecrated life, i.e., special societies in the Church whose members, called Religious, commit themselves by public vows to observe the evangelical counsels of poverty, chastity and obedience in a community kind of life in accordance with rules and constitutions approved by church authority.

The inspiration for the life of men and women Religious is the invitation extended by Christ, to follow Him with special dedication in a life like His own, which was that of a poor and chaste man under obedience to the Father.

In the earliest years of Christianity, some men and women committed themselves to the service of God in a special manner. In the third and fourth centuries, there were traces of a kind of religious profession, and the root idea of the religious life began to produce significant results in the solitary and community hermitages of Egypt and Syria under the influence of men like St. Paul of Thebes, St. Anthony the Abbot and St. Pachomius.

St. Basil, "Father of Monasticism in the East," exerted a deep and still continuing influence on the development of religious life among men and women. His opposite number in the West was St. Benedict, whose rule or counsels, dating from about 530, set the pattern of monastic life for men and women which prevailed for nearly six centuries and which still endures. Before his time, St. Augustine framed guidelines for community life which are still being followed by some men and women Religious.

MONASTIC INSTITUTES

Members of male monastic institutes, called monks, were the first to live a common life, and their form of life set the pattern for men Religious until the 13th century.

Monks can be clerics or laymen. They are attached for life to the monastery in which they profess their vows and have a stable form of life with emphasis on liturgical worship, contemplation and the internal concerns of their community. Major houses — monasteries, abbeys, conventual priories — are autonomous and under the direction of elected superiors, abbots and priors. A degree of monastic organization finds expression in confederations of houses. Monastic orders are the Benedictines, Cistercians, Trappists and Carthusians in the West, and Paulines, Antonians and Basilians in the East.

Contemplative institutes of women with solemn vows and some monastic-like features include the Poor Clares, Dominican Nuns of the Second Order of Perpetual Adoration, and Carmelites. Their manner of life remained the standard for women Religious until the 17th century.

MENDICANT ORDERS

Mendicant orders made their appearance early in the 13th century, with changes in established aspects of religious life associated with monastic institutes. The orders got their name from the Latin word for beggar, *mendicus*; their members originally relied on begging for support, and the orders bound themselves to the obligation of corporate poverty. Mendicants were freer than monks for works of the active ministry. They were also much more mobile, with a centralized form of government and organization into provinces, instead of autonomous monasteries and abbeys, as jurisdictional units. Mendicants include Dominicans, Franciscans, Augustinians, Carmelites, Trinitarians and the Servants of Mary.

OTHER INSTITUTES

A significant change in religious life developed in the 16th century when approval was given to several communities of men with simple vows rather than the solemn vows of monastics and mendicants. The Jesuits (Society of Jesus) and Barnabites were two of the new institutes; they were followed by others, like the Passionists, Redemptorists and Marists.

The Sisters of Charity, in 1633, were the first community of women with simple vows to gain church approval. Since that time, the number and variety of female communities have greatly increased. Women Religious, no longer restricted to the hidden life of prayer, became engaged in many kinds of work including education, health and social service, and missionary endeavor.

Clerical communities of men — i.e., those whose membership is predominantly composed of priests — are similarly active in many types of work. Their distinctive fields are education, home and foreign missions, retreats, special assignments and the communications media, as well as the internal life and conduct of their own communities. They also engage in the ordinary pastoral ministry which is the principal work of diocesan or secular priests. They are generally called regular clergy because of the rule of life (*regula* in Latin) they follow.

Non-clerical or lay institutes of men are the various brotherhoods whose non-ordained members (called lay brothers, or simply brothers) are engaged in educational and hospital work, missionary endeavors, and other special fields.

Some institutes of men have a special kind of status because their members, while living a common life like that which is characteristic of Religious, do not profess the vows of Religious. Examples are the Maryknoll Fathers, the Oratorians of St. Philip Neri, the Paulists and Sulpicians. They are called societies of apostolic life.

ESSENTIAL ELEMENTS OF RELIGIOUS LIFE

Following are excerpts from a document entitled "Essential Elements in the Church's Teaching on Religious Life as Applied to Institutes Dedicated to Works of the Apostolate." The document was released in June, 1983, by the Congregation for Religious and Secular Institutes. These excerpts embody the substance of key provisions of the Code of Canon Law on religious life.

Call and Consecration

"Religious life is a form of life to which some Christians, both clerical and lay, are freely called by God so that they may enjoy a special gift of grace in the life of the Church and may contribute each in his or her own way to the saving mission of the Church."

"The gift of religious vocation is rooted in the gift of baptism but is not given to all the baptized. It is freely given and unmerited, offered by God to those whom He chooses freely from among His people and for the sake of His people."

"In accepting God's gift of vocation, Religious respond to a divine call, dying to sin (cf. Rom. 6:11), renouncing the world and living for God alone. Their whole lives are dedicated to His service and they seek and love above all else 'God who has first loved us' (cf. 1 Jn. 4:10). The focus of their lives is the closer following of Christ."

"The dedication of the whole life of the Religious to God's service constitutes a special consecration. It is a consecration of the whole person which manifests in the Church a marriage effected by God, a sign of the future life. This consecration is by public vows, perpetual or temporary, the latter renewable on expiration. By their vows, Religious assume the observance of the three evangelical counsels (poverty, chastity, obedience); they are consecrated to God through the ministry of the Church; and they are incorporated into their institute with the rights and duties defined by law."

"Religious profession is made according to the formula of vows approved by the Holy See for each institute. The formula is common because all members undertake the same obligations and, when fully incorporated, have the same rights and duties."

"Considering its character and the ends proper to it, every institute should define in its constitutions the way in which the evangelical counsels of chastity, poverty and obedience are to be observed in its own particular way of life."

Community and Identity

"Community life, which is one of the marks of a religious institute, is proper to each religious family. It gathers all the members together in Christ and should be so defined that it becomes a source of mutual aid to all, while helping to fulfill the religious vocation of each. It should offer an example of reconciliation in Christ and of the communion that is rooted and founded in His love.''

"Religious should live in their own religious house, observing a common life. They should not live alone without serious reason, and should not do so if there is a community of their institute reasonably near. If, however, there is a question of prolonged absence, the major superior with the consent of his or her council may permit a Religious to live outside the houses of the institute for a just cause, within the limits of common law.''

"Religious should regard the following of Christ proposed in the Gospel and expressed in the constitutions of their institute as the supreme rule of life.''

"The constitutions are approved by competent ecclesiastical authority. For diocesan institutes, this is the local Ordinary; for pontifical institutes, the Holy See. Subsequent modifications and authentic interpretations are also reserved to the same authority.''

"By their religious profession, the members of an institute bind themselves to observe the constitutions faithfully and with love, for they recognize in them the way of life approved by the Church for the institute and the authentic expression of its spirit, tradition and law.''

The Three Vows

"The evangelical counsel of chastity embraced for the kingdom of heaven is a sign of the future life and a source of abundant fruitfulness in an undivided heart. It carries with it the obligation of perfect continence in celibacy.''

"Discretion should be used in all things that could be dangerous to the chastity of a consecrated person.''

"The evangelical counsel of poverty in imitation of Christ calls for a life poor in fact and in spirit, subject to work and led in frugality and detachment from material possessions. Its profession by vow for the Religious involves dependence and limitation in the use and disposition of temporalities according to the norms of the proper law of the institute.''

"By the vow of poverty, Religious give up the free use and disposal of goods having material value. Before first profession, they cede the administration of their goods to whomsoever they wish and, unless the constitutions determine otherwise, they freely dispose of their use and usufruct. Whatever the Religious acquires by personal industry, by gift or as a Religious, is acquired for the institute; whatever is acquired by way of pension, subsidy or insurance is also acquired for the institute unless the proper law states otherwise.''

"The evangelical counsel of obedience, lived in faith, is a loving following of Christ who was obedient unto death.''

"By their vow of obedience, Religious undertake to submit their will to legitimate superiors according to the constitutions. The constitutions themselves state who may give a formal command of obedience and in what circumstances.''

"Religious institutes are subject to the supreme authority of the Church in a particular manner. All Religious are obliged to obey the Holy Father as their highest superior in virtue of the vow of obedience.''

"Religious may not accept duties and offices outside their own institute without the permission of a lawful superior. Like clerics, they may not accept public offices which involve the exercise of civil power.''

Prayer, Apostolate, Witness

"The first and principal duty of Religious is assiduous union with God in prayer. They participate in the Eucharistic Sacrifice daily insofar as possible and approach the sacrament of penance frequently. The reading of sacred Scripture, time for mental prayer, the worthy celebration of the Liturgy of the Hours according to the prescriptions of proper law, devotion to the Blessed Virgin, and a special time for annual retreat are all part of the prayer of Religious.''

"Prayer should be both individual and communitarian.''

"The apostolate of all Religious consists first in the witness of their consecrated life, which they are bound to foster by prayer and penance.''

"The essential mission of those Religious undertaking apostolic works is the proclaiming of the word of God to those whom He places along their path, so as to lead them toward faith. Such a grace requires a profound union with the Lord, one which enables the Religious to transmit the message of the Incarnate Word in terms which today's world is able to understand.''

"Apostolic action is carried out in communion with the Church, and in the name and by the mandate of the Church.''

"Superiors and members should faithfully retain the mission and works proper to the institute. They should accommodate them with prudence to the needs of times and places.''

"In apostolic relations with bishops, Religious . . . have the special obligation of being attentive to the magisterium of the hierarchy and of facilitating for the bishops the exercise of the ministry of teaching and witnessing authentically to divine truth.''

"The witness of Religious is public. This public witness to Christ and to the Church implies separation from the world according to the character and purpose of each institute.''

"Religious should wear the religious garb of the institute, described in their proper law, as a sign of consecration and a witness of poverty.''

Formation and Government

"No one may be admitted to religious life without suitable preparation.''

"Conditions for validity of admission, for validity of novitiate, and for validity of temporary and perpetual profession are indicated in the common law of the Church and the proper law of each institute. So also are provisions for the place, time, program and guidance of the novitiate and the requirements for the director of novices."

"Authority to govern in religious institutes is invested in superiors who should exercise it according to the norms of common and proper law. This authority is received from God through the ministry of the Church. The authority of a superior at whatever level is personal and may not be taken over by a group. For a particular time and for a given purpose, it may be delegated to a designated person."

"Superiors should fulfill their office generously, building with their brothers or sisters a community in Christ in which God is sought and loved before everything. In their role of service, superiors have the particular duty of governing in accordance with the constitutions of their institute and of promoting the holiness of its members. In their person, superiors should be examples of fidelity to the magisterium of the Church and to the law and tradition of their institute. They should also foster the consecrated lives of their Religious by their care and correction, their support and their patience."

"Superiors must each have their own council, which assists them in fulfilling their responsibility. In addition to cases prescribed in the common law, proper law determines those cases in which the superior must obtain the consent or the advice of the council for validity of action."

SECULAR INSTITUTES

Secular institutes are societies of consecrated life in which members of the faithful — lay and clerical — strive for perfection and carry on apostolic works suitable to their talents and opportunities in the circumstances of their everyday lives in the world. Members profess the evangelical counsels by vows or other sacred bonds in accordance with the laws of their respective institutes.

The Second Vatican Council, in its *Decree on the Appropriate Renewal of Religious Life,* described the nature and purpose of secular institutes. "Secular institutes are not religious communities but they carry with them in the world a profession of evangelical counsels which is genuine and complete. . . . This profession confers a consecration on men and women, laity and clergy, who reside in the world. For this reason they should chiefly strive for total self-dedication to God, inspired by perfect charity. These institutes should preserve their proper and particular (secular) character . . . so that they may everywhere measure up successfully to that apostolate which they were designed to exercise, and which is both in the world and, in a sense, of the world."

Secular institutes, which originated in the latter part of the 18th century, were given full recognition and approval by Pope Pius XII in the 1947 apostolic constitution *Provida Mater Ecclesiae* and later documents; they are under the jurisdiction of the Congregation for Religious and Secular Institutes.

Interfaith Relations

Ecumenism is the movement of Christians and their church bodies toward the unity willed by Christ.

The modern ecumenical movement, which started about 1910 among Protestants and led to formation of the World Council of Churches in 1948, developed outside the mainstream of Catholic interest for many years. It has now become for Catholics as well one of the great religious facts of our time.

The magna charta of ecumenism for Catholics is a complex of several documents which include, in the first place, the *Decree on Ecumenism* promulgated by the Second Vatican Council Nov. 21, 1964. Other enactments underlying and expanding this decree are the *Dogmatic Constitution on the Church,* the *Decree on Eastern Catholic Churches* and the *Pastoral Constitution on the Church in the Modern World.*

The conciliar *Decree on Ecumenism* clearly states: "Promoting the restoration of unity among all Christians is one of the chief concerns of the Second Sacred Ecumenical Synod of the Vatican. The Church established by Christ is, indeed, one and unique. Yet many Christian communions present themselves to men as the true heritage of Jesus Christ. To be sure, all proclaim themselves to be disciples of the Lord, but their convictions clash and their paths diverge, as though Christ himself were divided. Without doubt, this discord openly contradicts the will of Christ, provides a stumbling block to the world and inflicts damage on the most holy cause of proclaiming the good news to every creature."

The Council recalled that "from her very beginnings there arose in this one and only Church of God certain rifts. . . . In subsequent centuries more widespread disagreements appeared and quite large communities became separated from full communion with the Catholic Church — developments for which, at times, men of both sides were to blame. However, one cannot impute the sin of separation to those who at present are born into these communities and are instilled therein with Christ's faith."

Some Common Elements

Despite these rifts and disagreements, "men who believe in Christ and have been properly baptized are brought into a certain, though imperfect, communion with the Catholic Church. Undoubtedly, the differences that exist in varying degrees between them and the Catholic Church — whether in doctrine and sometimes in discipline, or concerning the structure of the Church — do indeed, create many and sometimes serious obstacles to full ecclesiastical communion. These the ecumenical movement is striving to overcome."

"Moreover some, even very many, of the most significant elements or endowments which together go to build up and give life to the Church herself can exist outside the visible boundaries of the Catholic Church: the written word of God; the life of grace; faith, hope, and charity, along with other interior gifts of the Holy Spirit and visible elements. All of these, which come from Christ and lead back to Him, belong by right to the one Church of Christ.''

(In a later passage, the decree singled out a number of elements which the Catholic Church and other Christian churches have in common but not in complete agreement: confession of Christ as Lord and God and as mediator between God and man; belief in the Trinity; reverence for Scripture as the revealed word of God; baptism and the Lord's Supper; Christian life and worship; faith in action; concern with moral questions.)

"The brethren divided from us also carry out many of the sacred actions of the Christian religion. Undoubtedly, in ways that vary according to the condition of each church or community, these actions can truly engender a life of grace, and can be rightly described as capable of providing access to the community of salvation.''

"It follows that these separated Churches and Communities, though we believe they suffer from defects already mentioned, have by no means been deprived of significance and importance in the mystery of salvation. For the Spirit of Christ has not refrained from using them as means of salvation which derive their efficacy from the very fullness of grace and truth entrusted to the Catholic Church.''

Unity Lacking

"Nevertheless, our separated brethren, whether considered as individuals or as Communities and Churches, are not blessed with that unity which Jesus Christ wished to bestow on all those whom He has regenerated and vivified into one body and newness of life — that unity which the holy Scriptures and the revered tradition of the Church proclaim. For it is through Christ's Catholic Church alone, which is the all-embracing means of salvation, that the fullness of the means of salvation can be obtained. It was to the apostolic college alone, of which Peter is the head, that we believe our Lord entrusted all the blessings of the New Covenant, in order to establish on earth the one Body of Christ into which all those should be fully incorporated who already belong in any way to God's People.''

What the Movement Involves

"Today, in many parts of the world, under the inspiring grace of the Holy Spirit, multiple efforts are being expended through prayer, word, and action to attain that fullness of unity which Jesus Christ desires. This sacred Synod, therefore, exhorts all the Catholic faithful to recognize the signs of the times and to participate skillfully in the work of ecumenism.''

"The 'ecumenical movement' means those activities and enterprises which, according to various needs of the Church and opportune occasions, are started and organized for the fostering of unity among Christians. These are:

• "First, every effort to eliminate words, judgments, and actions which do not respond to the condition of separated brethren with truth and fairness and so make mutual relations between them more difficult.

• "Then, 'dialogue' between competent experts from different Churches and Communities [scholarly ecumenism].

• "In addition, these Communions cooperate more closely in whatever projects a Christian conscience demands for the common good [social ecumenism].

• "They also come together for common prayer, where this is permitted [spiritual ecumenism].

• "Finally, all are led to examine their own faithfulness to Christ's will for the Church and, wherever necessary, undertake with vigor the task of renewal and reform."

"It is evident that the work of preparing and reconciling those individuals who wish for full Catholic communion is of its nature distinct from ecumenical action. But there is no opposition between the two, since both proceed from the wondrous providence of God."

Primary Duty of Catholics

"In ecumenical work, Catholics must assuredly be concerned for their separated brethren, praying for them, keeping them informed about the Church, making the first approaches toward them. But their primary duty is to make an honest and careful appraisal of whatever needs to be renewed and achieved in the Catholic household itself, in order that its life may bear witness more loyally and luminously to the teachings and ordinances which have been handed down from Christ through the Apostles."

"Every Catholic must . . . aim at Christian perfection (cf. Jas. 1:4; Rom 12:1-2) and, each according to his station, play his part so that the Church . . . may daily be more purified and renewed, against the day when Christ will present her to himself in all her glory, without spot or wrinkle (cf. Eph. 5:27)."

"Catholics must joyfully acknowledge and esteem the truly Christian endowments from our common heritage which are to be found among our separated brethren."

"Nor should we forget that whatever is wrought by the grace of the Holy Spirit in the hearts of our separated brethren can contribute to our own edification. Whatever is truly Christian never conflicts with the genuine interests of the faith; indeed, it can always result in a more ample realization of the very mystery of Christ and the Church."

Participation in Worship

Norms concerning participation by Catholics in the worship of other Christian churches were sketched in the conciliar decree and elaborated in a number of other documents.

The norms encourage common prayer services for Christian unity and other intentions. Beyond that, they draw a distinction between separated churches of the Reformation tradition and separated Eastern churches, in view of doctrine and practice the Catholic Church has in common with the latter concerning the apostolic succession of bishops, holy orders, liturgy, and other credal matters.

Full participation by Catholics in official Protestant liturgies is prohibited, because it implies profession of the faith expressed in the liturgy.

Sacramental Discipline

Eucharistic communion was one of the subjects covered in the statement issued by the Vatican Secretariat for Promoting Christian Unity in 1973. The secretariat said, in part:

"There is an indissoluble link between the mystery of the Church and the mystery of the Eucharist, or between ecclesial and Eucharistic communion; the celebration of the Eucharist of itself signifies the fullness of profession of faith and ecclesial communion."

"Eucharistic communion practiced by those who are not in full ecclesial communion with each other cannot be the expression of that full unity which the Eucharist of its nature signifies and which in this case does not exist; for this reason such communion cannot be regarded as a means to be used to lead to full ecclesial communion."

Several key points of sacramental discipline with a bearing on interfaith relations are stated in Canon 844 of the Code of Canon Law (in *Code of Canon Law, Latin-English Translation*, by the Canon Law Society of America; copyright 1983).

"Catholic ministers may licitly administer the sacraments to Catholic members of the Christian faithful only and, likewise, the latter may licitly receive the sacraments only from Catholic ministers with due regard" (for the following three paragraphs and an exceptional case of baptism).

"Whenever necessity requires or genuine spiritual advantage suggests, and provided that the danger of error or indifferentism is avoided, it is lawful for the faithful for whom it is physically or morally impossible to approach a Catholic minister, to receive the sacraments of penance, Eucharist, and anointing of the sick from non-Catholic ministers in whose churches these sacraments are valid."

"Catholic ministers may licitly administer the sacraments of penance, Eucharist and anointing of the sick to members of the oriental churches which do not have full communion with the Catholic Church, if they ask on their own for the sacraments and are properly disposed. This holds also for members of other churches, which in the judgment of the Apostolic See are in the same condition as the oriental churches as far as these sacraments are concerned."

"If the danger of death is present or other grave necessity, in the judgment of the diocesan bishop or the conference of bishops, Catholic ministers may licitly administer these sacraments to other Christians who do not have full communion with the Catholic Church, who cannot approach a minister of their own community and on their own ask for it, provided they manifest Catholic faith in these sacraments and are properly disposed."

Common Prayer

Common prayer services as means of promoting Christian unity have been encouraged by the *Decree on Ecumenism,* subsequent documents and related practices. One of the recommended observances is the annual interfaith Week of Prayer for Christian Unity, January 18 to 25. The practice was begun in 1908 by Father Paul James Wattson, founder of the Anglican Society of the Atonement whose members were received into the Catholic Church with him a year later. The theme and texts for the observance are chosen by a mixed committee of representatives of the Catholic Church and the World Council of Churches. In the U.S., the observance is sponsored by the Faith and Order Department of the National Council of Churches of Christ and is endorsed by the Committee for Ecumenical and Interreligious Affairs, National Conference of Catholic Bishops.

Dialogues

In line with directives of the Second Vatican Council, representatives of the Catholic Church have been involved in recent years in dialogue with their counterparts of other churches. Official dialogues on a world level include those with Eastern Orthodox, Oriental Orthodox, Anglicans, Lutherans and Methodists. In the U.S., the Bishops' Committee for Ecumenical and Interreligious Affairs sponsors dialogues with Baptists (the American Baptist Convention, Southern Baptists), the Christian Church, the Disciples of Christ, the Episcopal Church, Lutherans, U.S.A., Methodists, Eastern Orthodox, Oriental Orthodox, Presbyterian and Reformed Churches.

These dialogue groups have produced a number of statements on doctrinal, moral, liturgical and historical subjects, reflecting various degrees of agreement and disagreement among participants in the talks.

Ecumenical Agencies

The Vatican Secretariat for Promoting Christian Unity is the top-level agency for Catholic ecumenical efforts. Its purposes are to provide guidance and, where necessary, coordination for ecumenical endeavors, and to establish and maintain relations with representatives of other

Christian churches for interfaith dialogue and action. The secretariat has relations with (but has declined membership in) the World Council of Churches, a worldwide fellowship of churches which acknowledges "Jesus Christ as Lord and Savior." While the secretariat and its counterparts in other ecclesial bodies and on other levels have focused primary attention on theological and other problems related to the quest for Christian unity, they have also begun, and in increasing measure, to emphasize the responsibilities of the churches for greater unity of witness and effort in areas of humanitarian need.

The U.S. Bishops' Committee for Ecumenical and Interreligious Affairs, established in 1964 as a standing committee of the National Conference of Catholic Bishops, maintains relations with other Christian churches and religious bodies on a national level, advises and assists dioceses in the development and application of ecumenical policies, and maintains liaison with the Vatican Secretariat for Promoting Christian Unity and Non-Christian Religions. The committee sponsors national consultations with other churches and confessional families. It has working relations with the National Council of Churches of Christ in the U.S.A., a cooperative organization of Protestant, Anglican and Orthodox bodies established in 1950, and is a member of its Faith and Order Commission.

Most dioceses in the U.S. have ecumenical commissions responsible for sponsoring and facilitating interfaith relations and action on local levels.

NON-CHRISTIAN RELIGIONS

The Second Vatican Council, in addition to the *Decree on Ecumenism* concerning the movement for unity among Christians, stated the mind of the Church on a similar matter in a *Declaration on the Relationship of the Church to Non-Christian Religions*. The following excerpts relate to the Jews, Hindus and Buddhists.

Spiritual Bond with Jews

"As this sacred Synod searches into the mystery of the Church, it recalls the spiritual bond linking the people of the New Covenant with Abraham's stock."

"For the Church of Christ acknowledges that, according to the mystery of God's saving design, the beginnings of her faith and her election are already found among the patriarchs, Moses, and the prophets. She professes that all who believe in Christ, Abraham's sons according to faith (cf. Gal. 3:7), are included in the same patriarch's call, and likewise that the salvation of the Church was mystically foreshadowed by the Chosen People's exodus from the land of bondage."

"The Church, therefore, cannot forget that she received the revelation of the Old Testament through the people with whom God in His inexpressible mercy deigned to establish the Ancient Covenant. Nor can she forget that she draws sustenance from the root of that good olive tree onto which have been grafted the wild olive branches of the Gentiles (cf. Rom. 11:17-24). Indeed, the Church believes that by His cross Christ, our Peace reconciled Jew and Gentile, making them both one in himself (cf. Eph 2:14-16).''

"The Jews still remain most dear to God because of their fathers, for He does not repent of the gifts He makes nor of the calls He issues (cf. Rom. 11:28-29). In company with the prophets and the same Apostle (Paul), the Church awaits that day, known to God alone, on which all peoples will address the Lord in a single voice and 'serve Him with one accord' (Zeph. 3:9; cf. Is. 66:23; Ps. 65:4; Rom. 11:11-32).''

"Since the spiritual patrimony common to Christians and Jews is thus so great, this sacred Synod wishes to foster and recommend that mutual understanding and respect which is the fruit above all of biblical and theological studies, and of brotherly dialogues.''

No Anti-Semitism

"True, authorities of the Jews and those who followed their lead pressed for the death of Christ (cf. Jn. 19:6); still, what happened in His passion cannot be blamed upon all the Jews then living, without distinction, nor upon the Jews of today. Although the Church is the new People of God, the Jews should not be presented as repudiated or cursed by God, as if such views followed from the holy Scriptures. All should take pains, then, lest in catechetical instruction and in the preaching of God's Word they teach anything out of harmony with the truth of the Gospel and the spirit of Christ.''

"The Church repudiates all persecutions against any man. Moreover, mindful of her common patrimony with the Jews, and motivated by the Gospel's spiritual love and by no political considerations, she deplores the hatred, persecutions, and displays of anti-Semitism directed against the Jews at any time and from any source.''

"The Church rejects, as foreign to the mind of Christ, any discrimination against men or harassment of them because of their race, color, condition of life, or religion.''

Both the Vatican and the National Conference of Catholic Bishops have set up commissions for the establishment and maintenance of relations with the Jews.

Moslems

The attitude of the Church toward Islam was stated as follows by the Second Vatican Council.

"Upon the Moslems, too, the Church looks with esteem. They adore one God, living and enduring, merciful and all-powerful, Maker of heaven and earth and Speaker to men. They strive to submit wholeheartedly even to His inscrutable decrees, just as did Abraham, with whom the Islamic faith is pleased to associate itself. Though they do not acknowledge Jesus as God, they revere Him as a prophet. They also honor Mary, His virgin mother; at times they call on her, with devotion. In addition they await the day of judgment when God will give each man his due after raising him up. Consequently, they prize the moral life, and give worship to God especially through prayer, almsgiving and fasting.''

"Although in the course of the centuries many quarrels and hostilities have arisen between Christians and Moslems, this most sacred Synod urges all to forget the past and to strive sincerely for mutual understanding. On behalf of all mankind, let them make common cause of safeguarding and fostering social justice, moral values, peace and freedom.''

Catholic-Moslem relations are the concern of a commission attached to the Vatican Secretariat for Non-Christians.

BUDDHISM AND HINDUISM

The conciliar declaration on non-Christian religions noted the following with respect to Hinduism and Buddhism.

"In Hinduism men contemplate the divine mystery and express it through an unspent fruitfulness of myths and through searching philosophical inquiry. They seek release from the anguish of our condition through ascetical practices or deep meditation or a loving, trusting flight toward God.''

"Buddhism in its multiple forms acknowledges the radical insufficiency of this shifting world. It teaches a path by which men, in a devout and confident spirit, can either reach a state of absolute freedom or obtain supreme enlightenment by their own efforts or by higher assistance.''

"Likewise, other religions to be found everywhere strive variously to answer the restless searchings of the human heart by proposing 'ways' which consist of teachings, rules of life, and sacred ceremonies.''

"The Catholic Church rejects nothing which is true and holy in these religions. She looks with sincere respect upon those ways of conduct and life, those rules and teachings which, though differing in many particulars from what she holds and sets forth, nevertheless often reflect a ray of that Truth which enlightens all men.''

The Church exhorts her sons to "acknowledge, preserve and promote the spiritual moral goods found among these men, as well as the values in their society and culture.''

Appendix

POPES: CHRONOLOGICAL LIST

Information includes the name of the pope, in many cases his name before becoming pope, his birthplace or country of origin, the date of accession to the papacy, and the date of the end of reign which, in all but a few cases, was the date of death. Double dates indicate times of election and coronation. Source: "Annuario Pontificio."

St. Peter (Simon Bar-Jonah): Bethsaida in Galilee; d. c. 64 or 67.

St. Linus: Tuscany; 67-76.

St. Anacletus (Cletus): Rome; 76-88.

St. Clement: Rome; 88-97.

St. Evaristus: Greece; 97-105.

St. Alexander I: Rome; 105-115.

St. Sixtus I: Rome; 115-125.

St. Telesphorus: Greece; 125-136.

St. Hyginus: Greece; 136-140.

St. Pius I: Aquileia; 140-155.

St. Anicetus: Syria; 155-166.

St. Soter: Campania; 166-175.

St. Eleutherius: Nicopolis in Epirus; 175-189.

Up to the time of St. Eleutherius, the years indicated for the beginning and end of pontificates are not absolutely certain. Also, up to the middle of the 11th century, there are some doubts about the exact days and months given in chronological tables.

St. Victor I: Africa; 189-199.

St. Zephyrinus: Rome; 199-217.

St. Callistus I: Rome; 217-222.

St. Urban I: Rome; 222-230.

St. Pontian: Rome; July 21, 230, to Sept. 28, 235.

St. Anterus: Greece; Nov. 21, 235, to Jan. 3, 236.

St. Fabian: Rome; Jan. 10, 236, to Jan. 20, 250.

St. Cornelius: Rome; Mar., 251, to June, 253.

St. Lucius I: Rome; June 25, 253, to Mar. 5, 254.

St. Stephen I: Rome; May 12, 254, to Aug. 2, 257.

St. Sixtus II: Greece; Aug. 30, 257, to Aug. 6, 258.

St. Dionysius: July 22, 259, to Dec. 26, 268.

St. Felix I: Rome; Jan. 5, 269, to Dec. 30, 274.

St. Eutychian: Luni; Jan. 4, 275, to Dec. 7, 283.

St. Caius: Dalmatia; Dec. 17, 283, to Apr. 22, 296.

St. Marcellinus: Rome; June 30, 296, to Oct. 25, 304.

St. Marcellus I: Rome; May 27, 308, or June 26, 308, to Jan. 16, 309.

St. Eusebius: Greece; Apr. 18, 309 or 310, to Aug. 17, 309 or 310.

St. Melchiades (Miltiades): Africa; July 2, 311, to Jan. 11, 314.

St. Sylvester I: Rome; Jan. 31, 314, to Dec. 31, 335. (Most of the popes before St. Sylvester I were martyrs.)

St. Marcus: Rome; Jan. 18, 336, to Oct. 7, 336.

St. Julius I: Rome; Feb. 6, 337, to Apr. 12, 352.

Liberius: Rome; May 17, 352, to Sept. 24, 366.

St. Damasus I: Spain; Oct. 1, 366, to Dec. 11, 384.

St. Siricius: Rome; Dec. 15, or 22 or 29, 384, to Nov. 26, 399.

St. Anastasius I: Rome; Nov. 27, 399, to Dec. 19, 401.

St. Innocent I: Albano; Dec. 22, 401, to Mar. 12, 417.

St. Zozimus: Greece; Mar. 18, 417, to Dec. 26, 418.

St. Boniface I: Rome; Dec. 28 or 29, 418, to Sept. 4, 422.

St. Celestine I: Campania; Sept. 10, 422, to July 27, 432.

St. Sixtus III: Rome; July 31, 432, to Aug. 19, 440.

St. Leo I (the Great): Tuscany; Sept. 29, 440, to Nov. 10, 461.

St. Hilary: Sardinia; Nov. 19, 461, to Feb. 29, 468.

St. Simplicius: Tivoli; Mar. 3, 468, to Mar. 10, 483.

St. Felix III (II): Rome; Mar. 13, 483, to Mar. 1, 492.

He should be called Felix II, and his successors of the same name should be numbered accordingly. The discrepancy in the numerical designation of popes named Felix was caused by the erroneous insertion in some lists of the name of St. Felix of Rome, a martyr.

St. Gelasius I: Africa; Mar. 1, 492, to Nov. 21, 496.

Anastasius II: Rome; Nov. 24, 496, to Nov. 19, 498.

St. Symmachus: Sardinia; Nov. 22, 498, to July 19, 514.

St. Hormisdas: Frosinone; July 20, 514, to Aug. 6, 523.

St. John I, Martyr: Tuscany; Aug. 13, 523, to May 18, 526.

St. Felix IV (III): Samnium; July 12, 526, to Sept. 22, 530.

Boniface II: Rome; Sept. 22, 530, to Oct. 17, 532.

John II: Rome; Jan. 2, 533, to May 8, 535.

John II was the first pope to change his name. His given name was Mercury.

St. Agapitus I: Rome; May 13, 535, to Apr. 22, 536.

St. Silverius, Martyr: Campania; June 1 or 8, 536, to Nov. 11, 537 (d. Dec. 2, 537).

St. Silverius was violently deposed in March, 537, and abdicated Nov. 11, 537. His successor, Vigilius, was not recognized as pope by all the Roman clergy until his abdication.

Vigilius: Rome; Mar. 29, 537, to June 7, 555.

Pelagius I: Rome; Apr. 16, 556, to Mar. 4, 561.

John III: Rome; July 17, 561, to July 13, 574.

Benedict I: Rome; June 2, 575, to July 30, 579.

Pelagius II: Rome; Nov. 26, 579, to Feb. 7, 590.

St. Gregory I (the Great): Rome; Sept. 3, 590, to Mar. 12, 604.

Sabinian: Blera in Tuscany; Sept. 13, 604, to Feb. 22, 606.

Boniface III: Rome; Feb. 19, 607, to Nov. 12, 607.

St. Boniface IV: Abruzzi; Aug. 25, 608, to May 8, 615.

St. Deusdedit (Adeodatus I): Rome; Oct. 19, 615, to Nov. 8, 618.

Boniface V: Naples; Dec. 23, 619, to Oct. 25, 625.

Honorius I: Campania; Oct. 27, 625, to Oct. 12, 638.

Severinus: Rome; May 28, 640, to Aug. 2, 640.

John IV: Dalmatia; Dec. 24, 640, to Oct. 12, 642.

Theodore I: Greece; Nov. 24, 642, to May 14, 649.

St. Martin I, Martyr: Todi; July, 649, to Sept. 16, 655 (in exile from June 17, 653).

St. Eugene I: Rome; Aug. 10, 654, to June 2, 657.

St. Eugene I was elected during the exile of St. Martin I, who is believed to have endorsed him as pope.

St. Vitalian: Segni; July 30, 657, to Jan. 27, 672.

Adeodatus II: Rome; Apr. 11, 672, to June 17, 676.

Donus: Rome; Nov. 2, 676, to Apr. 11, 678.

St. Agatho: Sicily; June 27, 678, to Jan. 10, 681.

St. Leo II: Sicily; Aug. 17, 682, to July 3, 683.

St. Benedict II: Rome; June 26, 684, to May 8, 685.

John V: Syria; July 23, 685, to Aug. 2, 686.

Conon: birthplace unknown; Oct. 21, 686, to Sept. 21, 687.

St. Sergius I: Syria; Dec. 15, 687, to Sept. 8, 701.

John VI: Greece; Oct. 30, 701, to Jan. 11, 705.

John VII: Greece; Mar. 1, 705, to Oct. 18, 707.

Sisinnius: Syria; Jan. 15, 708, to Feb. 4, 708.

Constantine: Syria; Mar. 25, 708, to Apr. 9, 715.

St. Gregory II: Rome; May 19, 715, to Feb. 11, 731.

St. Gregory III: Syria; Mar. 18, 731, to Nov., 741.

St. Zachary: Greece; Dec. 10, 741, to Mar. 22, 752.

Stephen II (III): Rome; Mar. 26, 752, to Apr. 26, 757.

After the death of St. Zachary, a Roman priest named Stephen was elected but died (four days later) before his consecration as bishop of Rome, which would have marked the beginning of his pontificate. Another Stephen was elected to succeed Zachary as Stephen II. (The first pope with this name was St. Stephen I, 254-57.) The ordinal III appears in parentheses after the name of Stephen II because the name of the earlier elected but deceased priest was included in some lists. Other Stephens have double numbers.

St. Paul I: Rome; Apr. (May 29), 757, to June 28, 767.

Stephen III (IV): Sicily; Aug. 1 (7), 768, to Jan. 24, 772.

Adrian I: Rome; Feb. 1 (9), 772, to Dec. 25, 795.

St. Leo III: Rome; Dec. 26 (27), 795, to June 12, 816.

Stephen IV (V): Rome; June 22, 816, to Jan. 24, 817.

St. Paschal I: Rome; Jan. 25, 817, to Feb. 11, 824.

Eugene II: Rome; Feb. (May), 824, to Aug., 827.

Valentine: Rome; Aug. 827, to Sept., 827.

Gregory IV: Rome; 827, to Jan., 844.

Sergius II: Rome; Jan., 844 to Jan. 27, 847.

St. Leo IV: Rome; Jan. (Apr. 10), 847, to July 17, 855.

Benedict III: Rome; July (Sept. 29), 855, to Apr. 17, 858.

St. Nicholas I (the Great): Rome; Apr. 24, 858, to Nov. 13, 867.

Adrian II: Rome; Dec. 14, 867, to Dec. 14, 872.

John VIII: Rome; Dec. 14, 872, to Dec. 16, 882.

Marinus I: Gallese; Dec. 16, 882, to May 15, 884.

St. Adrian III: Rome; May 17, 884, to Sept., 885. Cult confirmed June 2, 1891.

Stephen V (VI): Rome; Sept., 885, to Sept. 14, 891.

Formosus: Portus; Oct. 6, 891, to Apr. 4, 896.

Boniface VI: Rome; Apr., 896, to Apr., 896.

Stephen VI (VII): Rome; May, 896, to Aug., 897.

Romanus: Gallese; Aug., 897, to Nov., 897.

Theodore II: Rome; Dec., 897, to Dec., 897.

John IX: Tivoli; Jan., 898, to Jan., 900.

Benedict IV: Rome; Jan. (Feb.), 900, to July, 903.

Leo V: Ardea; July, 903, to Sept., 903.

Sergius III: Rome; Jan. 29, 904, to Apr. 14, 911.

Anastasius III: Rome; Apr., 911, to June, 913.

Landus: Sabina; July, 913, to Feb., 914.

John X: Tossignano (Imola); Mar., 914, to May, 928.

Leo VI: Rome; May, 928, to Dec., 928.

Stephen VII (VIII): Rome; Dec., 928, to Feb., 931.

John XI: Rome; Feb. (Mar.), 931, to Dec., 935.

Leo VII: Rome; Jan. 3, 936, to July 13, 939.

Stephen VIII (IX): Rome; July 14, 939, to Oct., 942.

Marinus II: Rome; Oct. 30, 942, to May, 946.

Agapitus II: Rome; May 10, 946, to Dec., 955.

John XII (Octavius): Tusculum; Dec. 16, 955, to May 14, 964 (date of his death).

Leo VIII: Rome; Dec. 4 (6), 963, to Mar. 1, 965.

Benedict V: Rome; May 22, 964, to July 4, 966.

Confusion exists concerning the legitimacy of claims to the pontificate by Leo VIII and Benedict V. John XII was deposed Dec. 4, 963, by a Roman council. If this deposition was invalid, Leo was an antipope. If the deposition of John was valid, Leo was the legitimate pope and Benedict was an antipope.

John XIII: Rome; Oct. 1, 965, to Sept. 6, 972.

Benedict VI: Rome; Jan. 19, 973, to June, 974.

Benedict VII: Rome; Oct. 974, to July 10, 983.

John XIV (Peter Campenora): Pavia, Dec., 983, to Aug. 20, 984.

John XV: Rome; Aug., 985, to Mar., 996.

Gregory V (Bruno of Carinthia): Saxony; May 3, 996, to Feb. 18, 999.

Sylvester II (Gerbert): Auvergne; Apr. 2, 999, to May 12, 1003.

John XVII (Siccone): Rome; June, 1003, to Dec., 1003.

John XVIII (Phasianus): Rome; Jan., 1004, to July, 1009.

Sergius IV (Peter): Rome; July 31, 1009, to May 12, 1012.

The custom of changing one's name on election to the papacy is generally considered to date from the time of Sergius IV. Before his time, several popes had changed their names. After his time, this became a regular practice, with few exceptions; e.g., Adrian VI and Marcellus II.

Benedict VIII (Theophylactus): Tusculum; May 18, 1012, to Apr. 9, 1024.

John XIX (Romanus): Tusculum; Apr. (May), 1024, to 1032.

Benedict IX (Theophylactus): Tusculum; 1032, to 1044.

Sylvester III (John): Rome; Jan. 20, 1045, to Feb. 10, 1045.

Sylvester III was an antipope if the forcible removal of Benedict IX in 1044 was not legitimate.

Benedict IX (second time): Apr. 10, 1045, to May 1, 1045.

Gregory VI (John Gratian): Rome; May 5, 1045, to Dec. 20, 1046.

Clement II (Suitger, Lord of Morsleben and Hornburg): Saxony; Dec. 24 (25), 1046, to Oct. 9, 1047.

If the resignation of Benedict IX in 1045 and his removal at the December, 1046, synod were not legitimate, Gregory VI and Clement II were antipopes.

Benedict IX (third time): Nov. 8, 1047, to July 17, 1048 (d. c. 1055).

Damasus II (Poppo): Bavaria; July 17, 1048, to Aug. 9, 1048.

St. Leo IX (Bruno): Alsace; Feb. 12, 1049, to Apr. 19, 1054.

Victor II (Gebhard): Swabia; Apr. 16, 1055, to July 28, 1057.

Stephen IX (X) (Frederick): Lorraine; Aug. 3, 1057, to Mar. 29, 1058.

Nicholas II (Gerard): Burgundy; Jan. 24, 1059, to July 27, 1061.

Alexander II (Anselmo da Baggio): Milan; Oct. 1, 1061, to Apr. 21, 1073.

St. Gregory VII (Hildebrand): Tuscany; Apr. 22 (June 30), 1073, to May 25, 1085.

Bl. Victor III (Dauferius; Desiderius): Benevento; May 24, 1086, to Sept. 16, 1087. Cult confirmed July 23, 1887.

Bl. Urban II (Otto di Lagery): France; Mar. 12, 1088, to July 29, 1099. Cult confirmed July 14, 1881.

Paschal II (Raniero): Ravenna; Aug. 13 (14), 1099, to Jan. 21, 1118.

Gelasius II (Giovanni Caetani): Gaeta; Jan. 24 (Mar. 10), 1118, to Jan. 28, 1119.

Callistus II (Guido of Burgundy): Burgundy; Feb. 2 (9), 1119, to Dec. 13, 1124.

Honorius II (Lamberto): Fiagnano (Imola); Dec. 15 (21), 1124, to Feb. 13, 1130.

Innocent II (Gregorio Papareschi): Rome; Feb. 14 (23), 1130, to Sept. 24, 1143.

Celestine II (Guido): Citta di Castello; Sept. 26 (Oct. 3), 1143, to Mar. 8, 1144.

Lucius II (Gerardo Caccianemici): Bologna; Mar. 12, 1144, to Feb. 15, 1145.

Bl. Eugene III (Bernardo Paganelli di Montemagno): Pisa; Feb. 15 (18), 1145, to July 8, 1153. Cult confirmed Oct. 3, 1872.

Anastasius IV (Corrado): Rome; July 12, 1153, to Dec, 3, 1154.

Adrian IV (Nicholas Breakspear): England; Dec. 4 (5), 1154, to Sept. 1, 1159.

Alexander III (Rolando Bandirelli): Siena; Sept. 7 (20), 1159, to Aug. 30, 1181.

Lucius III (Ubaldo Allucingoli): Lucca; Sept. 1 (6), 1181, to Sept. 25, 1185.

Urban III (Uberto Crivelli): Milan; Nov. 25 (Dec. 1), 1185, to Oct. 20, 1187.

Gregory VIII (Alberto de Morra): Benevento; Oct. 21 (25), 1187, to Dec. 17, 1187.

Clement III (Paolo Scolari): Rome; Dec. 19 (20), 1187, to Mar., 1191.

Celestine III (Giacinto Bobone): Rome; Mar. 30 (Apr. 14), 1191, to Jan. 8, 1198.

Innocent III (Lotario dei Conti di Segni): Anagni; Jan. 8 (Feb. 22), 1198, to July 16, 1216.

Honorius III (Cencio Savelli): Rome; July 18 (24), 1216, to Mar. 18, 1227.

Gregory IX (Ugolino, Count of Segni): Anagni; Mar. 19 (21), 1227, to Aug. 22, 1241.

Celestine IV (Goffredo Castiglioni): Milan; Oct. 25 (28), 1241, to Nov. 10, 1241.

Innocent IV (Sinibaldo Fieschi): Genoa; June 25 (28), 1243, to Dec. 7, 1254.

Alexander IV (Rinaldo, Count of Segni): Anagni; Dec. 12 (20), 1254, to May 25, 1261.

Urban IV (Jacques Pantaléon): Troyes; Aug. 29 (Sept. 4), 1261, to Oct. 2, 1264.

Clement IV (Guy Foulques or Guido le Gros): France; Feb. 5 (15), 1265, to Nov. 29, 1268.

Bl. Gregory X (Teobaldo Visconti): Piacenza; Sept. 1, 1271 (Mar. 27, 1272), to Jan. 10, 1276. Cult confirmed Sept. 12, 1713.

Bl. Innocent V (Peter of Tarentaise): Savoy; Jan. 21 (Feb. 22), 1276, to June 22, 1276. Cult confirmed Mar. 13, 1898.

Adrian V (Ottobono Fieschi): Genoa; July 11, 1276, to Aug. 18, 1276.

John XXI (Petrus Juliani or Petrus His-
panus): Portugal; Sept. 8 (20), 1276,
to May 20, 1277.

Elimination was made of the name of
John XX in an effort to rectify the numerical designation of popes named John. The
error dates back to the time of John XV.

Nicholas III (Giovanni Gaetano Orsini):
Rome; Nov. 25 (Dec. 26), 1277, to Aug.
22, 1280.

Martin IV (Simon de Brie): France; Feb.
22 (Mar. 23), 1281, to Mar. 28, 1285.

The names of Marinus 1 (882-84) and
Marinus II (942-46) were construed as
Martin. In view of these two pontificates
and the earlier reign of St. Martin I
(649-55), this pope was called Martin IV.

Honorius IV (Giacomo Savelli): Rome;
Apr. 2 (May 20), 1285, to Apr. 3, 1287.

Nicholas IV (Girolamo Masci): Ascoli;
Feb. 22, 1288, to Apr. 4, 1292.

St. Celestine V (Pietro del Murrone):
Isernia; July 5 (Aug. 29), 1294, to
Dec. 13, 1294; d. 1296. Canonized May
5, 1313.

Boniface VIII (Benedetto Caetani):
Anagni; Dec. 24, 1294 (Jan. 23, 1295),
to Oct. 11, 1303.

Bl. Benedict XI (Niccolo Boccasini):
Treviso; Oct. 22 (27), 1303, to July 7,
1304. Cult confirmed Apr. 24, 1736.

Clement V (Bertrand de Got): France;
June 5 (Nov. 14), 1305, to Apr. 20,
1314. (First of Avignon popes.)

John XXII (Jacques d'Euse): Cahors;
Aug. 7 (Sept. 5), 1316, to Dec. 4, 1334.

Benedict XII (Jacques Fournier):
France; Dec. 20, 1334 (Jan. 8, 1335),
to Apr. 25, 1342.

Clement VI (Pierre Roger): France; May
7 (19), 1342, to Dec. 6, 1352.

Innocent VI (Etienne Aubert): France;
Dec. 18 (30), 1352, to Sept. 12, 1362.

Bl. Urban V (Guillaume de Grimoard):
France; Sept. 28 (Nov. 6), 1362, to
Dec. 19, 1370. Cult confirmed Mar. 10,
1870.

Gregory XI (Pierre Roger de Beaufort):
France; Dec. 30, 1370 (Jan. 5, 1371),
to Mar. 26, 1378. (Last of Avignon
popes.)

Urban VI (Bartolomeo Prignano):
Naples; Apr. 8 (18), 1378, to Oct. 15,
1389. (See The Western Schism.)

Boniface IX (Pietro Tomacelli): Naples;
Nov. 2 (9), 1389, to Oct. 1, 1404.

Innocent VII (Cosma Migliorati): Sul-
mona; Oct. 17 (Nov. 11), 1404, to Nov.
6, 1406.

Gregory XII (Angelo Correr): Venice;
Nov. 30 (Dec. 19), 1406, to July 4,
1415, when he voluntarily resigned
from the papacy to permit the election of his successor. He died Oct. 18,
1417. (See The Western Schism,
below under Antipopes.)

Martin V (Oddone Colonna): Rome; Nov.
11 (21), 1417, to Feb. 20, 1431.

Eugene IV (Gabriele Condulmer): Venice; Mar. 3 (11), 1431, to Feb. 23, 1447.

Nicholas V (Tommaso Parentucelli):
Sarzana; Mar. 6 (19), 1447, to Mar.
24, 1455.

Callistus III (Alfonso Borgia): Jativa
(Valencia); Apr. 8 (20), 1455, to Aug.
6, 1458.

Pius II (Enea Silvio Piccolomini): Siena;
Aug. 19 (Sept. 3), 1458, to Aug. 15,
1464.

Paul II (Pietro Barbo): Venice; Aug. 30
(Sept. 16), 1464, to July 26, 1471.

Sixtus IV (Francesco della Rovere):
Savona; Aug. 9 (25), 1471, to Aug. 12,
1484.

Innocent VIII (Giovanni Battista Cibo):
Genoa; Aug. 29 (Sept. 12), 1484, to
July 25, 1492.

Alexander VI (Rodrigo Borgia): Jativa
(Valencia); Aug. 11 (26), 1492, to
Aug. 18, 1503.

Pius III (Francesco Todeschini-Pic-
colomini): Siena; Sept. 22 (Oct. 1, 8),
1503, to Oct. 18, 1503.

Julius II (Giuliano della Rovere): Savona;
Oct. 31 (Nov. 26), 1503, to Feb. 21,
1513.

Leo X (Giovanni de' Medici): Florence;
Mar. 9 (19), 1513, to Dec. 1, 1521.

Adrian VI (Adrian Florensz): Utrecht;
Jan. 9 (Aug. 31), 1522, to Sept. 14,
1523.

Clement VII (Giulio de' Medici): Florence; Nov. 19 (26), 1523, to Sept. 25,
1534.

Paul III (Alessandro Farnese): Rome;
Oct. 13 (Nov. 3), 1534, to Nov. 10,
1549.

Julius III (Giovanni Maria Ciocchi del
Monte): Rome; Feb. 7 (22), 1550, to
Mar. 23, 1555.

Marcellus II (Marcello Cervini): Montepulciano; Apr. 9 (10), 1555, to May 1, 1555.

Paul IV (Gian Pietro Carafa): Naples; May 23 (26), 1555, to Aug. 18, 1559.

Pius IV (Giovan Angelo de' Medici): Milan; Dec. 25, 1559 (Jan. 6, 1560), to Dec. 9, 1565.

St. Pius V (Antonio-Michele Ghislieri): Bosco (Alexandria); Jan. 7 (17), 1566, to May 1, 1572. Canonized May 22, 1712.

Gregory XIII (Ugo Buoncompagni): Bologna; May 13 (25), 1572, to Apr. 10, 1585.

Sixtus V (Felice Peretti): Grottammare (Ripatransone); Apr. 24 (May 1), 1585, to Aug. 27, 1590.

Urban VII (Giovanni Battista Castagna): Rome; Sept. 15, 1590, to Sept. 27, 1590.

Gregory XIV (Niccolo Sfondrati): Cremona; Dec. 5 (8), 1590, to Oct. 16, 1591.

Innocent IX (Giovanni Antonio Facchinetti): Bologna; Oct. 29 (Nov. 3), 1591, to Dec. 30, 1591.

Clement VIII (Ippolito Aldobrandini): Florence; Jan. 30 (Feb. 9), 1592, to Mar. 3, 1605.

Leo XI (Alessandro de' Medici): Florence; Apr. 1 (10), 1605, to Apr. 27, 1605.

Paul V (Camillo Borghese): Rome; May 16 (29), 1605, to Jan. 28, 1621.

Gregory XV (Alessandro Ludovisi): Bologna; Feb. 9 (14), 1621, to July 8, 1623.

Urban VIII (Maffeo Barberini): Florence; Aug. 6 (Sept. 29), 1623, to July 29, 1644.

Innocent X (Giovanni Battista Pamfili): Rome; Sept. 15 (Oct. 4), 1644, to Jan. 7, 1655.

Alexander VII (Fabio Chigi): Siena; Apr. 7 (18), 1655, to May 22, 1667.

Clement IX (Giulio Rospigliosi): Pistoia; June 20 (26), 1667, to Dec. 9, 1669.

Clement X (Emilio Altieri): Rome; Apr. 29 (May 11), 1670, to July 22, 1676.

Bl. Innocent XI (Benedetto Odescalchi): Como; Sept. 21 (Oct. 4), 1676, to Aug. 12, 1689.

Alexander VIII (Pietro Ottoboni): Venice; Oct. 6 (16), 1689, to Feb. 1, 1691.

Innocent XII (Antonio Pignatelli): Spinazzola; July 12 (15), 1691, to Sept. 27, 1700.

Clement XI (Giovanni Francesco Albani): Urbino; Nov. 23, 30 (Dec. 8), 1700, to Mar. 19, 1721.

Innocent XIII (Michelangelo dei Conti): Rome; May 8 (18), 1721, to Mar. 7, 1724.

Benedict XIII (Pietro Francesco — Vincenzo Maria — Orsini): Gravina (Bari); May 29 (June 4), 1724, to Feb. 21, 1730.

Clement XII (Lorenzo Corsini): Florence; July 12 (16), 1730, to Feb. 6, 1740.

Benedict XIV (Prospero Lambertini): Bologna; Aug. 17 (22), 1740, to May 3, 1758.

Clement XIII (Carlo Rezzonico): Venice; July 6 (16), 1758, to Feb. 2, 1769.

Clement XIV (Giovanni Vincenzo Antonio — Lorenzo — Ganganelli): Rimini; May 19, 28 (June 4), 1769, to Sept. 22, 1774.

Pius VI (Giovanni Angelo Braschi): Cesena; Feb. 15 (22), 1775, to Aug. 29, 1799.

Pius VII (Barnaba — Gregorio — Chiaramonti): Cesena; Mar. 14 (21), 1800, to Aug. 20, 1823.

Leo XII (Annibale della Genga): Genga (Fabriano); Sept. 28 (Oct. 5), 1823, to Feb. 10, 1829.

Pius VIII (Francesco Saverio Castiglioni): Cingoli; Mar. 31 (Apr. 5), 1829, to Nov. 30, 1830.

Gregory XVI (Bartolomeo Alberto — Mauro — Cappellari): Belluno; Feb. 2 (6), 1831, to June 1, 1846.

Pius IX (Giovanni M. Mastai Ferretti): Senigallia; June 16 (21), 1846, to Feb. 7, 1878.

Leo XIII (Gioacchino Pecci): Carpineto (Anagni); Feb. 20 (Mar. 3), 1878, to July 20, 1903.

St. Pius X (Giuseppe Sarto): Riese (Treviso); Aug. 4 (9), 1903, to Aug. 20, 1914. Canonized May 29, 1954.

Benedict XV (Giacomo della Chiesa): Genoa; Sept. 3 (6), 1914, to Jan. 22, 1922.

Pius XI (Achille Ratti): Desio (Milan); Feb. 6 (12), 1922, to Feb. 10, 1939.

Pius XII (Eugenio Pacelli): Rome; Mar. 2 (12), 1939, to Oct. 9, 1958.

John XXIII (Angelo Giuseppe Roncalli): Sotto il Monte (Bergamo); Oct. 28 (Nov. 4). 1958, to June 3, 1963.

Paul VI (Giovanni Battista Montini): Concessio (Brescia); June 21 (June 30), 1963, to Aug. 6, 1978.

John Paul I (Albino Luciani): Forno di Canale (Belluno); Aug. 26 (Sept. 3), 1978, to Sept. 28, 1978.

John Paul II (Karol Wojtyla): Wadowice, Poland; Oct. 16 (22), 1978. He is the first Polish pope and the first non-Italian pope since Adrian II (1522-23). By March, 1984, he had visited 39 countries on 20 foreign trips, had issued three encyclical letters, had convoked two assemblies of the Synod of Bishops and had promulgated and ordered into effect a revised Code of Canon Law.

Coat of Arms of Pope John Paul II:
Shield: blue with yellow cross and "M"
symbolizing devotion to the Blessed Virgin Mary.
Cross and keys: silver and gold. Sash and rope: red.

ANTIPOPES

This list of men who claimed or exercised the papal office in an uncanonical manner includes names, birthplaces and dates of alleged reigns. Source: "Annuario Pontificio."

St. Hippolytus: Rome; 217-235; was reconciled before his death.

Novatian: Rome; 251.

Felix II:.Rome; 355 to Nov. 22, 365.

Ursinus: 366-367.

Eulalius: Dec. 27 or 29, 418, to 419.

Lawrence: 498; 501-505. ⸱⸱

Dioscorus: Alexandria; Sept. 22, 530, to Oct. 14, 530.

Theodore: ended alleged reign, 687.

Paschal: ended alleged reign, 687.

Constantine: Nepi; June 28 (July 5), 767, to 769.

Philip: July 31, 768; retired to his monastery on the same day.

John: ended alleged reign, Jan., 844.

Anastasius: Aug., 855, to Sept., 855; d. 880.

Christopher: Rome; July or Sept., 903, to Jan., 904.

Boniface VII: Rome; June, 974, to July, 974; Aug., 984, to July, 985.

John XVI: Rossano; Apr., 997, to Feb., 998.

Gregory: ended alleged reign, 1012.

Benedict X: Rome; Apr. 5, 1058, to Jan. 24, 1059.

Honorius II: Verona; Oct. 28, 1061, to 1072.

Clement III: Parma; June 25, 1080 (Mar. 24, 1084), to Sept. 8, 1100.

Theodoric: ended alleged reign, 1100; d. 1102.

Albert: ended alleged reign, 1102.

Sylvester IV: Rome; Nov. 18, 1105, to 1111.

Gregory VIII: France; Mar. 8, 1118, to 1121.

Celestine II: Rome; ended alleged reign, Dec., 1124.

Anacletus II: Rome; Feb. 14 (23), 1130, to Jan. 25, 1138.

Victor IV: Mar., 1138, to May 29, 1138; submitted to Pope Innocent II.

Victor IV: Montecelio; Sept. 7 (Oct. 4), 1159, to Apr. 20, 1164; he did not recognize his predecessor (Victor IV, above).

Paschal III: Apr. 22 (26), 1164, to Sept. 20, 1168.

Callistus III: Arezzo; Sept., 1168, to Aug. 29, 1178; submitted to Pope Alexander III.

Innocent III: Sezze; Sept. 29, 1179, to 1180.

Nicholas V: Corvaro (Rieti); May 12 (22), 1328, to Aug. 25, 1330; d. Oct. 16, 1333.

Four antipopes of the Western Schism:

Clement VII: Sept. 20 (Oct. 31), 1378, to Sept. 16, 1394.

Benedict XIII: Aragon; Sept. 28 (Oct. 11), 1394, to May 23, 1423.

Alexander V: Crete; June 26 (July 7), 1409, to May 3, 1410.

John XXIII: Naples; May 17 (25), 1410, to May 29, 1415.

Felix V: Savoy; Nov. 5, 1439 (July 24, 1440), to April 7, 1449; d. 1451.

The Western Schism was a confused state of affairs which divided Christendom into two and then three papal obediences from 1378 to 1417

Urban VI, following transfer to Rome of the 70-year papal residence at Avignon, was elected pope Apr. 8, 1378, and reigned until his death in 1389. He was succeeded by Boniface IX (1389-1404), Innocent VII (1404-1406) and Gregory XII (1406-1415). These four are considered the legitimate popes of the period.

Some of the cardinals who chose Urban pope, dissatisfied with his conduct of the office, declared that his election was invalid. They proceeded to elect Clement VII, who claimed the papacy from 1378 to 1394. He was succeeded by Benedict XIII.

Prelates seeking to end the state of divided papal loyalties convoked the Council of Pisa which, without authority, found Gregory XII and Benedict XIII, in absentia, guilty on 30-odd charges of schism and heresy, deposed them, and elected a third claimant to the papacy, Alexander V (1409-1410). He was succeeded by John XXIII (1410-1415).

The schism was ended by the Council of Constance (1414-1418). This council, although originally called into session in an irregular manner, acquired authority after being convoked by Gregory XII in 1415. In its early irregular phase, it deposed John XXIII whose election to the papacy was uncanonical anyway. After being formally convoked, it accepted the abdication of Gregory in 1415 and dismissed the claims of Benedict XXIII two years later, thus clearing the way for the election of Martin V on Nov. 11, 1417.

Titles and Forms of Address

Given below are commonly used forms of address and salutation in letters to church dignitaries, priests and Religious. An appropriate conclusion for all of them is, "Yours respectfully."

Patriarchs: His Beatitude (full name), Patriarch of (see city); Your Beatitude.

Cardinals: His Eminence (first name) Cardinal (last name), or, His Eminence (full name); for heads of sees, follow with Archbishop or Bishop of (name of see); Your Eminence.

Archbishops and Bishops: Most Reverend (full name), Archbishop or Bishop of (name of see); Your Excellency or Dear Bishop (last name). Retired archbishops and bishops are usually addressed as: Most Reverend (full name), Former Archbishop or Bishop of (last see held).

Abbots: Right Reverend (full name, followed by initials of religious order), Abbot of (name of Abbey); Right Reverend Abbot or Dear Abbot (last name).

Monsignors (Protonotaries Apostolic, Prelates of Honor of His Holiness, Chaplains of His Holiness): Reverend Monsignor (full name); Reverend Monsignor or Dear Monsignor (last name).

Provincials of Religious Orders: Very Reverend (full name, followed by initials of order), Provincial of (title); Very Reverend and dear Father Provincial.

Diocesan Clergy: Reverend (full name), Reverend and dear Father or Dear Father (last name).

Religious Clergy: Reverend (full name, followed by initials of religious order); Dear Father (first name).

Transitional Deacons: Rev. Mr. (full name); Dear Mr. (last name).

Permanent Deacons: Mr. (full name); Dear Mr. (last name).

Brothers: Brother (full name, followed by initials of religious institute); Dear Brother (first name, usually).

Sisters: Sister (full name, followed by initials of religious institute); Dear Sister (first name).

General Index

A

Abbacies, 99, 102
Abbots, 99, 102
Abraham, 7
Abstinence, Days of, 77
Acolyte, 70
Acta Apostolicae Sedis, 112
Acta Sanctae Sedis, 112
Acts of the Apostles, 8
Actual Grace, 29-30
Actual Sin, 33
Ad Limina Visit, 101-102
Adam, 28, 29
Address, Titles and Forms of, 146
Adoration (*Latria*). 87
Advent, 75
Agatha, St., 79
Aged, Eucharistic Fast, 67
Agnes, St., 78
Alb, 56
Albert the Great, St., 22
Alexandrian Rite, 97, 98
All Saints, 83
All Souls, 83
Aloysius Gonzaga, St., 81
Alphonsus Liguori, St. 23
Altar, 60
Altar Cloth, 58
Ambo (Pulpit), 61
Ambrose, St., 23
Ambrosian Rite, 51
Ambry, 61
Amice, 56
Amos, 7
Analogy of Faith, 9
André Bessette, Bl., 78
Andrew, St., 14
Angelico, Fra, Equivalent Beatification, 88
Angels, 28
Angels, Guardian, 83
Angelus, 92-93
Ann, St. (Joachim and Ann), 81
Annuario Pontificio, 112
Annulment, Decree of, 73-74
Annunciation of the Lord, 79

Anointing of the Sick, 69
Anselm, St., 23
Anthony, St. (Abbot), 78, 124
Anthony, St. (of Padua), 23
Antiochene Rite, 97, 98
Antipopes, 145
Anti-Semitism, 136
Antonians, 124
Apostles, 14-16
  New Testament Writings, 8
  Successors, 2, 69, 99
  Transmission of Revelation, 3-4
Apostles' Creed, 27
Apostolate of Lay Persons, 120-121, 122-123
Apostolate of Religious, 128
Apostolic Administrator, 102
Apostolic Constitution, 12
Apostolic Delegates, 108
Apostolic Fathers, 22
Apostolic Nuncios, 108
Apostolic Penitentiary, 105
Apostolic See (Holy See)100
Apostolic Signatura, 105
Apostolic Succession, 2, 69, 99
Aquinas, Thomas, St., 26
Archangels, Feast, 83
Archbishops, 100-101
Archbishops ad Personam, 101
Archdiocese, 101
Armenian Rite, 97, 98
Arms Race, 43
Art Sacred, 50
Ascension of the Lord, 80
Ash Wednesday, 75, 79
Assumption, 82, 85
Athanasius, St., 23
Atonement, 33
Atonement, Society of the, 134
Audiences, Papal, 111-112
Augustine, St., 23, 124
Augustinians, 125
Authority, Religious Life, 129
Authority, Teaching, of Church (Magisterium), 5, 10-12
  Encyclicals, 12
  Infallibility, 10-12

Authority
of Ecumenical Councils, 17
Pope, 10-11
Sacred Scripture and, 5, 10
Auxiliary Bishop, 101
Avignon Residency of Papacy (Western Schism), 145

B

Babylonian Exile, 6, 7
Banns, 72
Baptism, 64-66
Baptism of the Lord, 78
Baptistery (Baptistry), 61-62
Barnabas, St., 14
Barnabites, 125
Basil the Great, St., 23, 124
Basilians, 124
Basilica, 62
Beatification, 88
Beatitudes, 32
Bede the Venerable, St., 23
Beliefs, Catholic, 27-30
See also Doctrine, Catholic
Bellarmine, Robert, St., 26, 32
Benedict, St., 81, 89, 124
Benedictines, 124
Benediction of Blessed Sacrament, 90
Benedictus, 49
Bernard of Clairvaux, St., 24
Bessette, André, Bl., 78
Bible, 6-9
Interpretation, 9
See also Revelation
Bible Service, 93
Biblical Commission, Pontifical, 106
Bination, 55
Bishops, 69, 99, 101-102
and Ecumenical Councils, 17
Authentic Teaching, 11
Conferences, 107
Congregation (Roman Curia), 105
Nomination, 101
Successors of the Apostles, 69, 99
Synod of, 102-103
Bishops, U.S., National Conference, 107
Committee for Ecumenical and Interreligious Affairs, 135
War and Peace Pastoral, 42
Blase, St., 79

Blessed Sacrament, Devotions, 90
See also Eucharist
Blessed Virgin Mary, 75, 85-86
Annunciation, 79
Assumption, 82, 85
Birth, 82
First Saturday Devotion, 93
Immaculate Conception, 84, 85
Immaculate Heart, 81
Presentation, 84
Purification, 79
Queenship, 82
Rosary (Devotion), 92
Rosary (Feast), 83
Solemnity, 78
Sorrows (Feast), 82
Visitation, 81
Blessings, 48
Bonaventure, St., 24
Boniface, St., 81
Borromeo, Charles, St., 83
Bosco, John, St., 78
Braga Rite, 51
Brébeuf, John de, St., 83
Breviary, 49
Brothers, 125
Buddhism, 137
Bulls, Papal, 12
Burial, Ecclesiastical, 48
Burse, 58
Byzantine Rite, 97

C

Cabrini. Frances Xavier, St., 84
Calendar, Church, 75-84
Feasts, 78-84
Candlemas Day (Presentation), 78
Candles, 62
Canon, Biblical, 6
Canon (of Mass), 54
Canon Law, Code of, 115-121
Sacramental Discipline, 133-134
Canonization, 87-88
Cardinals, College of, 100, 103-104
Categories, 103-104
Dean, 104
Eastern Patriarchs, 104
Retirement Age, 103
Voting Eligibility, 103
Carmelites, 124, 125
Carthusians, 124

Cassock, 57
Castelgandolfo, 110
Cathedral, 62
Catherine of Siena, St., 24
Catholic Church, 1-2, 28
  Apostolic Succession, 2, 69, 99
  Authority (Magisterium), 5, 10-12
  Beliefs, 27-30
  Creeds, 27
  Eastern, 94-98
  Hierarchy, 99-102
  Infallibility, 10-11
  Interfaith Relations, 130-137
  Law (Canon Law), 115-121
  Lay Persons in, 120-121
  Liturgical Year and Calendar, 75-77
  Liturgy, Rites, 47-51, 97-98
  Marks of, 1-2
  Marriage Doctrine, Laws, 71-74
  Moral Obligations, 31-33
  Organization, 99-103
  Penitential Discipline, 33-34
  Precepts, 32
  Pope, 10-11, 99-100
  Popes, List, 138-144
  Religious in, 124-125
  Revelation, 2, 3-5
  Sacraments, 28, 64-71
  Salvation and, 1, 30
  Social Doctrine, 35-46
  Theology, 13
Catholic Letters, 8
Cecilia, St., 84
Celibacy, 70-71
Chair of Peter (Feast), 79
Chalcedon, Council of, 18
Chaldean Rite, 97, 98
Chalice, 58
Chamber, Apostolic, 106
Chancery, Apostolic, 104
Chant, Gregorian, 49-50
Chapel, 62
Charity, Sisters of, 125
Charles Borromeo, St., 83
Chastity, Religious Life, 127
Chasuble, 56
Chasuble-Alb, 57
Chosen People, 6, 7
Christ, **see** Jesus Christ
Christ the King, Solemnity, 84

Christian Unity, Secretariat, 106, 133, 134-135
Christian Unity, Week of Prayer for, 134
  See also Ecumenism
Christianity and Social Progress, 35
Christmas, 84
Christmas Season, 75
Chronicles, 6
Chrysostom, John, St., 25
Church, Catholic, **see** Catholic Church
Church, Constitution on (Vatican II), 10-11, 11-12, 69, 70, 85-86, 87, 122
Church Building, 60-63
Church in Modern World, Constitution on (Vatican II), 36-44
Church-State Relations, 109
Churches, Particular, 99, 106-107
Ciborium, 58
Cincture, 56
Cistercians, 124
Clare, St., 82
Claver, Peter, St., 82
Clement I, St., 22
Clergy, Congregation for, 105
Coadjutor Archbishop, Bishop, 101
Code of Canon Law, 115-121, 133-134
Colors, Liturgical, 57
Colossians, 8
Commandments of God, 31
Communion, Holy, 67
  See also Eucharist
Communion of Saints, 28-29
Communion Rite, Mass, 54-55
Concelebration, 56
Conclave, 100
Conferences, Episcopal, 107
Confession, **see** Penance, Sacrament of
Confessional, 62
Confirmation, 66
Conscience, 33
Conscientious Objectors, 41
Consecration of Mass, 54
  of Priests, 67
Constance, Council of, 19, 145
Constantinople, Councils of, 18, 19
Contemplative Institutes, Religious, 124

Contrition, 33, 34
Conversion of St. Paul (Feast), 78
Cope, 57
Cor Unum, 106
Corinthians, 8
Cornelius, St., 82
Corporal, 58-59
Corporal Works of Mercy, 33
Corpus Christi (Feast), 80
Councils, Ecumenical, 17-21
Counsels, Evangelical, 126, 127-128
Covenant, Mosaic, 6
Covenant, New 8
Creation, 28
Creeds of Church, 27
Cremation, 48
Cross, Stations of the, 91-92
Cross, Triumph of the, 82
Crucifix, 62
Cruets, 62
Culture, Pontifical Council, 106
Curia, Roman, 104-106
Cyprian, St., 22, 82
Cyril and Methodius, Sts., 78, 89
Cyril of Alexandria, St., 24
Cyril of Jerusalem, St., 24

D

Dalmatic, 56
Daniel, 7
Dates, Old Testament, 7
David, King, 6, 7
Days of Prayer (Calendar), 77
Deacons, 70
Dead, Funeral Rites, Masses, 48, 56
Decalogue (Ten Commandments), 31
De Sales, Francis, St., 24
Devil (Satan), 28
Devil's Advocate, 88
Devotions, 90-93
Diaconate, Permanent, 70
Dialogues, Ecumenical, 134
Didymus (Thomas), 16
Dies Natalis, 76
Dioceses, 99, 106-107
Diplomacy, 108-109
Dispensation, 73
Divine Office (Liturgy of the Hours),
    48-49
Divorce, 73
Doctors, Church, 22-26

Doctrine, Catholic, 27-46
    Development of, 4
    Marian, 85-86
    Marriage, 71-74
    Social, 35-46
Doctrine of the Faith, Congregation,
    105
Dominic, St., 82
Dominicans, 125
    and Rosary Devotion, 92
Doxology (Mass), 53, 54
Dulia (Veneration of Saints), 87
Durocher, Marie Rose, Bl., 83
Duty, Easter, 67

E

Easter, 80
    Duty, 67
    Season, 76
    Triduum, 75-76
    Vigil, 76, 80astern Churches, Catho-
        lic, 94-98
    Celibacy, 71
    Decree (Vatican II), 94-97
    in U.S., 98
    Patriarchs, 95
    Rites, 51, 95, 97-98
    Sacraments, 95-96
Eastern Churches, Separated, 98
    Sacramental Discipline, 133-134
Eastern Ecumenism, 98
Ecclesiastes, Book of, 7
Ecumenical Councils, 17-21
Ecumenism, 130-135
    and Eucharistic Communion, 133
    Decree on (Vatican II), 98, 130-132
    Vatican Secretariat, 106, 133,
        134-135
Education, Catholic, Congregation
    for, 105
Election, Papal, 100
    Eligibility of Cardinals, 103
Elijah, 7
Elisha, 7
Elizabeth of Hungary, St., 84
Elizabeth Seton, St., 74
Elvira, Council of, 70
Encyclicals, Papal, 12
    Social, 35, 44-46
Enthronement of the Sacred Heart, 92
Eparch, 101

Ephesians, Epistle to, 8
Ephesus, Council of, 18
Ephraem, St., 24
Epiphany, 78
Episcopal Vicar, 101
Equality, 38
Esther, Book of, 6
Eucharist, 66-67
  Administration to Non-Catholics, 133-134
  and Ecumenism, 133
  Devotions Outside of Mass, 67, 90-91
  Extraordinary Ministers, 67
  Fast, 67
  Priest and, 67
  Reception, Conditions for, 67
  Reservation of, 67
  Viaticum, 67
  See also Mass
Eucharistic Congresses, 90-91
Eucharistic Liturgy, 54-55
Eucharistic Prayers, Mass, 54
Evangelical Counsels, Religious Life, 126, 127-128
Evangelists, 8, 14-16
Evangelization of Peoples, Congregation, 105
Eve, 28
Ex Cathedra, 11
Exarch, 101
Exegesis, 9
Exodus, Book of, 6, 7
Exsultet, 80
Extreme Unction, 69
Ezekiel, 7
Ezra, 6

F

Faith, Rule of, 28
Faithful, Rights and Obligations, 119-120
Fall, The, 28
Family, Council for the, 106
Family, Holy, 84
Fast, Eucharistic, 67
Fast Days, 77
Fathers, Church, 22-26
  Development of Doctrine, 4
Fatima, 93
Feasts in Calendar, 77, 78-84
Finger Towel, 59

First Friday, 93
First Saturday, 93
Flag, Papal, 111
Florence, Council of, 20
Formation, Religious Life, 128
Forty Hours Devotion, 90
Frances Xavier Cabrini, St., 84
Francis, St., of Assisi, 83, 89
Francis de Sales, St., 24
Francis Xavier, St., 84, 89
Franciscans, 125
Fridays, Penitential Observances, 77
Fruits of the Mass, 55
Funeral Rites, 48
  Masses, 56

G

Gabriel (Archangel), 83
Gad, 7
Galatians, Epistle to, 8
Gaudete Sunday, 57
General Absolution, 68
Genesis, Book of, 6
God, 27
Godparents (Sponsors), 66
Gonzaga, Aloysius, St., 81
Good Friday, 76, 80
Gospels, 8
  and Church Doctrine, 8, 35
  Synoptic, 8
Government, Church, 99-100
  Particular Churches, 106-107
  Roman Curia, 104-106
Grace, 29-30, 64
Gregorian Chant, 49-50
Gregorian Masses, 56
Gregory Nazianzen, St., 24
Gregory I, the Great, Pope St., 25, 50
Guadalupe, Our Lady of, 84

G

Habakkuk, 7
Habit, Religious, 57
Habitual Grace, 29
Haggai, 7
Hagiography, 88
Heaven, 29
Hebrews, Letter to, 8
Hell, 29
Hermeneutics, 8
Herod the Great, King, 7

Hierarchy, 99
Hinduism, 137
Holiness of the Church, 1-2
Holy Communion, 67
  See also Eucharist
Holy Days of Obligation, 76
Holy Family, Feast, 84
Holy Innocents, 84
Holy Orders, 69-70
Holy Saturday, 80
Holy See, 100
  Publications, 113
  Representatives, 108-109
Holy Spirit, 1-2, 3-5, 27-30
Holy Thursday, 75-76, 80
Holy Trinity, 27-28
Holy Water Fonts, 62
Holy Week, 75
Holy Year, 93
Homily, 53
Hosea, 7
Host, Consecrated, 67
Hours, Liturgy of the, 48-49
Human Rights, 37, 38
Humeral Veil, 58
Hypostatic Union, 28

I

Ignatius of Antioch, St., 83
Ignatius of Loyola, St., 82
Immaculate Conception, 84, 85
Immaculate Conception Shrine, U.S.,
  63
Immaculate Heart of Mary, 81
Impediments, Matrimonial, 73
Incarnation (Annunciation of the
  Lord), 79
Indulgence, 34
Infallibility, 10-11
Infancy Narratives, 8
Inspiration, Biblical, 3
Institutes, Secular, 129
Institutes of Consecrated Life, 124-125
Interfaith Relations, 130-137
Interpretation, Biblical, 9
Interregnum, 100
Intinction, 67
Irenaeus of Lyons, St., 22, 81
Isaac, 7

Isaac Jogues, St., 83
Isaiah, 7
Iscariot, Judas, 16
Isidore of Seville, St., 25
Isidore the Farmer, St., 81
Israel (Old Testament), 7
Italy-Vatican Concordat, 111

J

Jacob, 7
James the Greater, St., 14
James the Less, St., 14-15
  Letter, 8
Jeremiah, 7
Jerome, St., 25
Jerusalem, Temple at, 7
Jesuits, 125
Jesus Christ, 28
  Catholic Church, 1, 28
  in Gospels, 8
Jesus Christ, Feasts (Feasts of the
  Lord)
  Annunciation, 79
  Ascension, 80
  Baptism, 78
  Christ the King, 84
  Epiphany, 78
  Nativity (Christmas), 84
  Presentation, 78
  Resurrection (Easter), 80
  Sacred Heart, 80
  Transfiguration, 82
Jews, Commission for Relations with,
  106
  Revelation, Old Testament, 6-7
  Spiritual Bond with, 135-136
Joachim and Ann, Sts., 81
Job (Bible), 7
Joel, 7
Jogues, Isaac, St., 83
John, St., Apostle, Evangelist, 15
  Letters, 8
  Gospel, 8
John Baptist de la Salle, St., 79
John Bosco, St., 78
John Chrysostom, St., 25
John Damascene, St., 25
John de Brébeuf, St., 83
John Lateran, St., Basilica, 62, 110
  Feast of Dedication, 83

John Neumann, St., 74
  Forty Hours Devotion, 90
John of the Cross, St., 25
John Paul II, Pope, 144
  Encyclical on Work (*Laborem Exercens*), 44-46
  on Role of Theologians, 13
  Promulgation of Code of Canon Law, 116-117
John the Baptist, St., 8
  Feasts, 81, 82
John XXIII, Pope, 143
  Social Doctrine, 35
John Vianney, St., 82
Jonah, 7
Josaphat Kuncevyc, St., 84
Joseph, St., 79
Joshua, 6
Judah, Kingdom of, 7
Judas Iscariot, 16
Jude Thaddeus, St., 15
  Letter, 8
Judges, 6
Judgment, 29
Justice (Social Doctrine), 35-40
Justice and Peace Commission, 106
Justification, 29
Justin, St., 22, 81

K

Kateri Tekakwitha, Bl., 81
Kingdom of God, 8
Kings, Books of, 6
Kolbe, St. Maximilian, St., 82
Kuncevyc, St. Josaphat, 84

L

Laborem Exercens, Encyclical, 44-46
Laetare Sunday, 57
Laity, Council for the, 106
Laity in the Church, 120-123
  Apostolate of, Decree (Vatican II), 122-123
Lamentations, Book of, 7
Lateran Agreement, 111
Lateran Councils, 19, 20, 70
Latin (Roman) Rite, 51
Latria (Adoration), 87
Law, Canon, 115-121
Lawrence, St., 82

Lawrence of Brindisi, St., 25-26
Lay Brothers, 125
Lay Institutes of Men, 125
Lay Persons, 122
  Apostolate, 120, 122-123
  Rights and Obligations, 120-121
Lectern, 61
Lector, 70
Legates, Papal, 109
Lent, Season of, 75
Leo I, the Great, Pope St., 25
Leo XIII, Pope, 35, 143
Leonard of Port Maurice, St., 92
Letters, New Testament, 8
Leviticus, Book of, 6
Linens, Altar, 58-59
Litany, 93
Little Flower (St. Thérèse of Lisieux), 83
Liturgical Art, 50
  Colors, 57
  Music, 48
  Year, 75-84
Liturgy, 47-51
  Constitution on (Vatican II), 47, 48, 49, 50, 52, 86, 90
  Eucharistic, 54-55
Liturgy of the Hours, 48-49
Liturgy of the Word, 53
Lord's Day, 76
L'Osservatore Romano, 111
Lucy, St., 84
Luke, St., Evangelist, 15
  Acts of the Apostles, 8
  Gospel, 8
Luna (Lunette, Lunula), 58
Lyonnaise Rite, 51
Lyons, Councils of, 19

M

Maccabees, 6, 7
Magisterium (Teaching Authority), 5, 11-12, 17
Magnificat, 49
Malachi, 7
Marian Devotion, 85, 86
Marists, 125
Mark, St., Evangelist, 15
  Gospel, 8
Marriage (Matrimony), 71, 72-74
  Doctrine, 71

Marriage
  Laws of Church, 72-74
  Mixed, 74
Martha, St., 82
Martin of Tours, St., 83
Martyrology, 88
Marxism, 46
Mary, Mother of God, 85-86
  Devotion to, 75, 85, 86
  Devotions, 92-93
  Feasts, **see** Blessed Virgin Mary
  Titles of, 86
Mary Magdalene, St., 81
Maryknoll, 125
Mass, Eucharistic Sacrifice, 52-56
  Places for Celebration, 56, 60-61
  Vestments, Vessels, 56-58
Mass Obligation, 55, 76
Mass of the Lord's Supper, 75-76, 80
Matthew, St., Apostle, Evangelist, 15
  Gospel, 8
Mendicant Orders, 125
Mercy, Works of, 33
Merit, 30
Methodius, St. (Sts. Cyril and Metho-
  dius), 79, 89
Metropolitan Archbishop, 100
Micah, 7
Michael, Archangel, 83
Milan, Edict of, 60
Military Service, 41
Mitre, 58
Mixed Marriages, 74
Modern World, Church in the, Con-
  stitution (Vatican II), 36-44
Monastic Institutes, 124
Monsignor (Honorary Prelate), 102
Monstrance, 58
Moral Obligations, 31-34
Moslems, 106, 136-137
Motu Proprio, 12
Mount Carmel, Our Lady of. 81
Mozarabic Rite, 51
Music, Sacred, 48
Mysteries of the Rosary, 92
Mystical Body of Christ (Catholic
  Church), 1-2

N

Nahum, 7
Nathaniel, 14

National Conference of Catholic Bish-
  ops, U.S., 106
National Council of Churches of
  Christ, U.S.A., 135
Nativity (Christmas), 84
Nehemiah, 6
New Testament, 8-9
Nicaea, Councils of, 18, 19
Nicene Creed, 27
Nicholas, St., 84
Non-Believers, Secretariat, 106
Non-Christian Religions, Declaration
  on (Vatican II, 135-136, 137
Non-Christians, Secretariat, 106
Novena, 93
Nuclear Weapons, War, 42
Numbers, Book of, 6
Nunc Dimittis, 49
Nuncios, Papal, 108
Nuptial Mass, 56

O

Obadiah, 7
Obedience, Religious Life, 127
Obligations, Moral, 31-34
Octave of the Birth of the Lord (So-
  lemnity of Mary), 78
Offertory of Mass, 53
Old Testament, 3
  Books of, 6-7
  Dates, 7
Oratorians, 125
Oratory, 62
Ordinary of the Mass, 55
Ordinary Time (Calendar), 76
Orders (Sacrament), 69-70
Orders, Religious, 124, 125
Original Sin, 28, 29
Orthodox Churches, Eastern, 98
Orthodox Churches, Oriental, 98
Ostensorium, 58
Our Lady of Guadalupe, 84
Our Lady of Mount Carmel, 81
Our Lady of the Rosary, 83
Our Lady of Sorrows, 82

P

Pachomius, St., 124
Palatine Guard of Honor, 110
Pall, 59
Pallium, 58

Palm Sunday (Passion Sunday), 75, 79
Papal Audiences, 111-112
  Election, 100
  Flag, 111
  Representatives, 108-109
  Secretariat of State, 105
  States, 111
    See also Pope; Vatican City
Particular Churches, 106-107
Paschal (Easter) Season, 76
Paschal (Easter) Triduum, 75-76
Paschal (Easter) Vigil, 76
Passion Sunday, 75, 79
Passionists, 125
Paten, 58
Patriarchates, 97, 100
Patriarchs, 97, 100
  Cardinals, 104
Patriarchs, Old Testament, 7
Patrick, St., 79
Patron Saints, 89
Paul, St., Apostle, 15-16
  Letters, 8
Paul, St., Feast of Conversion, 78
  Solemnity (Sts. Peter and Paul), 81
Paul Miki and Companions, Sts., 79
Paul of Thebes, St., 124
Pauline Privilege, 73
Paulists, 125
Peace, 40
Penance (Penitence), 33-34
Penance (Sacrament), 67-68
  Individual Confession, 68
  Norms on General Absolutrion, 68
  Penitential Service, 68
Penitentiary, Apostolic, 105
Pentateuch. 6
Pentecost, 80
People of God, 1
Permanent Diaconate, 70
Peter, St., Apostle, First Pope, 16
  Letters, 8
Peter, St., Chair of, 79
Peter and Paul, Sts., 81
Peter Canisius, St., 26, 32
Peter Chrysologus, St., 26
Peter Claver, St., 82
Peter Damian, St., 26
Petrine Privilege, 73
Pews, 61

Philemon, Letter to, 8
Philip, St., Apostle, 16
Philip Neri, St., 81
Polycarp, St., 22, 79
Pontifical Biblical Commission, 106
Poor Clares, 124
Pope, 99-100
  Authority, Infallibility, 10-11
  Election, 100
  Representatives of, 108-109
Popes, Chronological List, 138-144
Popes, False (Antipopes), 145
Postulator, 88
Poverty, Religious Vow, 127
Prayer, Public, of Church (Liturgy of
    the Hours), 48-49
Prayer, Religous Life of, 128
Prayer of the Faithful, 53
Prayer over the Gifts, 54
Precepts of the Church, 32
Preface of the Mass, 54
Prefect Apostolic, 102
Prelates, 99, 102
Prelatures, 99
Presentation of Mary, 84
Presentation of the Lord, 78
Priests, 69-70
  and Daily Mass, 55
  Celebrants of Eucharist, 67
Primate, 101
Privilege of Faith (Petrine Privi-
    lege), 73
Promoter of the Faith, 88
Propagation of the Faith, Congrega-
    tion of, 105
Proper of Saints, 75, 76
Proper of Seasons, 75-76
Proper of the Mass, 55
Prophets, Old Testament, 7
Protonotaries Apostolic, 102
Provinces, Ecclesiastical, 107
Psalms, 7
Public Affairs of the Church, Council
    for, 105, 108
Publications, Vatican, 112-113
Pulpit, 61
Purgatory, 24
Purification (Presentation of the
    Lord), 74-75
Pyx, 58

Q

Quadragesimo Anno, Encyclical, 35
Queenship of Mary, 82

R

Radio, Vatican, 111
Raphael, Archangel, 83
Readings, Mass, 53
Readings, Office of (Liturgy of Hours), 49
Reconciliation, **see** Penance (Sacrament)
Reconciliation Room, 62
Red Mass, 56
Redeemer, 28
Regina Caeli, 93
Regular Clergy, 125
Relics, 89
Religious, 124-125
Religious Life, Elements, of, 126-128
Reliquary. 89
Representatives, Vatican, 108-109
Requiem Mass, 56
Rerum Novarum, Encyclical, 35
Resurrection (Easter), 80
Revelation, 3-5
  Constitution (Vatican II), 3-5, 9
    See also Bible
Revelation, Book of, 9
Rites, 50-51
Rites, Eastern, 51, 97-98
Robert Bellarmine, St., 26, 32
Rochet, 58
Rogation Days, 77
Roman Catholic Church, **see** Catholic Church
Roman Curia, 104-106
Roman Martyrology, 88
Roman Question, 111
Roman Rite, 51
Romans, Letter to, 8
Rosary, 92
  Feast, 83
Rota, Sacred Roman, 106
Rule of Faith, 28
Ruth, 6

S

Sacramentals, 48

Sacraments, 28, 64-71
  Administration to Non-Catholics, 133-134
  Congregation, 105
  Eastern Churches, 95-96
Sacred Heart, Solemnity, 80
Sacred Heart Devotion, 92
Sacrifice of Mass, **see** Mass
Saints, 14-16, 22-26, 87-89
  Canonization, 87-88
  Communion of, 28-29
    Congregation for Causes of, 88, 105
  in Calendar, 78-84
  Patrons, 89
  Relics, 89
  Veneration, 87
Salvation, 1, 28, 30
  Necessity of the Church, 1, 28
Salvation History, 30
Samuel, 6, 7
Sanctifying Grace, 29, 64
  See also Sacraments
Sanctuary, 60
Sanctuary Lamp, 62
Satan, 28
Saul, King, 6, 7
Schism, Western, 145
Scholastica, St., 79
Scripture and Tradition, 3-5
Secretariat of State, Vatican, 105
Secretariats (Roman Curia), 106
Secular Institutes, 129
  Congregation, 105
Secular Orders, 123
Seton, Elizabeth Ann, St., 78
Shrine, 62
Shrine, Immaculate Conception, U.S., 63
Sick, Anointing of, 69
Signatura, Apostolic, 105
Simeon, Canticle of, 49
Simon, St., 16
Sin, 33-34
  Original, 28, 29
  Penance, Sacrament of, 33, 67-68
Penitence, 33-34
Sirach, Book of, 7
Social Doctrine of the Church, 34-46
Societies of Apostolic Life, 125

Solemnity of Mary, 78
Solomon, King, 7
Sorrows, Our Lady of, 82
Spiritual Works of Mercy, 33
Sponsors, Baptismal, Confirmation, 66
Stamps, Vatican, 111
Stanislaus, St., 79
Stations Crucifix, 91
Stations of the Cross, 91-92
Statistics Office, Vatican, 106, 112
Statues, 61
Stephen, St., 84
Stipend, Mass, 55
Stole, 56
Sulpicians, 125
Sunday, 76
   Mass Obligation, 55, 76
Superiors, Religious, 129
Surplice, 58
Swiss Guards, 110
Synod of Bishops, 102-103
Synoptic Gospels, 8

T

Tabernacle, 61
Teaching Authority of the Church (Magisterium), 5, 10-12
Tekakwitha, Kateri, Bl., 81
Ten Commandments, 31
Teresa of Jesus, St., 26
Thaddeus, Jude, St., Apostle, 15
   Letter, 8
Theological Commission, International, 106
Theology, 13
Theotokos, 85, 86
Thérèse of Lisieux, St., 83, 89
Thessalonians, Letter to, 8
Third (Secular) Orders, 123
Thomas, St., Apostle, 16
Thomas Aquinas, St., 26
Timothy, St., 8
Titular Archbishop, Bishop, 101
Titus, Letter to, 8
Tobit, Book of, 6
Tradition, 3, 4-5
Transfiguration, 82
Trent, Council of, 20
   Canon of the Bible, 6

Trent, Council of
   Celibacy, 70
   Doctrine on Mass, 52
Tribunals of Roman Curia, 105-106
Triduum, 93
Triduum, Easter, 75-76
Trination, 55
Trinitarians, 125
Trinity, Holy, 27-28
   Solemnity, 80
Triumph of the Cross, 82
Trullo, Synod of, 71

U

United States, Relations with Vatican, 113-114
United States Catholic Conference, 107
Unity, Christian, 130-135

V

Vatican City, 110-114
   Concordat with Italy, 111
   Library, 111
   Philatelic Office, 111
   Press Office, 112-113
   Publications, 112
   Radio, 111
   Representatives, 108-109
   Secretariat of State, 105
   U.S. Relations with, 113-114
Vatican Council, First, 20
Vatican Council, Second, 20-21
   Church, Dogmatic Constitution, 10-11, 11-12, 69, 70, 85-86, 87, 122
   Church in the Modern World, Pastoral Constitution, 36-44
   Eastern Catholic Churches, Decree, 98, 130-132
   Ecumenism, Decree, 98, 130-132
   Laity, Apostolate of, Declaration, 122-123
   Liturgy, Constitution, 47, 48, 49, 50, 52, 86, 90
   Non-Christian Religions, Declaration, 135-136, 137
   Revelation, Divine, Constitution, 3-5, 9
Veil, 59
Veil, Humeral, 58
Venial Sin, 33

Vessels, Sacred, 58
Vestments, 56-58
Viaticum, 67
Vicar Apostolic, 102
Vicar General 102
Vicariates, 107
Vienne, Council, of, 19
Vigil, Easter, 76, 80
Vincent de Paul, St., 83
Visitation, 81
Vocation, 126
Vocations, 126
Votive Mass, 56
Vows of Religious, 124, 126, 127

W

War and Peace
   Church Teaching (Vatican II), 40-44
   U.S. Bishops Pastoral, 42
   Nuclear Weapons, 41
Wattson, Paul James, Rev., 134
Way of the Cross (Stations), 91-92
Week of Prayer for Christian Unity, 134

Weekdays (Church Calendar), 77
Western Schism, 145
Wisdom Books, Bible, 6-7
Work, Encyclical on (*Laborem Exercens*), 44-46
World Council of Churches, 135
Worship (Liturgy), 47-49
Worship, Divine, Congregation, 105
Worship, Eastern Churches, 272

X

Xavier, St. Francis, 84, 89

Y

Year, Holy, 93

Year, Liturgical (Calendar), 75-84

Z

Zechariah, 7
Zechariah, Canticle of (Benedictus), 49
Zephaniah, 7
Zucchetto, 58